Conversion in the Wesleyan Tradition

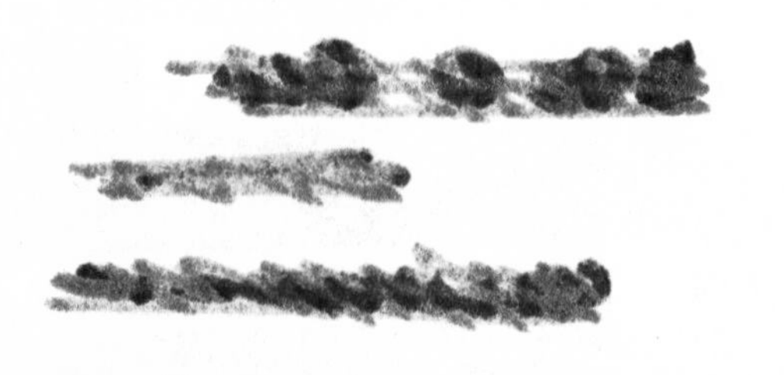

Conversion in the Wesleyan Tradition

Kenneth J. Collins
and
John H. Tyson

Abingdon Press
Nashville

CONVERSION IN THE WESLEYAN TRADITION

This book is printed on acid-free, recycled, elemental-chlorine–free paper.

Library of Congress Cataloging-in-Publication Data

Conversion in the Wesleyan tradition / [edited by] Kenneth J. Collins and John H. Tyson.
p. cm.
Includes bibliographical references and index.
ISBN 0-687-09107-1
1. Conversion—Methodist Church. 2. Methodist Church—Doctrines. I. Collins, Kenneth J. II. Tyson, John H., 1958-

BX8349.C64 C66 2001
248.2'4'08827—dc21

2001018837

Those noted KJV are from the King James Version.

01 02 03 04 05 06 07 08 09 — 10 9 8 7 6 5 4 3 2 1

MANUFACTURED IN THE UNITED STATES OF AMERICA

To the memory of
William Ragsdale Cannon

CONTENTS

Introduction

Conversion in the Wesleyan Tradition

Kenneth J. Collins

The reality of conversion well antedates the great and energetic eighteenth-century Methodist revival in the British Isles. Among the ancient Hebrews, for instance, the root *sûb* meant to turn, or in some cases, to return to the relationship with God, who had called forth the nation of Israel.[1] In the New Testament, the meanings of *sûb* were carried by two Greek words: *epistrephein* (and its cognates) and *metanoein*. The former term often described a literal turning of the person, while the latter entailed a change of outlook and a new direction. But when *epistrephein* was used in a religious context, especially in Acts and the Epistles, it too entailed a "change of outlook and a new direction given to life and to action."[2] As with their Hebrew antecedent, the Greek terms *epistrephein* and *metanoein* involved responding to an evoking, calling God—a God who invited men and women not only to participate in a much larger story but also to be known, in a covenantal way, as nothing less than the people of God.

A further distinction between the use of *epistrephein* and *metanoein* is actually indicative of the kind of ministry in which John Wesley himself engaged. *Epistrephein* was often used to refer to the first-time turning of unbelievers, that is, to initial repentance, while *metanoein* could refer to both rebellious sinners *and* to an apostate church. Indeed, Wesley never conceived of his mission of "spreading scriptural holiness across the land" simply in terms of the unchurched or unbelievers (though he reached many), but also in terms of those who, although they sat in pews on Sunday mornings, were spiritually asleep, self-satisfied, and who had unfortunately misunderstood the crucial importance of holy love. And in the twentieth century, E. Stanley Jones, the great missionary and evangelist, taught that "the acid test of the validity of a Christian church is whether it can not only convert people from the outside to membership but also produce conversion within its own membership. When it cannot do both, it is on its way out."[3]

The communion of churches today which look to Wesley as a theological mentor are, therefore, caught up in a larger story that embraces not only God's faithful actions toward the people of Israel but also the Most High's faithful activity in the life, death, and resurrection of Jesus Christ. The call to Christian conversion in the Wesleyan tradition is anything but provincial or narrow. On the contrary, it is an invitation to participate in the larger story of the church, of the *ekklesia*, of those who have been *called out* of the world to become a part of something far greater than themselves, even the very Body of Christ in whom is grace, mercy, and redemption. The movement, then, is away from sinful alienation and toward God as revealed in Jesus Christ. It is a "going beyond" sinful autonomy and self-curvature to become a real community, even the people of God. Martin Luther expressed the journey of Christian conversion well: "I live in God through faith and in my neighbor through love."[4]

Within the larger church, the Wesleyan communion of faith has had a rich and noble heritage of calling men and women to conversion and of urging those who have fallen from grace to beware of the deceitfulness of sin. From the eighteenth-century British revival among coal miners and the indigent to the flowering of Methodism on American soil, in black churches as well as in white ones, among the poor as among the middle class, the Methodist witness has been nothing less than prodigious. During the nineteenth century in this country, for example, Methodism employed camp meetings and other revivalistic techniques in order to introduce both the unawakened and the backslidden to the disciplined life of Methodism's class meetings and the rules of the United Societies, both of which were suitable structures for fostering repentance and conversion. Indeed, Methodism was the gateway to vital Christianity for so many on the American frontier that by mid-nineteenth century it had become the country's largest Protestant denomination.

Today, however, with the loss of some of the historic disciplines of Methodism (which had fostered both accountability and also spiritual earnestness) has come the concomitant loss of an emphasis on conversion and even on the use of "soteriological language." John Cobb, well known for his honesty and forthrightness, has noted a similar change as well:

> Unfortunately, the shift of attention away from the way of salvation in the work of major thinkers of the nineteenth century was accompanied by a fading of interest among Christians generally. The language in which the discussion was carried on then is rarely used now. The subtlety and rigor of thought of the Reformation in regard to Christian salvation has been largely lost, certainly among United Methodists. Psychological categories that have superseded theological ones in popular Protestantism are far less exact and carefully related to one another.[5]

Sensing this loss and realizing that those communions of faith which look to Wesley must give voice to the importance of conversion and transformation *now*, in an age sorely in need of renewal, several leading scholars approached me and asked if I would bring these issues before the broader community. Fortunately, I have been assisted in this endeavor by John H. Tyson, who has made important contributions at several points along the way. We have invited a number of scholars from a diversity of disciplines and ecclesiastical backgrounds (though most are United Methodist) to explore this salient topic in a timely and engaging way. Reflecting such diversity, the book is divided into four main parts: "Historical Perspectives: Wesley and the People Called Methodist," "Biblical Perspectives," "Theological Perspectives," and "Pastoral Perspectives."

The first part of the book, "Historical Perspectives: Wesley and the People Called Methodist," contains chapters from John H.

Tyson, Henry H. Knight III, Kenneth J. Collins, Douglas Strong, and Estrelda Alexander. It lays out, in a careful and evenhanded way, the significant role that conversion has played in Wesleyan churches in both Britain and America. Accordingly, in his "John Wesley's Conversion at Aldersgate," Tyson revisits the familiar, and well-contested, topic of Wesley's own conversion, bringing to it fresh insights, many of which have been culled from the most recent scholarship in Wesley studies. To illustrate, not only does Tyson, in a very inclusive way, explore a diversity of paradigms for the term *conversion* (moral, intellectual, and the like)[6] but he also employs Wesley's own idiom of "real Christianity," a theme which I have developed in my own work,[7] in order to bring greater clarity to Wesley's particular spiritual quest.

During the 1990s works on Wesley's doctrine of salvation emerged that placed a premium on process, on gradual, incremental development,[8] but neglected, in the eyes of some scholars, Wesley's equal emphasis on the "instantaneous" aspects of redemption. Here Wesley's well-crafted conjunction of *both* gradual *and* instantaneousness was in danger of being neglected, if not outright repudiated. This development would be all the more regrettable once it was realized that the instantaneous motif for Wesley functioned not simply in a chronological way but also, and perhaps more importantly, in a soteriological way. That is, this motif reflected the larger issue of faith and works, and it thus became Wesley's principal vehicle for underscoring not only the sheer gratuity of grace but also the crucial truth that it is God, not humanity, who both forgives sins and makes holy. In his sermon "The Scripture Way of Salvation," for example, as Wesley considers the way, the approach, toward entire sanctification, he observes:

> And by this token may you surely know whether you seek it by faith or by works. If by works, you want something to be done *first, before* you are sanctified. You think, "I must first *be* or *do* thus or thus." Then you are seeking it by works unto this day. If you seek it by faith, you may expect it *as you are*: and if as you are, then expect it *now*.[9]

Mindful of these developments, Henry Knight, in his "The Transformation of the Human Heart: The Place of Conversion in

Chapter 2

Wesley's Theology," insists that salvation, in Wesley's view, is *both* instantaneous *and* gradual. Indeed, Knight goes so far as to state that the "rejection of Wesley's emphasis on instantaneous moments of salvation . . . distorts his own position." Though this contemporary scholar has underscored the importance of the temporal elements in Wesley's doctrine of salvation, he nevertheless has been quite careful to avoid the error of thinking that Wesley's understanding of conversion was "decisionistic," a decision that would not only detract from the sheer gratuity of grace, upheld by the instantaneous motif itself, but that would also, in effect, leave the self very much at the center of its own spiritual life.

During the late 1980s and throughout the 1990s several Wesley scholars maintained that "the faith of a servant" unproblematically implied justification. Theodore Jennings, for example, actually obviated the whole question of Wesley's "conversion" at Aldersgate by claiming that it made little difference to Wesley whether he served God as a servant or as a son.[10] Randy Maddox, for his part, contended that Wesley finally came "to value the nascent faith of the 'servant of God' as justifying faith."[11] The effect of both of these judgments, in the eyes of some scholars,[12] was to lower Wesley's own soteriological standards, especially in terms of justification, the new birth that ever accompanies it, and conversion. My own work in the field has demonstrated that Wesley actually employed the phrase "the faith of a servant" not monolithically but in two key ways, one which implied justification (his "exceptions" or "exempt cases"), the other which did not (the spirit of bondage). In other words, on the one hand, the mature Wesley wanted to be sensitive, pastorally speaking, toward those who had the faith of a servant (in the sense of being under the spirit of bondage) in order not to discourage them, lest they would despair of God's future redeeming graces; but on the other hand, Wesley still maintained his standards regarding redemption. For though the "faith of a servant" in the sense just noted is indeed a measure of grace, as one is under the conviction of sin, it does not constitute what Wesley throughout his career (with some modifications along the way) called real, true, proper, or scriptural Christianity.

Since I have already explored the motif of real Christianity in my earlier works,[13] my contribution to the present volume, "John Wesley and the Fear of Death as a Standard of Conversion," takes a slightly different approach, but one that once again demonstrates Wesley's relatively high soteriological standards—standards that rightfully challenge us even today. Taking "There is therefore now no condemnation for those who are in Christ Jesus" (Rom. 8:1) as his guide, Wesley maintained throughout his career, and with much evidence, that one of the great liberties of the gospel is to be free not from all fear, of course, but from the fear "which has torment," from the kind that is painfully anxious with respect to "death, condemnation, and judgment." This is a freedom, predicated on the atoning work of Christ, that pertains even to a child of God, to the sons and daughters of the Most High. Indeed, when Wesley's many statements on this much neglected topic are applied to his own spiritual journey, a remarkable picture emerges, one that challenges the easy assumption that Wesley had justifying and regenerating faith while in Georgia.

Demonstrating that the motif of real Christianity was an idiom, a rhetoric, employed not simply by the father of Methodism but also by some of his American heirs, Douglas Strong's "A Real Christian Is an Abolitionist: Conversion and Antislavery Activism in Early American Methodism" recounts an engaging narrative crafted by Freeborn Garrettson in which Do-Justice and Professing Christian play leading roles. In the course of the story, Professing Christian undergoes a profound change, one that liberates him from the awful fear of death: "He freed his slaves and became an abolitionist, and his name changed from Professing Christian to Real Christian." Accordingly in his essay, Strong employs suitable historical materials, to call us contemporary Methodists and Wesleyans back to a much needed balance by demonstrating that the transition to being a real Christian entails not only personal depth but also social breadth. That is, a religion that transforms the heart with respect to its tempers or dispositions must ever find expression in love towards our neighbor—and on a number of different levels.

In a chapter that holds together the importance of *both* personal *and* social holiness, Alexander explores much of the same terrain as Strong (that is, the nineteenth-century American context), but with an important difference. While the earlier essay highlighted the transformation of being among slaveholders and taskmasters as they became convinced of the sinfulness not only of their own actions but also of the institutions in which they had participated, Alexander's essay invites us to share the perspective, the distinct vantage point, of the oppressed themselves as the grace of God, mediated to them through the Wesleyan tradition, issued in both liberation and renewal. Thus, through a consideration of the narratives of four courageous black women, Alexander demonstrates how conversion meant more to them than release from the power of sin; it also entailed deliverance from subservient positions. Put another way, these black women, as Alexander points out, found in their faith, conversion, and sanctification experiences "the energy and resolve to fight for a different kind of existence for themselves."

One of the truly remarkable things about these women is that they saw their identity not only as reflected in nineteenth-century American society, with all its injustices and humiliations, but also as it appeared in the sight of a holy God—what Luther called *Coram Deo*. And while it was the latter perspective of being related to the Most High that provided much of the wherewithal for the subsequent social struggle, it was also the same perspective in which these women had initially known themselves to be sinners. Indeed, as Alexander observes, "Their initial sense of the need of conversion . . . [came] from a sense of terrible uncleanness before God." Each of these women, then, had both the honesty and forthrightness to realize that though they were grievously oppressed in many ways, evil was not simply external to themselves, always a characteristic of "the other," but that in some important respects evil also lay within.

The placing of the next part, "Biblical Perspectives," in the second position and not in the opening one is not to suggest that the biblical material is not foundational, indeed normative, to this entire enterprise. Clearly, the stories of the Bible are not only chronologically prior to the Wesleyan story but they also provide the substance, the ethos, and even the orientation for the latter, as I have already indicated in my opening remarks. This particular arrangement, then, was chosen to take seriously the social location of our readers. It comes with the frank recognition that most

Christians (unless they are terribly individualistic and idiosyncratic) participate in hermeneutical communities, preferred ways of interpreting Scripture which, because of their value, are passed on from generation to generation. The content of these preferences constitute nothing less than tradition, what the great Reformation scholar Heiko Oberman has called "Tradition 1" in order to highlight Scripture as the "single" source of revelation (as opposed to "Tradition 2," which would argue for a dual source of revelation), while at the same time taking into account the significance of traditional ways of interpretation, ways that are ever oriented toward Scripture.[14] In the order of the parts of this book, then, chronological priority does not indicate valuational priority.

In the first essay of this part, " 'To Turn from Darkness to Light' (Acts 26:18): Conversion in the Narrative of Luke-Acts," Joel Green points out that the author of Luke-Acts has neither a "clearly delineated 'technology' of conversion," nor does he single out a "particular response as paradigmatic." And though the Third Evangelist evidently leaves open the form that conversion and repentance can take (thereby allowing for great diversity of experience), he nevertheless insists upon "the *necessity* of conversion for *both* Jew *and* Gentile."[15] The turning of conversion, the transformation it entails, then, is not optional, a requirement only for some people, the "sick souls" among us so to speak,[16] but it is a requisite for all people of whatever status or social location simply because, among other things, conversion in Luke-Acts is grounded in "the grand narrative of God's ancient and ongoing purpose." Conversion connects us to, and indeed invites us to become a participant in, God's faithful and redeeming acts on behalf of Israel and in the life, death, and resurrection of Jesus Christ, as noted earlier.[17] And though Green maintains that conversion orients us to a "vision of God and God's work," he is careful that this orientation be understood not simply in a doctrinal way but also, and more importantly, in a personal way. That is, in the end, we are directed not principally to proper teaching or doctrine—though teaching and doctrine are important—but to a person, even Jesus Christ, as Wesley himself had come to realize.[18]

Taking a slightly different approach, Ben Witherington III, in his "New Creation or New Birth? Conversion in the Johannine and

Pauline Literature," forges a conversation between the eighteenth century and the first, between historical Methodism and the biblical witness. Examining those texts that "were especially crucial to Wesley," Witherington pays particular attention to 1 John 3:9 and Romans 7:7-25. Of the former passage, he observes that "the Elder . . . seems to agree with Wesley, that victory over willful sin is possible if one abides in God." In this context, Witherington has carefully parsed the liberties that pertain even to a child of God (not confusing them with entire sanctification, which is a grace yet higher) by affirming the clear Wesleyan teaching that even a child of God is so far perfect as to be free from the *power* of sin.[19] To illustrate, in his sermon "Christian Perfection," Wesley elaborates: "In conformity therefore both to the doctrine of St. John, and to the whole tenor of the New Testament, we fix this conclusion: 'A Christian is so far perfect as not to commit sin.' "[20] Unfortunately, this liberty for which Christ died has been lost, for the most part, both in mainline Wesleyan churches, like The United Methodist Church, and in smaller holiness ones as well: in the former because they have, by and large, forsaken a "soteriological and theological orientation" in favor of an ethical and political one; in the latter because they have confused this gospel liberty, which pertains even to a son or daughter of God, with the graces of entire sanctification.[21]

Witherington's exegesis of the chief Pauline passage (Rom. 7:7-25) once again demonstrates not only the skills of this careful scholar but also his participation in a *Wesleyan* interpretive community. Like Wesley, and unlike some Lutheran and Reformed exegetes, Witherington agrees that the characteristics of the person portrayed in this passage ("I do not understand my own actions. For I do not do what I want, but I do the very thing I hate" [Rom. 7:15]) are *not* descriptive of those who are justified and born of God, but mark those who are still "under the law." Indeed, as Wesley himself points out (and Witherington cites this material): "To have spoken this of himself [that is, of the Apostle Paul], or any *true* believer, would have been foreign to the whole scope of his discourse."[22] What is common, then, in both the Johannine and Pauline material, as this contemporary New Testament scholar observes, is that nothing less than "a radical transformation of one's self is required in order to see the dominion of God."[23]

Since the next part, "Theological Perspectives," is conversant with many of the most recent developments in the broader Wesleyan community, it will be of special interest to many readers. In his "A Mutuality Model of Conversion," Barry L. Callen, influenced in large measure by Clark Pinnock's transition from Reformed evangelical presuppositions to more Wesleyan-Arminian ones, has underscored the salvific results "of taking seriously the concept of reciprocity." In this context, reciprocity is not an un-nuanced synergism that can easily devolve into a simple moralism. Instead, it is a "conjunctive" formulation that highlights not only the undeserved initiative of God (that is, the sheer gratuity of divine action) but also "the responding work of receiving and believing humans." Moreover, this reciprocity of divine initiative and human response, viewed in a larger setting of undeserved divine prevenient action, suggests the "openness" of God to human action and response in ways that earlier theological formulations (due to their particular understanding of divine omnipotence and impassibility) could not. Such understandings, then, can form a bridge between the Wesleyan community and Reformed evangelicals who are beginning to see, some for the very first time, the theological importance of the "Wesleyan-Arminian turn."

Few can doubt that John Wesley was a complex and careful thinker, especially in the area of salvation. The sophisticated theological synthesis that the Methodist leader painstakingly crafted throughout his career held together, without contradiction, the ideas of law and gospel; faith and holy living; grace and works; grace as both sheer unmerited favor and grace as empowerment; justification and sanctification; instantaneousness and process; grace as universal (prevenient) and grace as limited (saving actualization); divine initiative and human response; and finally, initial and final justification—elements that make up what can be termed a "conjunctive" theology.[24] Along these lines, in his "Conversion and Baptism in Wesleyan Spirituality," Ted Campbell explores yet another Wesleyan conjunction that embraces *both* sacramental *and* evangelical piety as they are reflected in Wesley's complex views on baptism.[25] Rejecting the notion that Wesley simply contradicted himself on this point, Campbell attempts to find the broader logic in which both a "catholic" piety ("remembering one's baptism as the ground of Christian hope") as well as an evangelical one ("the need for a fresh 'regeneration' even for those who were once regenerate in baptism") can find their rightful places. Viewing the sacrament of baptism as part of the "ordinary" ministry of the church and the necessity of preaching the new birth as part of its "extraordinary" ministry, Campbell notes that because it was a reform movement, historic Methodism necessarily emphasized preaching, albeit without neglecting baptism. Second, "contemporary Methodism is not in Wesley's place," Campbell cautions. As *churches*, "we have to take responsibility for the 'ordinary' as well as the 'extraordinary' means." The larger logic, then, of this scholar's resolution has very much to do with our own different social location.

William Abraham, one of the preeminent Methodist theologians of our age, bewails the fact that in liberal Protestantism "any appeal to conversion has dropped entirely from sight," while he applauds the "current recovery of nerve in embracing conversion." In an essay that is surely the most philosophical of the collection, Abraham poses the question, "Can we develop a vision of the knowledge of God that takes seriously the evidence of conversion but does so without eroding the place of divine revelation in the epistemology of theology?" Abraham knows that, for Wesley, "the Holy Spirit worked as a warrant for the claim that one is now a child of God," and that Wesley also articulated a "full-blown form of spiritual empiricism." For that reason, subsequent traditions which looked to the English leader as a theological mentor ran the risk of grounding divine revelation not in the canon of the church, Holy Scripture, but in human experience—whether that of individuals or of preferred groups—an unsuitable basis that could, and did, often result in division, theological decline, and its attendant malaise.

That "Pastoral Perspectives" is the last part of the book does not signify in any way that this section is least in importance. On the contrary, it can be argued that this is one of the most crucial sections since its burden is to render the theological and theoretical immensely practical. Put another way, "Pastoral Perspectives" seeks not only the explication of grace in its biblical, historical, and theological settings but also the instantiation, the actualization, of grace in the warp and woof of life, on both personal and social levels. Clearly, this is the challenge that clergy and laity, professor and student alike, all face.

In her "Conversion: Possibility and Expectation," an essay that ably demonstrates the promise of pastoral theology, Sondra Higgins Matthaei refers to the imbalance of some contemporary theologies in which "more attention has been given to Christian nurture and less to conversion." As a corrective, Matthaei calls for *both* conversion *and* nurture as essential in a "Wesleyan ecology of faith formation." And though conversion is that point at which our lives are radically changed when we "come to know God's forgiveness and salvation through Jesus Christ and experience . . . adoption as children of God," conversion is nevertheless a moment of transformation *and* a lifelong endeavor.[26] Rejecting many of the stereotypes of conversion that have occasionally surfaced in the Wesleyan community, Matthaei insists that it is not necessary for us to know the precise time of our conversion—a truth to which all who have participated in this present work would assent.[27] In a real sense, being converted to God as revealed in Jesus Christ is similar to falling in love: one may not know the exact time of its occurrence, but one does indeed know that a crucial—not a superficial—alteration of the heart and life has taken place.[28]

Matthaei's contribution is also valuable in undermining yet another stereotype that has emerged in the literature: that conversion is "individualistic," perhaps even "narcissistic." While there have been, no doubt, instances in American Methodism where conversion was indeed inordinately self-referential and neglectful of the importance of community and of the poor, this was never conversion at its best nor properly understood. In a real sense, conversion is a journey from self-centered alienation to loving fellowship, from sinful autonomy to an engaging community,[29] from preoccupation with self to concern for "the other," especially the very least of all. Beyond this, Matthaei illustrates the substance of this journey with her notion of "faith mentoring." That is, it is often key people, spiritual mentors, who introduce us to the riches of the Christian community. Faith mentors, such as Peter Böhler to John Wesley for example, serve as guides, models, guarantors, and mediators. In this setting, faith-to-faith relationships are critically important, and the church has a significant role to play in both conversion and nurture, for the grace of God often bears a human face.

Developing some of the same themes as Matthaei, but in a slightly different way, Gregory S. Clapper, in his chapter "From the 'Works of the Flesh' to the 'Fruit of the Spirit': Conversion and Spiritual Formation in the Wesleyan Tradition," insists that Christian conversion *and* spiritual formation must be nonnegotiable features of the life of our churches. Evangelistic activity, he cautions, is finally "not about getting 'decisions' but is concerned with producing *disciples*." So understood, Christian conversion should be seen as a "conversion to a lifetime of spiritual formation," where both personal and social holiness are embraced—an understanding that issues, once again, in a much needed balance.

In his essay "Embodying Conversion," Philip R. Meadows, a British Methodist, challenges his American counterparts. Well acquainted with the history of Methodism, both British and American, Meadows maintains that contemporary believers have "disembodied the gospel" by their failure to hold together Christian fellowship with the principles and practices of Methodism. "The early Methodist movement," Meadows affirms, "prudentially embodied the pursuit of scriptural holiness by having all its activities shaped, ordered, and connected by the end of converting sinners into saints."[30] This embodiment of the pursuit of holiness can be seen most clearly in the infrastructure of early Methodism with its class meetings, bands, and select societies,[31] in the Rules of the United Societies, and in the substance of the early Methodist hymns. William J. Abraham, in his essay, notes a similar dynamic: "We might say that early Methodism was a sensitive and carefully constructed spiritual machine for the production of conversion." Unfortunately, the telos, or goal, of scriptural holiness (often expressed in the need for conversion) has by and large been disconnected from the very practices of contemporary Methodist life. When this is done what can only remain is the form of religion without its power.

Part of the problem of this contemporary malaise, Meadows contends, is that the church has drunk deeply from a psychological worldview that has tended to shape an over-gradualist understanding of the gospel in many mainstream liberal Methodist churches. Not surprisingly, the "scandalous language of 'conversion' has largely been dropped in favor of . . . 'therapy.' " Like the counsel shared among the mental patients in *One Flew Over the Cuckoo's Nest*, it is best perhaps to tell the therapist not that you are well or something so bold as that you are healed, but only that you are "a little bit better today than you were yesterday." And while reconnecting the means of grace and corporate church life to scriptural holiness is clearly vital, if the means of grace become an end in themselves, we run the risk, Meadows cautions, of producing "just another breed of nominal Christians wearing the badge of a Methodist." The goal, however, is ever to produce "real Christians," marked by both the form and the power of the gospel.[32]

It is eminently fitting that a leader in Methodism such as William H. Willimon, who not only deeply loves the church but has also thought long and hard about its problems, should compose the conclusion to a work such as this. In a clear and distinct prophetic voice, Willimon laments the fact that United Methodists "are awfully accommodated, well situated, at ease in Zion." This is a church, he contends, that "has lost its conversionist roots, having settled comfortably into a characterization of the Christian life as continuous and synonymous with being a good person." Indeed, without an ongoing call to radical transformation, which holds the love *and* holiness of God together, "Methodism degenerates into insufferable, sentimental moralism in which the Christian life is depicted as simply another helpful means of making nice people even nicer." Conversion, on the other hand, is ever challenging and subversive. It is a "radical assault upon the conventional, officially sanctioned American faith that we are basically okay just as we are and that this world, for any of its faults, is all there is." Put another way, "conversion, being born again, transformed, regenerated, detoxified, is merely God's means of getting God's way with the world," Willimon reminds us. Conversion, in some sense, is the beginning of God's work with us, but there is far more work to be done. Willimon, therefore, invites us all to that labor, not to our own narrow plans, agendas, and concoctions, but to a rich participation in the ministry of God, a God of holy love.

And so *Conversion in the Wesleyan Tradition*, with its many authors from a diversity of traditions, is offered to the broader Wesleyan community—to mainline churches as well as to evangelical ones, to Methodists, Pentecostals, and Holiness folk alike—as a means to reflect critically on the genius of our broader tradition as well as on the elements that have played such a vital role within it. Though our voices have been distinct and, to a remarkable degree, unified for the sake of communicating some vital concerns, we do not imagine that ours are the only ones to be heard. Indeed, our common goal has ever been to spark a conversation within the broader Wesleyan community, to engender a rich dialogue about sin, grace, holiness, and transformation, the very elements of Wesley's own theological vocabulary. In God's grace, then, and in the holy love of the Most High, let the conversation begin.

Kenneth J. Collins
Pentecost, 2000

Part One

Historical Perspectives: Wesley and the People Called Methodist

Chapter One

John Wesley's Conversion at Aldersgate

John H. Tyson

Tensions Within the Aldersgate Conversion Paradigm

When John Wesley told his friends of his lack of saving faith prior to Aldersgate, they were stunned. Mr. Broughton, for example, objected at Blendon on April 25, 1738, that "he could never think that [Wesley] had not faith who had done and suffered such things." Even Wesley's brother, Charles, confidant and fellow laborer, was angry and complained that John "did not know what mischief [he] had done by talking thus." To these friends and family members, Wesley's testimony about his religious experience prior to Aldersgate was simply nonsense.[1] Prior to Aldersgate, Wesley had devoted his life to God, become a priest in the Church of England, and gone as a missionary to America. He was ardent, earnest, and exact in his devotion, and he encouraged and instructed others in the faith. Yet something happened that caused him to state he had not been a real Christian prior to May 1738. To many of Wesley's contemporaries, his new emphasis on the sudden and miraculous power of grace had the consequence of devaluing the sacraments, good works, and the notion of gradual sanctification. How could he say that his life of devoted service and tireless evangelism was prior to his conversion? The question remains alive for us today and rests on three central tensions.

First, is it appropriate to assert that Wesley was not a Christian and had never been converted prior to Aldersgate? Even he had problems answering this question in later life. Depending on what is meant by the term "conversion," many good theologians have argued that 1725 is a more appropriate date for Wesley's turning toward God, when he had a strong spiritual awakening and devoted his whole life to the Most High.[2] In other words, what constitutes conversion to Christianity? Is a particular and identifiable experience that results in a firm assurance that one is justified before God the only spiritual watershed that qualifies as conversion?

Second, what is the relationship of conversion and the sacraments? If Wesley was not truly converted until Aldersgate, are we to affirm that one can participate fully in the sacramental life of the church, as so many members of the Church of England did in Wesley's own day, and still not be a "real" Christian? Must the sacramental path of catechesis, baptism, and table fellowship, which assumes gradual growth in Christ, be accompanied by an experience of instantaneous conversion to result in authentic Christian formation? Does the notion of conversion subvert sacramental efficacy?

Third, does the Aldersgate paradigm of conversion result in unhelpful pastoral practices, namely the creation of unrealistic and discouraging expectations about conversion among the faithful?[3] If we encourage people to seek deliverance from the guilt and power of sin, which Wesley associates with conversion, do we court disappointment? Moreover, if power over willful sin does not come immediately after a cherished spiritual experience, does that mean the experience is not yet a conversion? Also, might not an emphasis on conversion divert people from doing the hard work of personal and spiritual growth, and instead leave them with the suggestion that God will solve all their problems for them without their full participation in the process? By using Wesley's Aldersgate experience as a paradigm for conversion, do we undercut the important work of gradual growth in holiness? Or, did Wesley perhaps hold a more sophisticated view of redemption, holding in tension both crisis and growth in grace, than many of his heirs?

In order to respond to these important questions we must move beyond our everyday conceptions of conversion as the touching of an individual by Christ and her or his consequent confession and repentance. To speak of conversion is not necessarily to reject models of Christian initiation and spiritual formation and its gradualist underpinnings, but it may require us to add to these perspectives Wesley's emphasis on the *actualization*, the instantiation, of saving grace. By looking for a broader conception of conversion, we can better identify and understand some of the ambiguities inherent within Wesley's evolving views of conversion, and we can better resolve some of the tensions that Wesley's conversion at Aldersgate suggest.

If we approach the narrative of Wesley's own spiritual pilgrimage, taking into account the numerous elements he holds in tension, we quickly recognize that there is more room than the continuing debates between liberal "gradualists" and evangelical "instantaneous-ists" allow. There are three competing descriptions of Wesley's conversion in the literature, and they should and can be brought into harmony. First, Wesley was baptized. For those who emphasize the efficacy of the sacraments, his baptism represents the moment of conversion (baptismal regeneration), and all subsequent acts of commitment simply supplement and deepen the transformative power of this act. This is one-half of the conjunction, Wesley's "catholic" view to which Ted A. Campbell refers in his contribution to this volume. Second, Wesley was moved to commit himself to ministry in 1725, and some claim this was his conversion. Finally, there is his Aldersgate experience in 1738, the other half of the conjunction, Wesley's "evangelical" view. I will look more closely at each of these possibilities below. As I do this I draw upon the vocabulary of developmental psychology in order to develop a rich, new understanding of conversion that can serve the church today. The work of James Fowler especially, but others as well, lets us place each of these experiences in one continuous narrative, with crucial points along the way, that frees us to support people who experience conversion in a variety of manners.

Wesley—Pre-1725

Until Wesley was twenty-two, his religious practice was largely outward and perfunctory. He said his prayers, attended church, read the Scriptures, received the Eucharist three times each year. While he knew himself to be guilty of sin, these "known sins" were rather unremarkable, and he exercised over all a very decent morality in connection with a fairly routine Christian commitment.[4] Using Fowler's terminology, we might say that Wesley had experienced a conversion of sorts, but only to the rather immature synthetic/conventional stage of faith.[5] It is not unusual for young people to reach this stage of faith. It is somewhat less usual to move beyond it.

Wesley's Conversion of 1725

In 1725, however, Wesley did experience a conversion beyond this conventional level. At this time he decided to undertake holy orders, and began to read certain authors in the Holy Living tradition, notably Thomas à Kempis and Jeremy Taylor. Wesley chaffed under their heavily moralistic yoke, but these writers profoundly nurtured and shaped his growing commitment to true holiness of heart and life. He began to realize that religion was not simply an outward thing, but that true religion springs from the heart and issues in loving and obedient actions. He developed a profound, personal, and inward understanding of the law of God—that God's law is to regulate not only one's outer behavior but one's inner dispositions as well. Referring to Taylor's *Holy Living and Dying* he wrote:

> In reading several parts of this book, I was exceedingly affected; that part in particular which relates to purity of intention. Instantly I resolved to dedicate all my life to God, all my thoughts, and words, and actions; being thoroughly convinced, there was no medium; but that every part of my life (not some only) must either be a sacrifice to God, or myself, that is, in effect, to the devil.[6]

Luke Tyerman called this period "the turning point" in Wesley's life.[7] Piette called it Wesley's conversion.[8] From this point forward, Wesley dedicated his entire life to God, and his subsequent life demonstrated that the conversion was profound and lasting. Wesley's experience in 1725 correlates to the conversion or faith-stage that Lonergan called "intellectual" conversion and that Conn called "critical" conversion.[9] In other words, Wesley at this time moved beyond the uncritical acceptance of an external authority that dictates morality to an internalized and critical appropriation of moral love. But a key question remains: Was Wesley at this point holy?

From 1725 to 1738, Wesley sought both freedom from the power of sin (often through the use of rules and resolutions) and assurance of his justification. Based upon the teachings of the Holy Living School, Wesley understood that his justification before God was dependent on the condition of sanctification, and he was very much aware that he had not yet found it.[10] Wesley sought a sense of peace with God and assurance of salvation. He believed these were available, and he knew they were not his. This knowledge and fear drove him powerfully. For this reason, Wesley could write quite forthrightly to the Rev. Dr. John Burton, one of the Georgia Trustees:

> My chief motive, to which all the rest are subordinate, is the hope of saving my own soul. I hope to learn the true sense of the gospel of Christ by preaching it to the heathens. . . . But I am assured, if I be once converted myself, he will then employ me both to strengthen my brethren and to preach his name to the Gentiles, that the very ends of the earth may see the salvation of our God.[11]

Wesley's Aldersgate Experience

Under Moravian influences, Wesley gradually moved away from thinking of faith as mere assent or obedience to doctrine; he also permanently and decisively moved away from assuming that sanctification must, or may, precede justification. Instead, he came to believe that justification must precede sanctification. In other words, he rejected the soteriological order of the Holy Living tradition and rediscovered the classical Anglican position. This shift involved several related steps. He moved away from the idea of Christ merely as example or head of the church, and toward the realization of Christ as personal savior whose blood was shed "for me." He moved toward the conviction that justifying faith is the one thing absolutely necessary for salvation, and realized that this faith is available to "thoroughly bruised" sinners. He came to believe that justifying faith is given to the unjust instantaneously by the Holy Spirit, and consists primarily in the conviction that "Jesus Christ died for me, and I am forgiven and reconciled through him."[12] Wesley came to believe that this faith implies a sense of forgiveness that one can feel tangibly, and that this faith brings with it the new birth, the power not to commit sin, and the witness of the Holy Spirit that one is now accepted as a son or daughter of God. For about two years Wesley wrestled with this new conception of justifying faith. He preached it during the spring of 1738. He received it himself on May 24, 1738:[13]

> In the evening I went very unwillingly to a society in Aldersgate Street, where one was reading Luther's Preface to the Epistle to the Romans. About a quarter before nine, while he was describing the change which God works in the heart through faith in Christ, I felt my heart strangely warmed. I felt I did trust in Christ, Christ alone for salvation, and an assurance was given me that he had taken away my sins, even *mine,* and saved *me* from the law of sin and death.[14]

This account is so simple, yet so profound. What Wesley describes having experienced is precisely the definition of justifying faith which he had been learning from the Moravians and quoting in his journal from the homily "Of Salvation." In this quiet moment, Wesley received that justifying faith he had sought so assiduously, and the assurance that faith implies. He then knew that Jesus was not only the Savior of the world (which had been Wesley's response to August Spangenberg's searching question, "Do you know Jesus?") but that Jesus was his own Savior as well. Wesley finally experienced what he had come to believe: that saving faith is a relationship of love and trust between a person and Jesus Christ, with holiness of heart and life as the necessary fruit of faith.

Prior to Aldersgate, Wesley already had in place a highly developed doctrine of sanctification, an appreciation for the necessity of obedience and active love of neighbor. After Aldersgate, he did not forget about sanctification but came to see the obligation to do good works as the necessary fruit of faith rather than its origin. Now Wesley could reconsider his journey in a different light. Looking back to his experience before meeting the Moravians, both he and Charles freely admitted that, prior to Aldersgate, their works had been the ground of their hope for salvation, a notion consistent with Wesley's subsequent self-perception as having had the faith of a servant, not of a son.

Of course, Wesley's new doctrine and experience of justification by faith raised almost as many personal and theological questions as it answered.[15] It took him several months and a visit to Germany to begin to sort things out, and at one point he feared he had lost his faith altogether.[16] For example, Wesley, in Lutheran fashion, struggled with the way the Moravians viewed righteousness, in all its forms, as imputed to those who lean on Christ in faith. While the Moravians expected the faithful to understand that they were fully "righteous in Christ" by faith through imputation, Wesley expected both imputed and actual imparted righteousness.[17] Over the years, Wesley worked out the question of degrees of faith, and the relationship between justification and sanctification, and between sanctification and Christian perfection. He also matured in his understanding of assurance.[18]

After 1738, Wesley spoke of the distinction between "real" Christians and "almost" Christians, and developed this theme, with some modifications along the way, throughout his career.[19] For example, in the sermon "The Almost Christian," which he preached at Oxford in 1741, Wesley described the "almost" Christian as one who excels in morality, uses the means of grace, and has a real desire to serve God but lacks both saving faith and the divine love of God and neighbor.[20] Even the most sincere "almost" Christians—those who lack saving faith, with its resulting complex of justification, the new birth, sanctification, and a measure of assurance—are heirs of hell. Since Wesley had not yet clarified the distinction between initial and entire sanctification, or a measure of assurance from full assurance, he tended to devalue the faith and work of "almost" Christians, hoping to motivate them to seek saving faith. Positively, he testified to his own experience of justification at Aldersgate as a model of conversion that all should seek. In his preaching and in the journals he prepared for publication, he emphasized what he had gained by his conversion. He described the identifying signs of the new birth as justifying faith, power over sin, peace with God, the witness of the Spirit that one is a child of God, and love of God and neighbor.

As late as 1760, Wesley still insisted that the new birth, which accompanies justifying faith, is absolutely necessary to salvation:

> For you will all drop into the pit together, into the nethermost hell. You will all lie together in the lake of fire, "the lake of fire burning with brimstone." Then at length you will see (but God grant you may see it before!) the necessity of holiness in order to glory—and consequently of the new birth, since none can be holy except he be born again.[21]

Wesley concluded this sermon by describing one who does no harm, but does good, keeps the commandments, and constantly attends church and sacrament: "But all this will not keep you from hell, except you be born again."[22] Wesley believed that those who lacked what he had received at Aldersgate, particularly justification and the new birth, would perish eternally.

Aldersgate and Wesley's Understanding of Conversion

It may be surprising for some to discover that conversion is not a word that Wesley used often (only about sixty times, and half of these were quotations from others), although it was a spiritual experience into which he led thousands of people.[23] Wesley used the word several times during his association with the Moravians, but he seldom used it thereafter.[24] This was probably because Wesley was almost constantly embroiled in theological controversies that necessitated the very precise use of terms. For example, for decades he argued with learned Anglican colleagues that justification implied not only orthodoxy and orthopraxy but the entire Pauline complex of justification by faith, the new birth, and a measure of assurance. Wesley knew very well that conversion was too fluid a term on which to base his arguments for justification. Under the circumstances, it was wise for Wesley to avoid speaking in terms of conversion.

This high threshold for conversion is seen in Wesley's standard definition of the word. In his *Complete English Dictionary,* he defined conversion as "a thorough change of heart and life from sin to holiness."[25] After 1738, Wesley believed it was impossible to experience a thorough change of heart and life from sin to holiness without experiencing the new birth, which is in turn dependent upon the exercise of justifying faith. Interconnected terms such as *conversion, justification, assurance,* and *new birth* defined Wesley's understanding of real Christianity, a topic that concerned him throughout his adult life. Wesley believed passionately that real Christianity was required of all believers, and that it was available to all. He wanted no one to stop short of this fully orbed Christian life. Yet he was very much aware that many sincere "almost" Christians did indeed stop short of real Christianity. What of those who never took the next step? What of those who served God in fear and diligence but never experienced justifying faith? Could Wesley hold together both pastoral sensitivity as he urged people to go into the deeper graces, and also his relatively high standards in terms of redemption?

As early as 1754, we see harbingers of change concerning Wesley's opinion of the eternal state of those who had not experienced justifying faith and the new birth. In his *Explanatory Notes upon the New Testament,* Wesley discussed servants of God, that is, people of faith who sincerely endeavor to worship and serve God according to the light they have but who have not exercised saving faith. These are said to have the "faith of a servant," and Wesley asserted that they have been "accepted": "*But in every nation he that feareth God and worketh righteousness . . . is accepted of him*—through Christ, though he knows him not. . . . He is in the favour of God, whether enjoying his written word and ordinances or not."[26]

Wesley still had not applied this line of thinking to "almost" Christians, as evidenced in his 1760 sermon on the new birth. Nevertheless, a revolution in Wesley's soteriology was under way, for he would eventually conclude that sincere "almost" Christians, whom he now termed more positively as servants of God (as distinguished from children of God) are accepted for the light and grace that they have, even though they are not justified![27]

This line of thinking shows clearly in the journal emendations he made in 1774 and 1775. In the original entry for February 1, 1738, he lamented, "But what have I learned in the meantime? Why (what I the least of all suspected), that I who went to America to convert others, was never myself converted to God."[28] In 1774 he added the remark to this entry: "I am not sure of this." This reflects the ambivalence the mature Wesley felt about the meaning of conversion as it applies to servants of God. Wesley knew very well that the Old and New Testament verbs translated as "conversion" can refer to personal or corporate repentance from a specific act of wrongdoing and disobedience, or they can refer to the Pauline cluster of justification, sanctification, assurance, and the new birth. But when Wesley had originally made his journal entry in 1738, his method was to denigrate the state of those whom he soon designated "almost" Christians in an effort to motivate them to become real Christians.

Gradually, Wesley had come to realize that it was both more helpful and more truthful to admit that many "almost" Christians had already entered into a sincere and acceptable relationship with God, and indeed they had undergone some degree of *shub* and *metanoia.* This is not conversion in the Pauline sense, and it is not conversion in the sense that Wesley favors, but it is conversion in the sense of repentance and a degree of obedience.[29]

The mature Wesley declared that it should be "well observed" that all those who "fear God and work righteousness" are "at that very moment in a state of acceptance," and "the wrath of God" no longer "abideth upon him," even though that person is "only a *servant* of God, not properly a *son*" of God.[30] Was Wesley saying here that those who lack justifying faith are nevertheless justified due to their good works? No, he was not. Wesley's understanding of degrees of faith simply came into full play.[31] Justification is a renewed relationship with God in which a person *realizes* that he or she is pardoned, forgiven, loved, and accepted by God. It is part of a total conversion experience, which normally includes saving faith, the new birth, and a measure of assurance. The servant of God, however, has none of these experiences. Nevertheless, the servant of God who fears God and works righteousness is "in a degree 'accepted with him' " but does not know it.[32] The mature Wesley was suggesting that although justification is the reality of pardon, justification can be distinguished from acceptance in that God's acceptance of the servant can occur apart from the normal complex of saving faith, initial sanctification, the new birth, and a measure of assurance. For Wesley, justification always occurs as one aspect *within* this Pauline complex. Wesley's use of the word "acceptance" in the case of the servant of God indicates a unilateral action on God's part that is not comprehended or enjoyed by the person, and that is not attended by the other graces which transform one from a servant to a child of God. This marks a significant difference in his use of the terms *acceptance* and *justification*. John Cobb puts the distinction well:

> Justification is not simply the objective fact that God pardons, nor is it simply a cognitive belief that this is so. It involves an experience of being pardoned or knowing ourselves as pardoned—the sort of experience Wesley had at Aldersgate. It is not just the knowledge that Christ has taken away our guilt. It involves also becoming experientially free from that guilt.[33]

So the servant of God still serves in fear and anxiety, does not have the peace of God, and does not experience the love of God shed abroad in the heart crying, "Abba, Father." The servant of God is accepted but not justified, because justification is more than acceptance; it is a restored relationship of reciprocal love and confidence. The servant of God remains in an infant state of salvation, on the "porch" of redemption, properly speaking.[34]

A Wesleyan Conception of Conversion for Today

As Wesley grew older, he used the term "conversion" less because it was imprecise, but not because he was any less passionate about leading others into the conversion experience, which he called real Christianity. I wonder whether the same can always be said for us. Sometimes our ministry seems to bear a greater resemblance to Wesley's before Aldersgate than after. Prior to Aldersgate, Wesley preached a great deal and had little success. After Aldersgate, he began to preach on justification by faith (conversion), and the word spread like fire among the stubble.

Judging from the denominational records, we United

Methodists, for example, excel in engaging our members in the gradual growth in sanctification, but we are losing our ability to play midwife to the new birth. Worse, there is room to fear that we have left that messy and humbling chore to other denominations less wed to middle-class prosperity than The United Methodist Church and whose spiritual birthrates are booming, while we spend most of our time in the mortuary.[35] For several decades it has been tempting for Methodists (as well as other mainline denominations) to dismiss conversion as a simplistic and unsophisticated concept better left to ignorant and emotional people. This not only contributes to the steady decrease in our membership rolls but is un-Wesleyan as well.

The mature Wesley's understanding of conversion will serve us better. Wesley never lifted his focus from leading others to the threshold of real Christianity, and then beyond, to Christian perfection. But he did learn, in a very pastoral way, to appreciate the reality and the value of degrees of faith and, implicitly, degrees of conversion. Without encouraging servants of God to be content with their degree of conversion, he learned to affirm their progress while enthusiastically pointing the way to a higher actualization of grace. With this in mind, let us return to some of the questions with which we began this essay.

Was it appropriate for Wesley to say he had never been a Christian prior to Aldersgate? Probably not, for the term can be understood in a number of ways, not simply theologically but also sociologically. Indeed, it is because the Christian life prior to the exercise of justifying faith is in some sense Christian that Wesley found it necessary to use an intensifying adjective when speaking of real Christianity. Prior to Aldersgate, and indeed prior to 1725, Wesley had certainly thought of himself as a Christian. The events of 1738 simply demonstrated to him that his earlier level of conversion and spiritual growth was weak and immature in comparison with what it could become. Nevertheless, the young Wesley was consciously involved in the sacraments, catechesis, worship, fellowship, and prayer of the church. He had made no profound renunciation of the faith; to the contrary, he continued to grow in it.[36] An immature Christian he may have been prior to Aldersgate, but a Christian, in some sense, he was from his baptism.

Nevertheless, if we ask whether Wesley was a real Christian from his baptism, we would answer no. The term "real, or proper, Christian" is a specialized designation Wesley developed for those who had experienced not only acceptance but also justification, the new birth, and a measure of assurance, and he did not have these prior to Aldersgate.

What about the question of Wesley's conversion? Would it be appropriate to say that Wesley had never been converted prior to Aldersgate? As we have seen, Wesley himself had difficulty with this question, for he remarked in his journal in 1738 that he had never been converted, and then commented in 1774 that he was not sure of this.[37] Wesley never really resolved this ambiguity, which only demonstrates his general dissatisfaction with the term. It is clear that at one time Wesley had associated conversion exclusively with justification. But he knew that the word could be construed legitimately in other ways, as illustrated by the words *shub* and *metanoia* in the Scriptures. In the end, Wesley wanted to facilitate conversion, but his terminology of *justification, sanctification, servants of God,* and *children of God* worked toward this end with greater clarity and precision. Again, I turn to the terminology of developmental psychology because it gives latitude for the wide range of conversion experiences that are suggested in Scripture and are observable in Christian experience. Wesley clearly had conversion experiences prior to Aldersgate, although the content of those experiences did not include justifying faith. Wesley's earliest conversion experiences were transvalued in 1725, and his conversion in 1725 was transvalued by his conversion to real Christianity at Aldersgate when he exercised justifying faith. A soteriology that includes degrees of conversion is not inconsistent with Wesley's insistence on degrees of faith. Such a view does not diminish the importance of Aldersgate, but highlights and clarifies its significance. It also helps ameliorate the tension between a sacramental and an evangelical soteriology.

Our third question was about the relationship of conversion to a sacramental soteriology. It is well known that Wesley faced a cultural situation in which nearly everyone was baptized but many clearly were Christians in name only. Many were not living within the gracious sacramental covenant into which they had been initiated. They had "sinned their grace away."[38] How could he awaken them? How could he make them realize that they did not possess the thing they assumed so lightly was theirs? To do this, Wesley developed his rhetoric of the "almost" Christian and the real Christian. As he defined these levels of faith, he helped his listeners realize that many of them had not yet reached the standards of the "almost" Christian, let alone the real Christian. Yet such an approach sets up very real tensions with sacramental theology, since it suggests that the sacraments alone are not sufficient to salvation. Acknowledging that there are degrees of conversion through which the sacramental life nurtures and shepherds us removes this tension. That is, conversion to real Christianity is not something that happens automatically through the sacraments, but neither is it something that happens in spite of them. Rather, the sacraments are meant to assist us to conversion to real Christianity and then on to perfection in love. The sacramental life of the church provides the structure within which conversion occurs. Sacrament without conversion is a sham, and conversion without sacrament is not fully Christian. Participation in the sacraments may come before or after one's conversion, but the two should never be long separated. A sacramental soteriology is invigorated by an emphasis on conversions.

Finally, we started this chapter by acknowledging that it is possible to claim too much for conversion, which can result in a great deal of confusion, despair, and spiritual torpor for those who are young in the faith. An "Aldersgatism" that defers the personal responsibilities of spiritual growth to some future and mysterious gift of conversion does little to encourage Christian maturity and does much to harm it. To deny our measure of faith, no matter how weak, because it falls short of Wesley's descriptions of real Christianity may lead to despair and would be all too tragic. Acknowledging the reality of degrees of faith and acceptance might be helpful in addressing this problem. The mature Wesley himself offered this kind of spiritual guidance by dropping the rhetoric of damnation for the servants of God, and by encouraging them diligently to use the means of grace as they seek the faith of a child of God. He also acknowledged the role of infirmities of mind and body which might prevent those with justifying faith from enjoying the full experience of that faith. We could choose to view this as another instance of Wesley's tacit move toward acknowledging different kinds of conversion. Such a move can be helpful for pastoral ministry today.

By acknowledging a diversity of "conversions" as well as degrees of faith and acceptance, pastors could lead their people to the next level of faith (and thereby maintain soteriological standards) in an atmosphere that seeks diligently and responsibly the transforming power of God without denigrating the sincerity, reality, and power of earlier conversions. The medical and psychological model we have for some physical and spiritual disorders is in some degree allowed for by Wesley's allowance of "infirmities" of mind or body which can block the justified from the full experience of their faith, assurance in particular.

In conclusion, affirming Aldersgate as the occasion of Wesley's true conversion sets up many soteriological tensions. But they are worthwhile tensions: the balance of pastoral sensitivity and the standards of Christian redemption, which, for many Christians, point to the existence of multiple moments of conversion; the importance of participation in sacramental life; and the gradual outworking of holiness. Acknowledging that individuals may experience several conversions (in the process of becoming fully Christian) harmonizes the rich variety of tensions that Wesley's theology, and authentic Christian living, suggest.

Aldersgate is a paradigm of the conversion experience, but it does not have to be the only one.[39] Many Methodists find the story of Wesley's "strangely warmed heart" a compelling narrative that resonates with their own sense of how the Spirit of God has wrought change in their lives. When Wesley acknowledged the importance of the faith of a servant of God, he introduced another description of the experience of conversion, one that also resonates with many believers—both then and now. By asserting that servants of God are no longer under condemnation but are accepted by God, Wesley encouraged servants of God to seek the faith of children of God. We may all wish for the clarity and assurance of a conversion experience like Wesley had at Aldersgate. Those who receive such a gift should be humble and filled with gratitude. For many, the moment is less remarkable and dramatic.

Those who move through the degrees of faith more slowly are not thereby exempt from discipleship or from the holiness that is *necessary* to see the Lord, and we should not denigrate their earlier faith, informed principally by prevenient grace. Pastoral ministry must help believers identify the measure of faith they have been given, while spurring them on to greater levels of sanctification, for God is the source of grace that works among us to transform God's people into one holy priesthood.

Chapter Two

The Transformation of the Human Heart: The Place of Conversion in Wesley's Theology

Henry H. Knight III

For John Wesley salvation was both instantaneous and gradual. Even a cursory examination of his writings on the subject reveals this. Yet this has not kept interpreters of Wesley from arguing over which was more central in his thought and practice; even less has it prevented his theological descendents from promoting one at the expense of the other.

More than any other question, the question of the significance of Wesley's Aldersgate experience has focused the issue. The development of nineteenth-century revivalism, with its emphasis on instantaneous conversion, led to a highlighting of Aldersgate as Wesley's conversion experience.[1] The tendency was to neglect the gradual aspects of Wesley's salvation story on either side of Aldersgate.[2] Recent decades have witnessed a reaction against this interpretation. The rediscovery of the Wesleyan themes of Christian formation by way of spiritual disciplines and accountability has led many to diminish or reject outright both the conversionist reading of Aldersgate and the importance of instantaneous conversion in Wesley's theology.[3]

As one who has contributed to this recovery of Christian formation in Wesley,[4] I certainly endorse this new concern for means of grace and spiritual disciplines. Yet the rejection of Wesley's emphasis on instantaneous moments in salvation not only distorts his own position but also can be detrimental to the theology and practice of those of us who seek to learn from him. A more theologically fruitful course is to ask why Wesley insists salvation is both instantaneous and gradual, and what role conversion plays within his soteriology as a whole.

What Conversion Is and What It Is Not

In order to examine its role in Wesley's theology we must first clarify what Wesley means by *conversion.* In particular, it is crucial to distinguish Wesley's understanding from that of later revivalism. There are at least four errors of interpretation to be avoided, each of which tends to reduce conversion to a single element, and in some cases to define that element in ways different from Wesley.

The first is to equate conversion with regeneration. Ole Borgen, in his critique of interpreters of Wesley who equate the two, rightly insists that conversion for Wesley is much broader, encompassing the gift of faith, justification, regeneration (or new birth), and the witness of the Spirit.[5] These elements constitute conversion in both Wesley's theology and Wesley's experience at Aldersgate.

It should be noted that Wesley himself does not use the word *conversion* often (as it is not a common scriptural term),[6] or always consistently. Sometimes he links it to *repentance,* and at other times to *sanctification.*[7] This imprecision means care must be taken in citing Wesley, and indicates that he did not consider "conversion" to be as clear in meaning as "justification" or "regeneration." But for our purposes, conversion is a useful term to denote the four elements mentioned above, which for Wesley normally occur together in a single moment.

Second, if treating conversion and regeneration as synonymous is an error, then equating conversion and justification is an even greater error. For Wesley, justification was another word for pardon,[8] and was itself a transformative gift of God. However, it was not the goal of the Christian life—which was the renewal of the human heart in love, a process of sanctification begun with regeneration and culminating in Christian perfection. Wesley's commitment to holiness of heart and life made him a strong critic of preaching that confused salvation with pardon for sin:

> I find more profit in sermons on either good tempers, or good works, than in what are vulgarly called Gospel sermons. . . . Let but a pert, self-sufficient animal, that has neither sense nor grace, bawl out something about Christ, or his blood, or justification by faith, and his hearers cry out, "What a fine Gospel sermon!" Surely the Methodists have not so learned Christ! We know no Gospel without salvation from sin.[9]

A third error is to confuse conversion with a human decision to believe. The revivalism of the nineteenth and twentieth centuries, while by no means denying conversion as a work of God, called for hearers to make an immediate decision in response to the preached word. Those who did were considered converted. This is in contrast to Wesley's own practice, in which those responding to the message would be enrolled in a class meeting; conversion would be a subsequent event following the faithful practice of spiritual disciplines, often two years after joining the class.[10]

Wesley's understanding of conversion is not decisionistic; the focus is always on divine agency, not human. That is, conversion is first and foremost an act of God that is transformative in its effects. Thus, for Wesley justification is "that great work which God does *for us,* in forgiving our sins," while the new birth is that "great work which God does *in us,* in renewing our fallen nature."[11] Likewise the witness of the Spirit "is given by the Spirit of God to and with our spirit. He is the person testifying."[12]

Even faith is a gift of God, as Wesley explains: "Undoubtedly faith is the *work of God;* and yet it is the *duty of man* to believe . . . *if* he will, though not *when* he will. If he seek faith in the appointed ways, sooner or later the power of the Lord will be present, whereby (1) God works, and by *His* power (2) man believes."[13] Thus it is the action of God that enables a person to have faith. Certainly it is a human decision to believe once God has acted and, enabled by prevenient grace, it is also a human decision to seek this faith through the appointed means. But the claim that one cannot believe *when* one wills sets even this far apart from the decisionist conversionism of the next two centuries (and the admonition to seek faith by the appointed means shows the intrinsic linkage for Wesley of instantaneous and gradual salvation).

A fourth error is to identify conversion with having an experience, that is, with having certain feelings. Wesley's Aldersgate account lends itself to this misunderstanding when he speaks of his heart as "strangely warmed."[14] Yet Wesley does not make this experience normative for others. While it is frequently the case that feelings of various kinds accompany conversion, they are not necessary to conversion nor do they constitute it.

What normally accompanies conversion is a witness of the Spirit, which Wesley defines as "an inward impression on the soul, whereby the Spirit of God directly 'witnesses to my spirit that I am a child of God'; that Jesus Christ hath loved me, and given himself for me; that all my sins are blotted out, and I, even I, am reconciled to God."[15] The witness of the Spirit is more an inner conviction than a feeling; it corresponds to Wesley's language describing Aldersgate, which immediately follows the account of his heart being "strangely warmed."

What this underscores again is Wesley's insistence that conversion is primarily an instantaneous act of God, and only partially and secondarily involves human action in response. Conversion is most fundamentally a multifaceted transformation of the human heart, whose immediate goal is to enable persons to know and love God, and ultimately aims toward their perfection in love.

Epistemological Transformation: The Gift of Faith

Wesley's primary stated reason for insisting on instantaneous conversion is that this is the way God seems to work, both in Scripture and in the experience of the majority of persons who became Christians in his day. In 1738 it was from Peter Böhler that Wesley first encountered the idea that faith was an instantaneous gift of God. It was the instantaneousness of the work that troubled Wesley:

> I could not understand how this faith should be given in a moment; how a man could *at once* be thus turned from darkness to light, from sin and misery to righteousness and joy in the Holy Ghost. I searched the Scriptures again . . . but to my

> utter astonishment found scarce any instances there of other than *instantaneous* conversions—scarce any other so slow as that of St. Paul, who was three days in the pangs of the new birth.[16]

Even so, Wesley was not convinced the biblical pattern still reflected God's ordinary manner of working until Böhler brought several witnesses who gave accounts of instantaneous conversion.

These first few witnesses would be supplemented with hundreds more throughout Wesley's ministry. As he assured "John Smith" in 1745, "I am acquainted with more than twelve or thirteen hundred persons whom I believe *to be truly pious* . . . who have severally testified to me with their own mouths that they *do know* the day when the love of God was first shed abroad in their hearts."[17] Wesley never wavered in his belief that most conversions were instantaneous, nor did his experience give him reason to think otherwise.

Wesley is likewise clear as to why conversion is instantaneous: salvation is by faith, and faith is a gift of God. Faith for Wesley is not primarily assent to truth. Rather, as he explains to "John Smith," it "is a divine conviction of invisible things; a supernatural conviction of the things of God, with a filial confidence in his love."[18] That is, faith is both a "spiritual sense,"[19] enabling us to know God's love, and an abiding trust in that love. Faith has an epistemological function in Wesley's theology, and thereby makes the Christian life possible. "For we can't rightly serve God unless we love him. And we can't love him unless we know him; neither can we know God, unless by faith."[20]

Such faith is not a human possibility. The power of sin effectively prevents both knowledge of and trust in God. While those under the power of sin may well believe that there is a God, they remain "only practical atheists" who "have not acquainted themselves with him, neither have any fellowship with him. . . ."[21] They are either oblivious to their condition, unable to know reality other than that with which they are already acquainted, or, if convicted, actively seek to know that which they as yet do not. Wesley depicts this ignorance as having "a thick veil" between the one under sin and the "invisible world";[22] what is needed is for the veil to be removed so that our capacity to know God can function properly.

Only God can remove the veil and enable us to know God. Wesley insists: "No man is able to work it in himself. . . . It requires no less power thus to quicken a dead soul than to raise a body that lies in the grave. It is a new creation; and none can create a soul anew, but he who at first created the heavens and the earth."[23] That is, the gift of faith is an act of God that is essentially transformative, not only creating the possibility of knowing God but also re-creating the knower as well.

Wesley underscores this emphasis on the power of God by insisting conversion is miraculous. "I think a miracle is a work of omnipotence, wrought by the supernatural power of God," he writes "John Smith." "Now if the conversion of sinners to holiness is not such a work, I cannot tell what is."[24] He even goes so far as to say that "at the moment of our conversion," God acts "irresistibly"[25]—a statement made in a treatise largely designed to deny the Calvinist insistence that grace is irresistible.

In Wesley's view, all grace is transformative, whether it is instantaneous or gradual. What is distinctive about an instantaneous work of grace is the nature of the transformation. An instantaneous work creates in the life of the recipient a new possibility that did not previously exist and could not emerge from preexisting factors. This is conveyed by Wesley's use of terms like *miracle, omnipotence,* and *irresistible,* as well as his analogies with creation and resurrection. The gradual work then builds on the new life that the instantaneous work has brought into existence.

We have seen this already in his understanding of faith as a spiritual sense: the veil is removed and the believer finds himself or herself inhabiting a spiritual reality of which he or she was hitherto unaware. Such faith enables one to know God as opposed to only knowing about God; it is the epistemological precondition for both a transformative encounter and a growing relationship.

Relational Transformation: Justification

The ultimate goal of conversion for Wesley is holiness or Christian perfection. Justification and the new birth are the elements of instantaneous conversion that enable one to grow in sanctification and thus move toward that goal. Both justification and the new birth are instantaneous because each consists of a transformative act that only God can do. Justification is a change in our relationship with God, while new birth is a transformation of the heart. As Wesley notes, "Justification implies only a relative, the new birth a real, change." Thus the "former changes our outward relation to God, so that of enemies we become children; by the latter our inmost souls are changed, so that of sinners we become saints."[26]

In Wesley's mature theology, justification marks the transition between having the "faith of a servant" and the "faith of a child of God." As Wesley states, this is a significant change from what he believed at the beginning to be the Methodist awakening:

> Indeed nearly fifty years ago, when the preachers commonly called Methodists began to preach that grand scriptural doctrine, salvation by faith, they were not sufficiently apprised of the difference between a servant and a child of God. They did not clearly understand that even one "who feared God, and worketh righteousness, is accepted of him."[27]

While Wesley is clear that simply assenting to Christian truth is not in itself saving faith, he is convinced that the faith of a servant "brings eternal salvation to all those that keep it to the end." Thus the one who possesses the faith of a servant "is at that very moment in a state of acceptance."[28]

What those with the faith of a servant are not is justified—that is, they do not have the "*faith* of the children of God," which comes by God "*revealing* his only-begotten Son in their hearts." In other words, they do not have the witness of the Spirit, wherein the Holy Spirit witnesses to their spirit that they are children of God.[29]

This brings us to an admitted difficulty in interpreting Wesley. In the passages I have just cited, he never uses the word *justification.* Because of that, one could make the following argument: To be justified is to be accepted by God, and to be accepted implies as well that one is forgiven. Those with the faith of a servant are accepted, therefore they are justified and their sins are forgiven. Their not *experiencing* forgiveness in no way negates their *being* forgiven, and therefore justified.[30]

There are passages in Wesley's writings that seem to support such an argument. First, as early as 1747 Wesley distinguishes between forgiveness and the assurance of forgiveness:

> Because, if justifying faith *necessarily* implies such an explicit sense of pardon, then everyone who has it not, and everyone so long as he has it not, is under the wrath and . . . curse of God. But this is a supposition contrary to Scripture as well as to experience. . . . Again. The assertion that justifying faith is a sense of pardon is contrary to *reason*; it is flatly *absurd*. For how can *a sense of our having received pardon* be the *condition* of our receiving it?[31]

Second, Wesley typically links justification and acceptance, defining justification as "pardon," "the forgiveness of all our sins, and (what is necessarily implied therein) our acceptance with God."[32] Thus if those with the faith of a servant are accepted, they seemingly must be justified as well.

Yet this way of construing justification creates more difficulties than it solves. To extend justification to the faith of a servant contradicts Wesley's insistence that "at the same time that we are justified, yea, in that very moment, *sanctification* begins. In that instant we are 'born again'. . . ."[33] Rather than weaken or abandon Wesley's contention that justification and new birth occur together, I would distinguish between justification and acceptance. That is, while justification does necessarily imply acceptance, Wesley came to believe that the faith of a servant prior to justification also implies acceptance. Those with this faith are accepted because, enabled by grace, they are responding to the grace they have received.[34] What they have not yet received is justifying grace; and that is what they are seeking as they attend their class meetings and attempt to keep the Methodist discipline.

As I noted earlier, Wesley also came to believe that while justifying grace normally brought with it an assurance, it did not do so necessarily. While Wesley continued to insist that the witness of the Spirit is a normal element in conversion to be both sought and expected, he also held that the indirect "witness of our own spirit" could infer that one is both justified and regenerated even without the direct witness.[35]

Wesley could make this distinction because justification is an act of God. It is sought by the awakened sinner who has the servant faith, and promised to those who seek it—"unless the servants of God halt by the way, they will receive the adoption of sons"[36]—but the timing is God's. Wesley's insistence that justification is instantaneous ultimately rests on both the nature of the act itself (one is either forgiven or one is not) and on the divine agency that accomplishes it.

Yet there is a necessary human role in justification, and that is to accept it by faith. Thus "faith is the condition, and the only condition of justification. . . . [N]one is justified but he that believes; without faith no man is justified."[37] As we have seen, faith itself is a gift of God, a spiritual sense enabling us to know the love and forgiveness of God. But thereby enabled, it is also a human act of trusting in God, without which we are not justified.

This distinction between divine and human agency is important lest we see our believing in some way causing our justification rather than receiving it as a gift. Salvation, according to Wesley, is by grace alone. At the same time, salvation is essentially relational, necessarily involving grace-enabled human response in both faith and obedience. Thus, although "some infer, that repentance and faith are mere gifts as remission of sins," this is not so; "for man co-operates in the former, but not in the latter. God alone forgives sins."[38]

The immediate effect of justification is to transform the faith of a servant into the faith of a child of God. The relationship with God is fundamentally altered, from obedience to God out of fear (servant) to a response out of both fear and love (child); with sanctification the love grows until perfect love (Christian perfection) casts out fear.

Justification, then, is an encounter with God whose effects are not only forensic but also transformative, both as to our relationship with God and our motivation for obedience. The forensic element—forgiveness that removes the guilt of sin—at the same time removes the barrier that sin has placed between God and us. Combined with the gratitude evoked by the love of God in providing for our forgiveness through the cross of Jesus Christ, this removal of guilt enables a new relationship marked by love. That is why Wesley states, regarding justification and the new birth: "In order of time neither of these is before the other. . . . But in order of thinking, as it is termed, justification precedes the new birth. We first conceive his wrath to be turned away, and then his Spirit to work in our hearts."[39] The turning away of God's wrath in justification is more than pardon; it creates the new relationship of the faith of a child that will both enable and characterize sanctification. It is in this way that justification and sanctification, though distinct works of God, are nonetheless intrinsically linked.

Affective Transformation: The New Birth

The new birth is the central element in the drama of human redemption. It is the point in which the human heart itself is transformed by the Holy Spirit, the beginning of a process of sanctification that culminates in another decisive work of the Spirit—Christian perfection. It is thus both the precondition for and the actual beginning of God's re-creation of persons in love.

Wesley's language describing the new birth is remarkably consistent. Again and again he insists that this "instantaneous change" brings "a peace that passeth all understanding, a joy unspeakable, full of glory, the love of God and all mankind filling the heart, and power over all sin."[40] Among these elements that constitute the new birth, the latter two are most significant. Love for God and neighbor, and power over sin are directly related to both the content and goal of salvation. They also are reciprocally related to each other, as the presence of love necessarily entails power over sin and the concomitant end of sin's power over us.

We can best understand the necessity of the new birth by examining Wesley's understanding of the human condition. We were created in the image of God, and most especially in God's moral image: " 'God is love': accordingly man at his creation was full of love, which was the sole principle of all his tempers, thoughts, words, and actions. God is full of justice, mercy, and truth: so was man as he came from the hands of his Creator."[41]

With the Fall, Adam "lost the life of God" as "he was separated from him in union with whom his spiritual life consisted." He "lost both the knowledge and the love of God, without which the image of God would not subsist." He became "unholy as well as unhappy," sinking "into pride and self-will, the very image of the devil, and into sensual appetites and desires, the image of the beasts that perish."[42]

In this description of the human predicament we see the necessity of the gift of faith for restoring our ability to know God, and of justification, which restores the relationship with God that enables our spiritual life. Yet we also see why these are not sufficient. Human nature itself has been corrupted through unholy tempers that now govern the heart. When we are convicted of sin, we can desire to change, and indeed can alter our behavior to a degree; but in the end we find we cannot break this power of sin over our lives. "This," says Wesley, "is the foundation of the new birth—the entire corruption of our nature."[43] It requires a transformation of the heart itself, and that only God can do.

What we believe about fallen humanity will inevitably affect our belief about the nature of salvation. If we do not understand human nature to be entirely corrupted, then there is no need for the kind of new birth Wesley envisions. Salvation could be conceived as gradual with no instantaneous transformation. But if, like Wesley, we see the heart as entirely corrupted, then a transformative act of God becomes the necessary precondition for gradual growth in sanctification, that is, for the Christian life itself. For Wesley the new birth is in fact "a part of sanctification"; "it is the gate of it, the entrance into it."[44]

As the entrance into sanctification, the new birth decisively changes the fundamental dispositions of the heart. It is, says Wesley, that "change wrought in the whole soul by the almighty Spirit of God" in which "love of the world is changed into love of God, pride into humility, passion into meekness; hatred, envy, malice, into a sincere, tender, disinterested love for all mankind."[45]

It is here that holy affection and tempers begin to supplant the unholy, and love for God and neighbor take root and begin to govern the heart.[46] Just as conviction of sin with the faith of a servant brought with it a change in external behavior, the new birth with the faith of a child of God brings with it a new set of internal dispositions. As it is on the basis of the gift of faith that we can grow in the knowledge of God, so it is on the basis of the gift of a new birth that we can grow in the love of God.

In this way God begins the work of restoring the image of God in the human heart. This restoration is finally accomplished by Christian perfection, a second instantaneous transformation in which the corruption is entirely healed and love for God and neighbor fully governs the heart and life. For Wesley "nothing short of this is Christian religion," which involves "a restoration not only to the favour, but likewise to the image of God" and implies "not barely deliverance from sin but the being filled with the fullness of God."[47]

I have argued that conversion is normally instantaneous because it is essentially a complex of interrelated transformative acts of God, accomplishing that which we, due to our fallen nature, cannot.[48] Conversion is an encounter with God's love that lays a new foundation relationally and dispositionally, enabling subsequent growth in the Christian life. Given the entire corruption of the moral image of God and God's intention to fully restore that image in this life, only the re-creative power of the Holy Spirit is sufficient for such a task. Thus salvation cannot be conceived as only gradual; it must also involve instantaneous transformation.

In light of this it might be asked why salvation could not be completely instantaneous—if it is ultimately through the creative power of God, why does God not do it all at once? Wesley himself seems to have been tempted by this line of thought, initially confusing the new birth with Christian perfection.[49] The answer has to do with God's purpose in restoring humanity to the moral image of God. As God freely loves us, and has done so even unto death on a cross, so God seeks a people who will also love in freedom. So while both conversion and Christian perfection are seemingly irresistible as acts of God, they come only to those who desire and are open to receive them, that is, those who are responding to the gradual work of God in their lives. Likewise, conversion and Christian perfection are retained only by those who continue to grow in grace daily. The gradual work of salvation before and after conversion consists of an ongoing relationship with God; the instantaneous work of conversion provides a new foundation in the human heart that transforms the relationship from that of a servant to that of a child of God.

Wesley's soteriology recognized both divine and human agencies in a way that neither diminished God's love and power nor denied human sin and finitude. He took full account of the effects of the entire corruption of the human heart, while insisting that the promise of Christian perfection has fulfillment in this life. To lose the integration of instantaneous and gradual aspects of salvation risks unraveling these central elements of Wesley's theology. Such an impoverishment could lead to a false optimism or, more likely, a this-worldly despair that settles for far less than the salvation promised by God.

Chapter Three

John Wesley and the Fear of Death as a Standard of Conversion

Kenneth J. Collins

As an adept spiritual counselor, John Wesley realized that the lure of inbred sin was so strong, even among the children of God, that unless certain normative elements were in place to keep believers spiritually honest, they would quickly fall under the power of self-deception and delusion once more. To prevent this malaise, Wesley underscored the importance of three elements as conducive to both honesty and spiritual health. First of all, Wesley emphasized that a conscience rightly informed by the Word of God, especially the moral law, is a gift of grace that holds in place a "true knowledge of ourselves."[1] Second, in a way that George Whitefield had not, Wesley appreciated the value of the accountability and truthfulness required in small groups such as the classes, bands, and select societies that were an integral part of Methodist discipline and practice. Indeed, one of the probing questions asked of all band members, for example, was this: "Do you desire that in doing this [participating in the bands] we should come as close as possible, that we should cut to the quick, and search your heart to the bottom?"[2] This rigorous, and at times uncomfortable, sort of questioning bespeaks of the third element, namely, the pastoral practice of both John and Charles Wesley to gauge the spiritual estate of the Methodists by inquiring whether they were afraid to die, that is, whether they were willing to depart and be with Christ.[3]

Though hardly appreciated by contemporary scholarship, the motif of the fear of death as an indicator of one's spiritual condition surfaces repeatedly in the writings of John Wesley. As Martin Schmidt has pointed out in a chapter ("The Conversion") of his work *John Wesley: A Theological Biography*:

> Once again it was the fear of death which aroused in [Wesley] ultimate questions. The possibility of death indeed runs like a recurring theme through the whole period of his spiritual development. During his student days he was brought sharply up against the fact of death by the passing of friends and acquaintances: John Griffith, William Morgan, and a young girl whose name we do not know had died almost before his own eyes. On each occasion he was sharply confronted by the question of "conversion," that complete turning to God.[4]

However, before tracing the motif of the fear of death and its relationship to Wesley's understanding of conversion and real Christianity in his writings, a few distinctions are in order lest there be misunderstanding. In a letter dated January 15, 1731, Wesley maintains that not all fear of death is negative and that some fear is actually necessary for the continuation of life: "But if pain and the fear of death were extinguished," he observes, "no animal could long subsist."[5] In this context, then, fear of death is not indicative of a problematic existential or spiritual condition; instead, it is a remarkable and useful "intuition" to sustain and preserve life, an intuition that characterizes all believers no matter how holy. In contrast, the negative senses of the fear of death from which believers can rightly expect to be delivered are enumerated in Wesley's *A Farther Appeal to Men of Reason and Religion*, published in 1745. Wesley notes:

> Men commonly fear death, first because of leaving their worldly goods and pleasures; [second], for fear of the pains of death; and, [third], for fear of perpetual damnation. But none of these causes trouble good men, because they stay themselves by *true* faith, perfect charity, and sure hope of endless joy and bliss everlasting.[6]

Though Wesley maintains that people of true faith are not marked by the fear of death in any of the senses just enumerated, he nevertheless was sensitive enough to distinguish between fear of the prospect of physical pain in the dying process itself and the fear of perpetual damnation. Such a judgment is substantiated by Wesley's pastoral care for the sick and dying, especially in terms of the alleviation of pain,[7] as well as his repeated—and almost exclusive—emphasis in his writings on fear in the third sense: fear of judgment and eternal loss.

Wesley, Before Aldersgate, Fears Death

On October 14, 1735, John Wesley, along with his brother Charles, who was recently ordained, headed out for Gravesend to depart for Georgia. Accompanying them were Benjamin Ingham of Queen's College, Oxford, and Charles Delamotte, the son of a London merchant. At the Gravesend dock, the four boarded the *Simmonds* along with twenty-six Moravians and others. Though the *Simmonds* was a seaworthy vessel, Atlantic crossings in the eighteenth century could be quite dangerous. The sheer length of the voyage, in this case several months, allowed for the likelihood that the vessel would be pummeled by Atlantic storms that invariably arose during this season. On November 23, for instance, Wesley lay in his cabin only to be awakened by the tossing of the ship and the roaring of the wind, both of which showed him that he was, to use his own words, "unwilling to die."[8]

Though the voyage had been relatively smooth during December, the weather deteriorated in January 1736. Indeed, several powerful storms gathered in the Atlantic and buffeted the *Simmonds* during the period of January 17 through 25. On the first day of this ordeal, Wesley recounted in his journal that "the sea broke over us from stem to stern, burst through the windows of the state cabin where three or four of us were, and covered us all over, though a bureau sheltered me from the main shock."[9] And nature, so powerful and awesome, once again evoked a response of fear from Wesley: "[I was] very uncertain whether I should wake alive, and much ashamed of my unwillingness to die." Yet another storm appeared during the evening of January 23, and

Wesley confessed in his journal: "I could not but say to myself, 'How is it that thou hast no faith?' being still unwilling to die."[10] But the most powerful and frightening of all the storms en route to Georgia did not occur until two days later. The vivid detail of Wesley's journal account, together with his several judgments, demonstrate that this storm in particular had left an indelible impression on the anxious traveler. Wesley recalls:

> In the midst of the psalm wherewith their service began the sea broke over, split the mainsail in pieces, covered the ship, and poured in between the decks, as if the great deep had already swallowed us up. A terrible screaming began among the English. The Germans calmly sung on. I asked one of them afterwards, "Was you not afraid?" He answered, "I thank God, no." I asked, "But were not your women and children afraid?" He replied mildly, "No; our women and children are not afraid to die."[11]

So taken was Wesley with the Moravian courage and serenity in the face of such great danger that he appended to this account: "This was the most glorious day which I have ever hitherto seen."[12]

Upon later reflection, Wesley drew a connection between the powers of nature and the state of one's soul. "I can conceive no difference comparable to that between a smooth and a rough sea," he writes, "except that which is between a mind calmed by the love of God and one torn up by the storms of earthly passions."[13] Moreover, in July 1736, when Wesley was in America, he experienced a horrific thunderstorm and confessed in his journal, once again, that he was "not fit to die."[14] And a couple of weeks later, while he was on a boat crossing the neck of St. Helena Sound, off the coast of South Carolina, Wesley encountered yet another ominous storm. So furious were the wind and rain that they collapsed the mast of the ship, terrifying all on board. Of this incident, Wesley concluded with respect to himself, "How is it that thou hadst no faith?"[15]

After the collapse of his Georgia ministry, Wesley boarded the *Samuel,* of which Captain Percy was the commander. On Christmas Eve the ship sailed over Charleston bar and soon lost sight of land. A few days later Wesley experienced what today might be referred to as an anxiety attack: "Finding the unaccountable apprehensions of I know not what danger (the wind being small, and the sea smooth), . . . I cried earnestly for help, and it pleased God as in a moment to restore peace to my soul."[16] In the wake of this unsettling incident, Wesley observed that "whoever is uneasy on any account (bodily pain alone excepted) carries in himself his own conviction that he is so far an unbeliever." More particularly, Wesley added: "Is he uneasy at the apprehension of death? Then he believeth not that 'to die is gain.'"[17] Beyond this, shortly before Wesley arrived in England he connected the three elements of the truthfulness of the gospel, being a real Christian, and the fear of death in a way that expressed his own spiritual condition:

> Whoever sees me, sees I *would* be a Christian. Therefore "are my ways not like other men's ways." Therefore I have been, I am, I am content to be, "a by-word, a proverb of reproach." But in a storm I think, "What if the gospel be not true?" Then thou art of all men most foolish. For what hast thou given thy goods, thy ease, thy friends, thy reputation, thy country, thy life? For what art thou wandering over the face of the earth? A dream, "a cunningly devised fable"? O who will deliver me from this fear of death![18]

Wesley, After Aldersgate, No Longer Fears Death

Around the time Wesley received assurance of his justification and regeneration at Aldersgate, Wesley's own fear of death dissipated, never again to emerge in his journal, though he continued to apply this standard of spiritual health to others.[19] Still very much in the first flush of his Aldersgate experience, Wesley appeared before the venerable of Oxford University, at St. Mary's Church on June 11, 1738, and delivered a sermon that Albert Outler has rightly termed Wesley's "evangelical manifesto."[20] On that day, Wesley boldly proclaimed to all who would hear the liberties of the gospel, of which one was surely freedom from both guilt and sinful fear. "Not indeed from a filial fear of offending," Wesley cautioned, "but from all servile fear, from that 'fear which hath torment,' from fear of punishment, from fear of the wrath of God."[21] A couple of months later, while Wesley was visiting the Moravian community at Herrnhut, he noted, with apparent approval, Christian David's association of conversion with being set free from the spirit of fear: "Yet they were not properly *converted;* and they were not *delivered from* the spirit of fear; they had not *new hearts;* neither had they received the 'gift of the Holy Ghost.' "[22]

Six years later, when Wesley preached his last sermon at St. Mary's, Oxford (probably because he had referred to those assembled as a "generation of *triflers;* triflers with God, with one another, and with your own souls"[23]), he not only proclaimed that one who is justified and born of God is free from the fear of death, but he also linked this fear, a fear that has torment, specifically with the spirit of bondage. In his sermon "Scriptural Christianity," for example, Wesley elaborates:

> He [the Christian believer] feared not what man could do unto him, knowing the very hairs of his head were all numbered. He feared not all the powers of darkness, whom God was daily bruising under his feet. Least of all was he afraid to die; nay, he desired to "depart, and to be with Christ"; (Phil.i.23;) who, "through death, had destroyed him that had the power of death, even the devil; and delivered them who, through fear of death, were all their lifetime," till then, "subject to bondage."[24]

And the following year, in his treatise *A Farther Appeal to Men of Reason and Religion,* Wesley associates the fear of death, the spirit of bondage, and the Jewish dispensation in a way that underscores the liberty of the gospel, especially when he points out that " 'the Jews were subject to the fear of death, and lived in consequence of it in a state of bondage.' "[25]

But perhaps the best and most lucid explication of the connection between the fear of death and the spirit of bondage is found in Wesley's sermon "The Spirit of Bondage and of Adoption," which was written in 1746. In this sermon, Wesley explores the "legal state," that spiritual condition prior to the liberating and empowering graces of the gospel. Indeed, the one "under the law" finds that "sin let loose upon the soul . . . is perfect misery," Wesley notes. "He feels . . . fear of death, as being to him the gate of hell, the entrance of death eternal."[26] Interestingly enough, Wesley explores this bondage, energized by the fear of death and the dominion of sin, in terms of the duplicity, the division of the will, which is articulated by the apostle Paul in the seventh chapter of Romans: "For that which I do, I allow not; for what I would, I do not; but what I hate, that I do." Again, those under a spirit of bondage feel sorrow and remorse; they fear death, the devil, and humanity. They desire to break free from the chains of sin but cannot, and their cry of despair is typified by the Pauline expression: "O wretched man that I am, who shall deliver me from the body of this death?"[27] And in considering the spiritual estate of the person under such enslaving powers, Wesley affirms: "Such is the bondage under which [one] groan[s]; such the tyranny of [a] hard [task]master."[28]

Wesley's exploration of the motif of the fear of death, as well as its linkage to the spirit of bondage, was not merely an early emphasis, but one that continued throughout his career. For instance, in 1750, in his sermon "The Original, Nature, Properties, and Use of the Law," Wesley cautions the reader about being "entangled again with the yoke of bondage," and he counsels that one should "abhor sin far more than death or hell; abhor sin itself far more than the punishment of it."[29] That same year, in his sermon "Satan's Devices," the Methodist leader reminds those who have become the sons and daughters of God that "if your eye be not steadily fixed on him who hath borne all your sins, he will bring you again under that 'fear of death,' whereby you was so long 'subject unto bondage.' "[30] In fact, in his sermon "The Wilderness State" (1760), Wesley chronicles the slow and subtle descent into sin, and the reemergence of a spirit of fear:

> We begin to doubt whether we ever did find in our hearts the real testimony of the Spirit. Whether we did not rather deceive our own souls, and mistake the voice of nature for the voice of God. . . . And these doubts are again joined with servile fear, with that "fear" which "hath torment." We fear the wrath of God, even as before we believed; we fear lest we should be cast out of his presence; and thence sink again into that fear of death from which we were before wholly delivered.[31]

Moreover, while on a preaching tour in Ireland in 1762, Wesley evidently witnessed at Waterford the execution of four young men convicted of breaking into houses, and he exclaimed in his journal: "O what but love can cast out the fear of death! And how inexpressibly miserable is that bondage!"[32] In 1772, Wesley dined with one who, as he put it, was "completely miserable through 'the spirit of bondage' and, in particular, through the fear of death."[33]

Beyond this considerable evidence, and much more could be cited, Wesley's letter to Thomas Davenport in 1781 is especially significant because in it Wesley reveals quite clearly that the spirit of bondage—that "legal faith" that is under the power or dominion of sin and is therefore plagued by the fear of death and judgment—is not, and cannot be, justifying faith. Wesley explains:

> You are in the hands of a wise Physician, who is lancing your sores in order to heal them. He has *given* you now *the spirit of fear.* But it is in order to *the spirit of love and of a sound mind.* You have now *received the spirit of bondage.* Is it not the forerunner of the Spirit of adoption? He is not afar off. Look up! And expect Him to cry in your heart, Abba, Father! He is nigh that justifieth.[34]

Others may have confused the spirit of bondage with justifying faith. Clearly, Wesley did not.

As a mature and sensitive pastor, Wesley did not want to discourage those under the spirit of bondage lest they would despair of ever receiving justifying and regenerating graces; so he freely acknowledged that the conviction associated with this fearful spirit did indeed mark a measure of grace as well as a species of faith. Perhaps even more important, in his sermon "On the Discoveries of Faith" (1788), Wesley underscores the connection between the spirit of bondage unto fear and the faith of a servant, demonstrating once again that such faith, understood in its broad sense, is not justifying faith.[35] "Exhort him to press on by all possible means, till he passes 'from faith to faith; from the faith of a *servant* to the faith of a *son;* from the spirit of bondage unto fear, to the spirit of childlike love.' "[36] This is not to deny, of course, that Wesley actually understood the faith of a servant in two key ways. One sense of this faith—what Wesley termed the "exempt cases" or "exceptions," and which may be called the narrow sense—is indeed characterized by both justifying and regenerating graces, though not by assurance. However, whenever Wesley explored the faith of a servant in the broad sense (that is, in relation to the fear of death and the spirit of bondage), it never constituted justifying faith.[37] Therefore the assumption held by some contemporary Wesley scholars, that the "faith of a servant" is unproblematically justifying faith in each and every instance, not only fails to take into account that Wesley actually employed this phrase in two ways but also has the unfortunate effect of lowering Wesley's high standards for the proper Christian faith.

Justification, Regeneration, and Assurance as Deliverance from the Fear of Death

The preceding pages have demonstrated that Wesley explored the motif of the fear of death in terms of the spirit of bondage, a spirit that, because it is under the power or dominion of sin, fails to enjoy the deeper graces of God. But Wesley also considered this motif in a more positive fashion and linked deliverance from the fear of death with justification, the new birth, and a measure of assurance, the same three elements that constitute what Wesley termed *conversion*.

In November 1738, for example, Wesley recorded in his journal the experience of John Lancaster, who was justified by God's grace, having received the forgiveness of sins, and who maintained: "From that hour I have never been afraid to die."[38] In 1744, in his sermon "Scriptural Christianity," Wesley declared that one who was justified by faith in Christ had peace: "He feared not all the powers of darkness, whom God was daily bruising under his feet. Least of all was he afraid to die; nay, he desired to 'depart and to be with Christ' (Phil. 1:23)." A few years later, Wesley marveled at the transformation of John Roberts, a burglar, who sought repentance and the forgiveness of sins with the salutary result that he soon declared "the burden of sin was gone; that the fear of death was utterly taken away, and it returned no more."[39] In 1756, Wesley noted in his journal the experience of Richard Varley, who was about to be executed at York for the crime of highway robbery. The condemned man had received the remission of sins recently and therefore wrote to his suffering wife just hours before his death that Christ "has taken away the sting of death, and I am prepared to meet my God."[40] And in 1781, in his sermon "The End of Christ's Coming," Wesley affirmed, in the words of the apostle Paul, that "being justified by faith, we have peace with God through our Lord Jesus Christ." He then added: "That peace . . . which delivers us from all perplexing doubts, from all tormenting fears, and in particular from that 'fear of death whereby we were all our life-time subject to bondage.' "[41]

As forestated, Wesley linked freedom from the fear of death not only with the graces of justification but also with those of the new birth and assurance. In 1745, for instance, Wesley took note of the experience of Molly Thomas who, after she had received the assurance that her sins were forgiven, gave evidence that the power of the fear of death was broken.[42] During this same period, Wesley also considered the witness of Mary Cook who, though gravely ill, professed to her mother, "I am happy, I am happy . . . I am assured of God's love to my soul. I am not afraid to die."[43] The following year, in his sermon "The Way to the Kingdom," Wesley articulated the great liberties enjoyed by the children of God, even babes in Christ, who had a measure of assurance: "It is a peace that banishes . . . fear," Wesley exclaimed. "All such fear as hath torment; the fear of the wrath of God, the fear of hell, the fear of the devil, and, in particular, the fear of death."[44] And in terms of regeneration itself Wesley maintained, in his sermon "The Law Established Through Faith, Discourse I," that a child of God is no longer under the Mosaic institution, and so "he is delivered from the wrath and curse of God, from all sense of guilt and condemnation, and from all that horror and fear of death and hell whereby he was 'all his life' before subject to bondage.' "[45] Beyond this, late in his career, in his sermon "Heavenly Treasure in Earthen Vessels" (1790), Wesley once again proclaimed the grace and liberty entailed in the new birth:

> The persons concerning whom he is here speaking are those that are born of God, those that, "being justified by faith," have now "redemption in the blood of Jesus, even the forgive-

> ness of sins"; those who enjoy that peace of God which passeth all understanding. . . . This then is the treasure which they have received, a faith of the operation of God, a peace which sets them above the fear of death, and enables them in everything to be content.[46]

The Fear of Death as a Test of Christian Experience

Since Wesley explored the fear of death repeatedly in terms of the spirit of bondage, and since he marked the liberation from such fear and slavery in terms of justification, the new birth, and assurance (conversion), it is not surprising that Wesley painstakingly recorded in his journal numerous accounts of people who had been delivered from just such a fear. Among other things, Wesley seems to have taken a special interest in the experiences of children. Entries in his journal include the dates of 1745, 1746, 1750, and 1764. In 1764, for instance, Wesley marveled at the faith of a five- or six-year-old child who had "many serious thoughts about death and judgment" but who received a measure of the love of God.[47] Beyond this, Wesley took special note of the testimony of Dr. Annesley, his maternal grandfather. Indeed, Wesley's mother, Susanna, remarked to her inquiring and curious son that a little before her father's death, her father "had no darkness, no fear, no doubt at all of his being 'accepted in the Beloved.' "[48] Add to this the substance of Wesley's preaching on several occasions—for instance, in 1759 at Robinhood's-Bay, where he proclaimed: "No man is delivered from the fear of death but he that fears God"[49]—and a picture of Wesley begins to emerge as one who did indeed employ the question of whether one had been set free from the fear of death as a gauge of genuine Christian experience.

Wesley realized that the Methodists, like other Christians, ran the risk of taking comfort in the *form* of religion without its *power.* In other words, quite real was the temptation to assure *themselves* that all was well with their souls precisely because they had vigorously undertaken works of piety, mercy, and the like; or because they had used all the means of grace assiduously; or because, leaning on that broken reed, "they were not as bad as other people." In "A Word to a Protestant," Wesley cautions:

> How do you hope to be saved? by doing thus and thus? by doing no harm, and paying every man his own, and saying your prayers, and going to church and sacrament? Alas! alas! Now you have thrown off the mask: This is Popery barefaced. You may just as well speak plain, and say, "I trust to be saved by the merit of my own works."[50]

Accordingly, in order to dispel the spiritual stupor that could easily encompass the soul in its many and sinful attempts at self-justification (where the work of inward religion, the religion of the heart, would be viewed as a "pious indulgence," or as a "needless extravagance"), Wesley applied the corrective of his probing query: "But are you afraid to die, are you willing to depart and be with Christ?" To be sure, just as with the illuminating and accusatory power of the moral law, such an uncomfortable question, through the grace of the Holy Spirit, could cut to the quick and break through the layers of self-deception and self-justification in which the sinful soul had placed its trust. Wesley, therefore, invited the Methodists to undertake the painful existential and spiritual work often entailed in dispositional change, a change that would, through the empowering grace of God, instantiate the holy tempers of love in the believing soul.

Furthermore, so intent was Wesley in making the question of whether one had been set free from the fear of death one of his more important soteriological standards that he specifically explored this probe in terms of his well-worked motif of real Christianity.[51] Thus, in his *Farther Appeal to Men of Reason and Religion*, Wesley quotes from a "Sermon Against the Fear of Death" and agrees that "a true Christian man is not afraid to die."[52] Elsewhere, in "A Thought on Necessity," Wesley exclaims: "O what advantage has a Christian (a real Christian) over an Infidel! He sees God! Consequently . . . he tramples on inexorable fate, and fear, and death, and hell!"[53] But perhaps the best example of the explicit association of freedom from the fear of death with the real or proper Christian faith is found in Wesley's spiritual counsel to Ms. Cummins late in his career: "O make haste! Be a Christian, a real Bible Christian now! You may say, 'Nay, I am a Christian already.' I fear not. (See how freely I speak.) A Christian is not afraid to die. Are not you? Do you desire to depart and to be with

Christ?"[54] So then, if Wesley affirmed in the 1770s that a real Christian is not afraid to die, then what does that make him while he was in Georgia forty years earlier? Remember his terror during those powerful Atlantic storms!

The motifs of the fear of death and real Christianity together demonstrate that Wesley lacked the proper Christian faith while he was in Georgia. Ignoring this has, in turn, allowed some contemporary Wesley scholarship to misprize Wesley's own spiritual journey and soteriological standards, and, in extreme cases, to "debunk" or at least to minimize unjustly the significance of Wesley's experience at Aldersgate.[55] On the contrary, and in light of considerable evidence, it must now be affirmed that Aldersgate was not only the time of Wesley's justification and regeneration, but also the occasion upon which he was delivered from the sinful fear of death. At Aldersgate, then, Wesley received, through the sheer grace of God, not the spirit of bondage unto fear, but the spirit of adoption, even the spirit of a child of God, whereby he could now cry, "Abba, Father."

Chapter Four

A Real Christian Is an Abolitionist: Conversion and Antislavery Activism in Early American Methodism

Douglas Strong

It was a June day in 1775, just two months after the battles of Lexington and Concord. The citizens of Harford County, Maryland—like their counterparts in the rest of British North America—were preoccupied with politics and military preparation. Freeborn Garrettson,[1] a prosperous young slaveowner, a devout Anglican, and "a professed friend to the American cause," had plans to spend the day with his neighbors attending a "general review" of the local unit of the Maryland militia. At daybreak, however, Garrettson was aroused from sleep "by an awful voice [saying], 'Awake, sinner, for you are not prepared to die.' " Instantly, Garrettson was "smitten with conviction." He hastened out of bed and cried out, "Lord have mercy on my soul!"[2]

Garrettson did not go to the military parade that day. Instead, he devoted his morning to meditative prayer, and in the afternoon he attended a meeting held by the Methodists—a group he had visited before. After soul searching, Garrettson determined that he possessed "a form of godliness" but lacked genuine faith in Christ. Visibly shaken, Garrettson sought counsel from his Anglican pastor. The minister tried to convince him that his current spiritual condition was adequate, since he led "an upright life." Methodists, the pastor explained to Garrettson, "carried matters too far" by insisting that Christians needed to turn from sin consciously and experience an assurance of regeneration. But it was precisely the Methodists' soteriological distinction between nominal faith and saving faith that Garrettson found to be persuasive in reference to his own life. Garrettson believed that he needed to know "sensibly" that his sins were forgiven. Soon, Garrettson experienced the conversion he had been seeking—but only by submitting to God's gracious initiative. He vowed to God to "part with all and become a humble follower of thine."[3]

Despite this powerful experience of divine favor, the next few days were not easy ones for Garrettson. He was still distressed about his relationship with God. He felt emotionally despondent, though he was uncertain about the cause of his despair. Somehow his conversion seemed incomplete. He had experienced the new birth, but perhaps there was something more for him to do; perhaps his life was not as morally "upright" as he had previously supposed. Theologically, he was arriving at the Methodist understanding that an initiatory experience of Christ was only the beginning of a sanctified life. After spending some time by himself, with only his Bible to accompany him, Garrettson suddenly received spiritual clarity from God: "It is not right for you to keep your fellow creatures in bondage; you must let the oppressed go free." Garrettson paused a minute and then replied, "Lord, the oppressed shall go free." Later, he wrote that at the very time he gave his slaves their liberty, he too felt "at liberty" to experience the joy of his salvation.

> Had I the tongue of an angel, I could not fully describe what I felt: all my dejection and that melancholy gloom, which preyed upon me, vanished in a moment: a divine sweetness ran through my whole frame—O! in what a wonderful manner was my poor soul set into the depths of my Redeemer's love! . . . I . . . now . . . wished to spread my Redeemer's glory to the ends of the world.[4]

Not surprisingly, Garrettson soon began traveling as a Methodist itinerant, eventually becoming second only to Francis Asbury as a leader of early American Methodism. He corresponded regularly with John Wesley and became one of the interpreters of Wesleyan doctrine and practice for the American church. Through the years, Garrettson was known for his evangelistic zeal, his advocacy in behalf of greater democratic usages within the Methodist Episcopal institutional structure, and his unceasing remonstration against slavery. Combining biblical ideas with the democratic ideas of the American Revolution, he frequently contrasted the freedom of the gospel to the bondage of the world—whether bondage to sin or bondage to human despots.[5]

Besides preaching against slavery, Garrettson also wrote an antislavery tract—in the form of a moral allegory—directed toward those slaveholders who claimed to be Christians. In this tract, a fictional abolitionist named Do-Justice confronted a slaveowner named Professing Christian.[6] Do-Justice challenged Professing Christian to examine his life in order to determine if he actually had saving faith. In Garrettson's mind, the enslavement of other people indicated one's continued enslavement to sin, thus negating the possibility of a living, sanctifying relationship with God. At the end of the story, Professing Christian was converted to genuine faith in Christ. He freed his slaves and became an abolitionist, and his name changed from Professing Christian to Real Christian.[7]

Garrettson's use of the phrase "real Christian" was indicative of his dependence on Wesley as a theological mentor. Wesley often spoke about "real Christianity" as a way of designating vital regenerative faith in contrast to nominal or formalistic religion. Real Christians, Wesley taught, had a conscious assurance of divine acceptance.[8] Wesley wrote, for instance, that "every Christian believer has a perceptible testimony of God's Spirit that he is a child of God." But genuine faith entailed more than just spiritual experience; it included a sanctified lifestyle. Wesley contended that a person who wished to "be a real Christian [should] . . . 'deny himself, . . . and take up his cross daily, and follow [Jesus].' "[9] Wesley also employed the phrase "real Christian" in conjunction with the freedom that justified believers receive from their captivity to evil. In his commentary on Romans 8:15,[10] Wesley stated that real Christians were those who "have not received the spirit of bondage."[11]

Such descriptions resonated with Garrettson's twofold interest in conversion and antislavery. Garrettson discovered a way to bring together Wesley's theology with the democratic ideology prevalent in the early republic. As a result, he took the Wesleyan concept of the new birth, viewed as one's initial sanctification leading the believer to a life of holiness, and interpreted it in relation to the American context. For Garrettson (like Wesley before him), a real Christian was one who was converted to Christ; and, since conversion necessarily implied disengagement from the sin of slavery, then, according to Garrettson, a real Christian was also an abolitionist.[12]

Many other Methodists in the revolutionary period, steeped in the democratic idiom of the day, linked the Wesleyan understanding of conversion directly to their commitment to abolition. Consequently, the Methodist Episcopal Church in its early days maintained a strong position against slaveholding. During the succeeding years, however, this uncompromising position was whittled away. A number of historians have offered explanations for the abandonment of abolitionist standards among antebellum American Methodists. They note that the rise of sectionalism and the desire to expand the church in the South caused denominational leaders to surrender the church's antislavery principles.[13]

While these sociopolitical and ecclesiastical factors help to explain the decline of antislavery among American Methodists, it is also important to take into account certain changes in theological emphasis regarding the consequences of salvation. That is, the specific moral effects expected from one's conversion changed in the early decades of the nineteenth century. Methodists altered one of the key demands required of convicted sinners who hoped to be saved and of regenerated believers who hoped to be sanctified—the demand to renounce slavery. As a result, by the 1840s, only a few of Garrettson's denominational heirs retained the original American Methodist viewpoint that antislavery was an integral part of the order of salvation.

The Early American Methodist Understanding of Conversion

But what was the American Methodist belief and practice regarding conversion?[14] It is important to remember that Methodism in America began with the evangelistic preaching of laypeople such as Robert Strawbridge, Thomas Webb, and Barbara Heck. Due to the scarcity of ordained clergy and to the non-Anglican roots of many of the movement's followers, American Methodism—to a greater degree than its English sibling—tended to neglect the sacerdotal aspects of ministry. Even the liturgical forms that Wesley had suggested in his Sunday Service generally were replaced by more extemporaneous modes of prayer and preaching.[15] This informal and conversionistic orientation of Methodist church life corresponded to the predominant evangelical ethos of the early republic. Indeed, evangelicalism became the unofficial religious establishment in the new nation, so much so that when Robert Baird attempted to write a comprehensive description of "religion in the United States" in 1844, he concluded that nearly all denominations of significance adhered to one fundamental concept: that a conversion experience was normative for Christian belief. By the antebellum period, Americans who presumed themselves to be religious were expected to be able to narrate a spiritual transformation in specifically evangelical terms.[16]

For Methodists, this evangelical conversionism had a communal context; that is, the medium for their conversion experiences was usually a gathering or "conference" of some sort. Methodists seemed to have a distinctive affinity for group meetings. Although men and women who were convicted of their sins sometimes took a meditative walk in the woods or spent solitary time in prayer, the formative defining moments of conversion usually occurred in an associational setting, such as a class meeting, prayer meeting, quarterly conference, love feast, watchnight service, or camp meeting.[17]

Paradoxically, these corporate times of prayer, singing, exhortation, biblical exposition, testimony, and mutual accountability were also opportunities for affirming an individual's sense of worth, and particularly the self-worth of those excluded from the power structures of the broader society, such as women, slaves, poor laborers, and young people. Contemporary accounts indicate that youth and young adults were especially attracted to Methodist meetings because at such events their spiritual experiences were authenticated.[18] Historian Lester Ruth has determined that these expressions of fellowship became the "dominant aspect of early Methodist ecclesiology" and served as the primary agency for experiencing divine grace.[19]

American Methodists congregated because, according to their own statements, they received acceptance from their Christian brothers and sisters, and from God. In fact, these two features of Methodist spirituality were closely linked. The familial Christian companionship of prayer meetings, class meetings, and camp meetings—often referred to as a "melting time"—was an important instrumental means for believers to experience the intimacy of God's Spirit. Similarly, a consciousness of God's presence enabled Methodists to sense closeness among God's people. James Horton, a preaching associate of Freeborn Garrettson, exhibited this interrelationship between the divine and human community in an ecstatic way at a love feast:

> While the brethren were passing the bread and water around . . . I was greatly blessed—my soul so filled with the love of God, that for some time I was lost to all that was passing around me. It appeared to me that I was taken up into heaven . . . and there I saw the shining happy millions flaming around his throne in such immortal beauty that my tongue cannot describe it. . . . When I came to my recollection, I was standing up on my seat with my hands uplifted, and when I looked down upon the people around me, they looked like the shining ones in whose company I seemed to be the moment before in the heavenly world.[20]

The converting grace that American Methodists received at their various meetings bore witness to a vital sense of God's immediacy, a present experience of Christ. For instance, after his conversion, antislavery advocate John G. Fee announced to a convention of religiously inclined (but slaveholding) Kentucky politicians that "there is a personal God—not a mere force in nature." Fee rejected the notion of a remote and uninvolved divinity, the conventional view of many deistically influenced churchmen. Methodists renounced the concept of an impassible deity in favor of an image of an active, living God—one who encourages human emotion and empathizes with the human predicament. Along this line,

Marcus Swift, a Methodist abolitionist, stated that God's omnipotence and benevolent moral character gives "Him a most perfect knowledge of the slave's sorrows, and utterly forbids the idea that He remains unaffected by them." When Christians pray on behalf of the oppressed, Swift declared, "we know that the burden of our supplications accord with all the blessed emotions of His holy nature."[21]

Similarly, the experience of Laura Smith, a young woman from Niagara County, New York, illustrates the Methodist inclination for a vital piety in which believers had interpersonal communion with an accessible and even approachable God. Smith's attendance at Methodist prayer meetings worried her parents because the denomination had a reputation for "overheated zeal" and "excitement," in contrast to the "settled principles" and reasoned pursuit of understanding that they believed should prevail in all religious matters. In spite of her parents' concerns, Smith continued to go to Methodist meetings and was converted to faith in Christ. She came to believe that God worked in human hearts directly and personally, a belief that provided the theological basis for her incarnational activism as an advocate for fugitive slaves. Smith also expressed the opinion that church members "should become united [to their congregations] by heart-felt experience" rather than by "the system of birthright membership," which she had known as a child.[22]

Though subjective, the "heart-felt" experiences to which Smith, Swift, and other early Methodists were referring had specific objective content, based on their perception of evangelical beliefs and their dependence on the testimony of Scripture. For instance, similar to the experiences of many other Methodists, Smith's conversion transpired only after "the Bible became [her] daily companion." She was spiritually formed by the text of the New Testament, as transmitted by Methodist preaching and teaching. Thus, even though early American Methodists expressed fervent and almost mystical experiences, they were nonetheless grounded on a firm scriptural foundation that was derived from Wesleyan doctrine and biblical interpretation. Today's United Methodists sometimes speak about the normative theological role of "experience" (within the Wesleyan quadrilateral) as if it were merely the sum total of events or influences in one's life. Early American

Methodists were not so generic in their theological understanding of experience. Eighteenth- and nineteenth-century men and women knew that a truly Christian experience was a biblically formed assurance of the pardoning and regenerating love of God through Jesus, and that is what they meant when they spoke of a "real" Christianity.[23]

In the early republic, a description of the theological content of Methodist spirituality always included a depiction of the process of receiving God's grace. This process consisted of three experiential steps: repentance, the new birth, and holiness—which Asbury explained as "the operations of the eternal Spirit of God, in its convincing, converting, and sanctifying influences." Sometimes, as in this explanation by Asbury, Methodists used the term "conversion" to refer solely to the new birth, and at other times to the entire series of experiences, from repentance through sanctification.[24]

The first step toward salvation was taken when potential Christians were convicted (or "convinced") by God of the thoroughgoing effects of their sin. Asbury stated that a Methodist preacher's first task was to "convince the sinner of his dangerous condition. . . . He must set forth the depth of original sin, and show the sinner how far he is gone from original righteousness." Following Asbury's advice, itinerant circuit riders exhorted people "to quit their sins and pray to God to convert their souls." [25] By God's grace, this conviction of sin led men and women to repent, thus preparing them for the new birth.

The second experiential step in the American Methodist morphology of conversion took place the moment the sinner accepted God's grace, when a person received forgiveness of sins and was pardoned. This spiritual event was often referred to as the actual experience of conversion, and resulted in the assurance of a gracious Presence. Theologically, Methodists interpreted the pardoning work of God in classical Protestant terms as "justification," the time when God "saved their souls." But in addition to the justifying work that God accomplished for the believer at conversion, Methodists also spoke of God's new creation that occurred within the believer, the new life in Christ that began with regeneration.[26]

This rendering of the first two steps of Christian conversion—conviction of sin and the new birth—is strikingly similar to the description of conversion as portrayed by Baptists, Presbyterians, Disciples of Christ, and other evangelicals in the early republic. Some scholars, in fact, have commented that Methodist conversion narratives were not very different from those of other Americans.[27] But it was what followed the new birth—sanctification, the third step in the conversion process—that made Methodists unique among American evangelicals.[28] Methodists expected new believers to move beyond the preliminary experiences of their salvation and to ask themselves what it was they were being saved for. What was God's call on their lives? To what were Christians converted?

"Real Religion Is Real Holiness": The "Thorough Conversion" of American Methodists

Francis Asbury commented that *"real religion is real holiness. . . .* All sensations without a strong disposition for holiness are but delusive."[29] Asbury was describing the essential connection between an affective assurance of faith and sanctified action. He believed that the "real religion" of spiritual experience should result in the equally real evidence of a transformed life and a transformed society. With that conviction in hand, the leaders of the young denomination boldly declared that the purpose of Methodism in America was to reform the continent and to spread Scriptural holiness throughout the land. Methodists taught that the new creation in Christ led to holy living, or in theological terms, that regeneration was the beginning of sanctification. They appropriated Wesley's understanding of conversion as a born-again experience that, by God's grace, inaugurated a lifelong inculcation of "holy tempers." Sanctification, then, was simply an extension of conversion—not different from, but a natural continuation of, one's new birth.

What were the specific distinctives of holy living required of American Methodists? One important character trait of the men and women who responded to God's grace was the compelling urge to evangelize. According to Freeborn Garrettson, his conversion created in him an incentive "to spread my Redeemer's glory to the ends of the world." Likewise, after her joyous experience of justifying grace, Laura Smith "had a lifelong desire to invite to this gospel feast others, especially my young associates."[30]

It was also expected that the words and actions of each Christian disciple seeking sanctification would conform to biblical standards of behavior (as interpreted by the *Discipline*). Consequently, believers often spoke of their need for "consecration" and greater "faithfulness in the performance of known duty." In his General Rules, Wesley provided an outline of ethical principles so that Methodists on both sides of the Atlantic would be equipped with a plan for benevolent activism considered foundational for Christian holiness. But even with Wesley's guidelines in place, Americans practiced their social ethics in their own way. Certain aspects of the United States setting gave rise to differences between the British and American articulations of Methodist sanctification. In particular, the pervasiveness of democratic thought in the early republic profoundly influenced American religious ideas and institutions. Methodists regularly referred to their sanctification experience, for example, as the occasion when they were "set at liberty" from slavery to sin, inviting a comparison to social and political movements for liberty from oppression. "As vital piety spreads," Garrettson wrote, drawing a parallel between the growth of affective Christian faith and the increase of moral virtue in the United States, "so will a spirit of freedom." Such references to both spiritual and physical freedom were commonplace in the religious narratives of American Methodists.[31]

The engrafting of democratic ideals onto the Wesleyan view of conversion resulted in a characteristically American conception of the proper expression of holiness. This amalgam of Methodist and democratic values eventuated in a kind of Christianization of the Enlightenment principles of equality, human potential, and personal autonomy. American evangelicals commonly used democratic language to describe God's design for a sanctified society: for example, reformist principles reflected the "gospel of impartial love"; the abolition of class, race, and gender distinctions resulted in a "leveling" of society; and the biblical Golden Rule was defined in terms of the relations between the varied social strata of the United States.[32]

The American commitment to both sanctification and democracy found resonance in the Methodist theological emphasis on humanity's equal access to God regardless of one's race or social status. Employing democratic phraseology in conjunction with the phraseology Christians used to describe the intimacy they felt toward fellow believers at camp meetings, antebellum Methodists wrote that "prejudices against colored people . . . soon melted away" in the new Christian community formed by the Spirit. Methodists in the United States also urged greater democratization in the church's institutional structures, for ecclesiastical bondage could be just as restricting as political bondage. Garrettson, for instance, struggled for years to encourage the Methodist Episcopal Church to practice a more egalitarian polity. Similarly, some Methodists were worried that an individual's "personal identity and rights [could] be swallowed up in the power and general government of a [denominational] connexion."[33]

Most significantly, the joining of holiness ideas with American democratic commitments resulted in antislavery agitation. From its inception, the Methodist movement spoke out against the cruelties of human enslavement. Wesley viewed slavery as an abominable evil, and his strongly worded sentiments on the subject became an example for generations of his followers. As forceful as his opposition was to slavery, however, his most significant writing on the issue, *Thoughts Upon Slavery,* was a derivative piece that he borrowed primarily from a pamphlet written by the Quaker Anthony Benezet.[34] Wesley never explicitly connected his ethical position on the subject of slavery to his soteriology, at least not in the definitive way that American Methodists did. It was Garrettson and other revolutionary era Methodists in the United States who first described antislavery as constitutive to the order of salvation.[35]

American Methodist abolitionist commitments were stated in reference to both the experience of the new birth and to the experience of sanctification. Early Methodists often associated their regenerative experience of justification with their acceptance of antislavery principles. Even as late as the antebellum period there were some Methodists (as well as other American evangelicals) who identified a linkage between regeneration and antislavery. In the words of one activist: "From the hour of my spiritual birth I have been an Abolitionist."[36]

Other Methodists needed further spiritual motivation in order for them to become committed to antislavery; they identified abolition with the sanctification experience. Theologically, such a connection made sense; for them, antislavery activism became the evidence of the effectual outworking of conversion, the substantive demonstration of regenerated living. Garrettson, for example, believed that it was "a Christian's privilege to love God with an undivided heart and his neighbor as himself, [but] not while he willfully or willingly keeps slaves in bondage." Emancipation became a practical manifestation of the power of divine love.[37]

Although all Wesleyans agreed that conversion had immediate ethical consequences, by the mid-nineteenth century only a relatively small group of American Methodists made the specific application of holiness to antislavery. This theological departure from the original Methodist position connecting conversion with abolition was as significant a factor in the church's compromise on slavery as the rise of sectional struggles, and the spread of racist ideology during the early republic and antebellum period. As Methodists in both the South and certain parts of the North became firmly entrenched in their defense of slavery, so other Methodists became just as adamant in their opposition to slavery. Abolitionist rhetoric became increasingly inflammatory, which encouraged the opposition to justify theologically their attachment to slavery. In response to these polarized positions, most Methodists abandoned their earlier theological commitment to antislavery for fear of being labeled as rabid abolitionists. According to the foremost historian of Methodist attitudes toward slavery, by the 1830s and 1840s "the historic antislavery faith" of Freeborn Garrettson and other Wesleyan forbears had declined considerably.[38]

Nonetheless, a few antebellum Methodists retained the original vision. While revolutionary era Methodists focused their antislavery efforts on manumission, by the 1840s those Methodists who were abolitionists focused their involvement on political action. They applied the doctrine of entire sanctification to the quest for antislavery voting, antislavery legislation, and the election of candidates. But whatever their particular tactical angle, the theological component of Methodist abolitionism remained the same: that is, antislavery was considered to be an essential element of conversion. Indeed, abolitionists viewed their antislavery activism as evidence of a "thorough conversion."[39]

Smith's spiritual autobiography offers us an example of a person from the later period who experienced a rather typical Methodist conversion and who then demonstrated the "historic antislavery faith" characteristic of Garrettson. While visiting a prayer meeting with her Methodist uncle, Smith heard a young woman who was no older than herself testify that she "earnestly sought the Lord, and found Jesus so precious in the forgiveness of her sins." The Methodist practice of allowing the public testimony of young people impressed Smith and convinced her that "God was no respecter of persons," that is, God did not make distinctions or play favorites. Smith was affirmed as one of God's beloved despite her lowly position in society as a youth. That very evening, Smith resolved to "receive an evidence that [she was] the Lord's child. [She] wanted to realize that peace and joy those men and women expressed in that meeting." In the context of intimate fellowship, Smith had witnessed Christian believers who had a vital experience of God's immediacy—a real Christianity. She, too, wanted that "evidence" of faith, but she needed "light to dispel [her] darkness and doubt."

> In this despairing state . . . I exclaimed, O, what a sin-stricken world is this! . . . Is there no balm in Gilead? Is there no physician there to heal this sin-stricken world, this sin-sick soul of mine? Like a flash the answer came, Yes, Jesus is that balm; he shed his own precious blood for me on Calvary, that I might live now, and for evermore! Yes, the healing balm is applied, and I *am saved*! O, what a fountain is opened for cleansing! My peace was like an overflowing river. . . . I stood a monument of amazing mercy, praising God with every breath. All nature praising, instead of mourning as it did a few moments before. O, how changed the scene! . . . O, what a leveling of all nations of the earth was this [spiritual] baptism. I had been prejudiced against the Irish people. . . . But now every soul seemed so precious, I thought I could toil all my life long if I could become instrumental in bringing one soul to the Savior who

> died to save sinners. . . . Jesus shed his blood to redeem all who would by faith accept salvation so freely. The African and Indian races were alike objects of redeeming love.[40]

Smith's narrative illustrates many standard elements of American Methodist conversions. Drawn to the Methodists by the quality of their interpersonal interactions, she felt a validation of her personhood. At the same time, Smith was convicted of her sin. Through grace, she received pardon and an assurance of salvation. The pardon for her sins signified the beginning of God's new creation in her soul; indeed, all of nature changed before her eyes. This new creation led her toward holiness, which immediately effected in her a longing to evangelize. Smith's new life also caused a transformation of her formerly prejudicial attitudes toward Irish, African, and Native American people; she explained her transformation by using the characteristic democratic description of the "leveling" of inequalities. The acceptance that Smith felt from God and from her Methodist friends (since neither were "respecters of persons") allowed her the spiritual freedom to be accepting of others.

Several years later, after her marriage and a move to Michigan, Laura Smith Haviland began to live out her commitment to sanctified antislavery action more vigorously. This commitment was derived from her earlier experience of the new birth and her dedication to American ideas of democracy. She fearlessly conducted runaway slaves on the Underground Railroad, joined a fledgling abolitionist denomination (the Wesleyan Methodist Connection), and opened the only interracial school in Michigan. The foundational principle of her school was "the perfect equality of all." Its purpose was to lead black and white students to an experience of regeneration and "to inculcate personal freedom as the spirit of American government."[41] Clearly, the "real religion" that Haviland experienced in her conversion had definite implications for a sanctified life—a holiness expressed tangibly by her antislavery activism.

Chapter Five

Conversion and Sanctification in Nineteenth-century African American Wesleyan Women

Estrelda Alexander

The life stories of four extraordinary nineteenth-century black women in the Wesleyan and Holiness traditions provide us with an understanding of conversion as more than a release from the power of sin. For them, conversion was also a liberation from the restraints that kept them, as black women, in subservient positions in both the church and society. These exemplary pioneer women leaders and preachers—Jarena Lee, Julia Foote, Zilpha Elaw, and Amanda Berry Smith—were empowered through their conversion and later sanctification not only to live what they considered godly lives but also to challenge openly the vestiges of sexism and racism within their religious communities, as well as in the unbearably oppressive system of slavery and in segregated American society.

The lives of these four women span the period of U.S. history from the decade after the Revolutionary War to the years just prior to World War I (Lee was born in 1783; Smith died in 1913). They lived at a time in which America was experiencing rapid change in its political and social realities. Along with transformation in industry, geographical boundaries, ethnic identity, and other areas of the culture, the status of women in American society was in flux. For the most part, that status spiraled to heights undreamed of a century earlier. Women received the right to vote, moved from the home to the public workplace in great numbers, and won other "rights" that had been denied them for many centuries. Christian women were often at the forefront of these battles.

However, the status of African American women improved much more slowly than that of white women. Although African American women gained emancipation, their economic rights and possibilities for advancement remained limited. While taking on some leadership roles in the church and community, these women remained subject to the dominance of African American men as well. Further, they were not able to benefit fully from the hard-won battle for women's suffrage; and the women's rights movements that brought qualitative improvements to the everyday lives of most white women in America did not extend to women of color. Yet Lee, Foote, Elaw, and Smith, and many other black women like them, found in their faith, conversion, and sanctification experiences the energy and resolve to fight for a different kind of existence for themselves, their children, and their communities.

The earliest of these women, Jarena Lee (b. 1783), a lay leader in Richard Allen's fledging African Methodist Episcopal (AME) Church, a traveling evangelist, and, apparently, the first woman in that denomination to be allowed to preach publicly, was also involved in the abolition movement. Zilpha Elaw (b. 1790), probably the least known of the four, was, according to Andrews, one of the first women field missionaries of any race to pursue her calling without the support of a denomination or supervisory board. For a short time she ran a school for black children in Burlington, New Jersey. Her missionary travels took her to England, but before emancipation, she also courageously ventured into the southern states to preach to slaves, at great risk to her own life and liberty. Julia Foote (b. 1823) was the first African American woman to be ordained a deacon, and the second to be ordained an elder in the African Methodist Episcopal Zion (AMEZ) Church and therefore in the Wesleyan tradition. She began her ministry by holding evangelistic meetings in her own home; by the end of her ministry she had traveled and preached up and down the eastern coast of the United States and the western frontier of the United States and Canada. Amanda Berry Smith (1837–1915) was an outstanding evangelist whose preaching engagements on the Holiness camp-meeting circuit took her not only throughout the United States but also to Europe, Africa, and Asia. She was one of the first women ministers to attend a general assembly of the AME church (though she was not accepted as a delegate), and in her later years she founded a home for orphans.

As we will see below, their individual stories vary in details. Most notably, Smith was born a slave, though her family was later set free; Foote, Elaw, and Lee, however, were born free women in the North. Foote and Lee exercised their ministries among the various branches of the people called Methodist, while Elaw and Smith participated in Holiness churches. Despite these differences, several common themes are woven through the fabric of these extraordinary women's lives, tying them together sociologically and theologically. First, they all shared a deep spirituality and uncommon moral strength. These characteristics were born out of a personal encounter with the God who was the source of energy and resolve for their relentless struggle to bring about change for black slaves before Emancipation, for black women in society more generally, and for women in the religious sphere of the fledgling black wing of the Wesleyan Methodist and Holiness movements.

Second, all four women consciously strove for conversion. Their initial sense of the need for conversion was not awakened by a deep love for God or a desire to please God, but from a sense of terrible uncleanness before God. This was true even though these women experienced conversion at an early age—prior to attaining what many would call full womanhood (though their harsh circumstances forced them to take on the responsibilities of adulthood before they should have been expected to). Conversion served to make them aware that they were accepted by God and that God forgave their sins, ameliorating their initial sense of dread. However, it did not always bring them complete peace with God; for these four women, conversion was just a beginning.

Third, the spiritual awareness or conviction that conversion brought about in them is a common thread. Again, this awareness did not free them entirely from dread or doubt concerning their ultimate status before God. It led them, instead, to an intensified confrontation with sin—a spiritual power they understood as personified in Satan himself. The graphic depiction each has provided of her dramatic contests with the very personification of evil might lead some to credit the women with having an overactive imagination. However, within the ethos of the African American religious traditions that are rooted in the slave spirituality of their parents and, in turn, in African traditional religion, such narratives were common, even expected. Their religious tradition encouraged strong belief in the reality of the involvement of the spirit world—both good and evil spirits—in the everyday lives of living people.[1] In their struggles, these women—not an angel or God—argued directly with Satan himself over the condition of their souls and their resolve to be free from the power of his evil intent. Yet they relied on God to deliver them from the tempter, for they sensed that they were no match for such a powerful and evil foe.

Fourth, the intensity of their struggle with Satan and sin, and its continuation after conversion, caused them to sense a need for sanctification—or what Foote would refer to as "full salvation"[2]—and to pursue this sanctification with full vigor. The initial joy and peace of their conversion experience stimulated in them an awareness of the forgiveness of sins that they had previously committed. But along with the ensuing battle with the perceived powers of evil, it awoke in them a conviction of their own inability to live a sin-free life. They felt trapped between desiring to please God and facing the reality that, for them, it was humanly impossible to do so consistently. The more their desire to please God grew, the more frustrated they became with what they saw as an unattainable goal of sin-free living within their own energies and resolve. All four of these women refused to rest until they obtained the blessed assurance of this full salvation.

Finally, this struggle and ultimate victory birthed in each woman a sense of divine calling and destiny beyond the strictly determined roles that varied for each of them as individuals and yet were similarly constrictive for them as black women. Each woman would contend that conversion made her aware of a new reality—that she was in fact one of God's dear children. The women also contend that sanctification gave them the courage to pursue their perceived calling without the need to be accepted by those who could not see beyond their dark skin and their female-gendered bodies.

There is not sufficient space here to examine the substantial accomplishments of these four women in detail. Their lives are sufficiently documented within their biographies and autobiographies.[3] However, a brief outline of their accomplishments does help us better understand their experiences of conversion and, subsequently, how they integrated social and spiritual concerns. These women certainly do not represent the average black woman of their day (or of any race or time, for that matter) either within the Holiness movement, the Wesleyan tradition, the broader church, or society in general. However, their electrifying stories shed light on our understanding of what the experiences of conversion and sanctification meant in the lives of nineteenth- and early twentieth-century black women in the Wesleyan Methodist and Holiness traditions.

Jarena Lee

For Jarena Lee, the first woman preacher in the African Methodist Episcopal Church, the conversion struggle began at the early age of seven and lasted fourteen years. Convicted by a lie she told to her mistress, Lee experienced what she later described as "the Spirit of God mov[ing] through [her] conscience" and telling her that she was a "wretched sinner."[4] This experience left her with a deep sense of guilt that probably lingered near the surface of her consciousness throughout her young life. Later she affirmed that "the Spirit of the Lord never entirely forsook me, but continued . . . striving with me," perhaps in an unconscious way throughout her entire young life. Her sense of guilt resurfaced again and again during this time and figured prominently in her struggle until "[God's] gracious power converted [her] soul."[5]

At the age of twenty-one, Lee went to a Presbyterian service with some friends. She was put off by the solemnity of the preaching and worship style and, after several months of attendance, was determined that this was not the kind of church to which she wanted to belong. However, the solemn preaching brought renewed conviction of her sinfulness that instigated a period of intense spiritual struggle and led her to such despair that she considered suicide.[6] Soon after that, she began attending Methodist worship services at which Richard Allen, founding bishop of the African Methodist Episcopal Church, presided and preached. Three weeks after the day she first heard Allen, she attended another service in which he preached, and responded to his invitation for "such as felt a desire to flee the wrath to come, to unite on trial with [the congregation]." As she put it:

> My soul was gloriously converted to God. . . . That instant, it appeared to me, as if a garment, which had entirely enveloped my whole person, even to my fingers' end, split at the crown of my head, and was stripped away from me, passing like a shadow from my sight—when the glory of God seemed to cover me instead.
>
> That moment, though hundreds were present, I did leap to my feet and declare that God, for Christ's sake, had pardoned the sins of my soul. Great was the ecstacy [sic] of my mind, for I felt that not only the sin of *malice* was pardoned, but all other sins were swept away together.[7]

After her initial spiritual experience, which Lee considered conversion, she experienced a moment of great joy and peace. But this soon gave way to a prolonged period of doubt, of struggle with Satan himself. As she describes it: "From the day on . . . until the hour of my deliverance, I was . . . buffeted by that enemy of all righteousness—the devil."[8]

Her struggle with Satan lasted four years. This internal, spiritual warfare filled her again with suicidal thoughts.[9] According to her, one reason for the prolonged length of her struggle was that "[her] parents had no knowledge of God" that they could pass on to her. In fact, before her conversion, Lee felt herself totally ignorant of the basics of Christian faith, even of the fact that Christ had died for her sins and those of the rest of the world.[10]

Her inner struggles over the state of her soul were so real and intense that they made her physically ill. In retrospect, the illness might have seemed to be one of the most fortuitous acts of providence in her young life. Through it she came into contact with a black doctor who was a member of the Methodist society, and through him with William Scott, "a certain Colored man . . . [who] had taken much time in visiting the sick and distressed of our color."[11] Through this association she came to learn about the doctrine of sanctification that finally brought about the release for which she had sought so long. Following his instruction and encouragement, she began to pray specifically and earnestly for sanctification.

> I had struggled long and hard, but found not the desire of my heart. When I rose from my knees, there seemed a voice speaking to me, as I yet stood in a leaning posture—"Ask for sanctification." When to my surprise, I recollected that I had not even thought of it in my whole prayer. It would seem Satan had hidden the very object from my mind, for which I had purposely kneeled to pray. But when this voice whispered in my heart, saying, "Pray for sanctification," I again bowed . . . and said, "Lord *sanctify* my soul for Christ's sake." That very instant, as if lightning had darted through me, I sprang to my feet, and cried, "The Lord has sanctified my soul!" . . . No sooner had I cried out . . . than there seemed another voice behind me, saying, "No, it is too great a work to be done." But another spirit said, "Bow down for the witness—I received it—*thou art sanctified!*"[12]

Four or five years after her sanctification, Lee heard another voice distinctly tell her, "Go and preach the Gospel!" And with that a new chapter for women in black Methodism began.

Zilpha Elaw

In 1790, Zilpha Elaw was born a free woman in Pennsylvania to deeply religious parents who conducted daily devotions in their home. Both parents died by the time she reached adolescence; however, sometime before his death, her father had placed Elaw in a Quaker home that she described as not outwardly religious. Reflecting in her memoirs on her experience before conversion, Elaw described a time when, even as a young teenager, she felt herself "to be so exceedingly sinful that [she] was certain of meeting with condemnation at the bar of God." Given to dreams and visions, even at a young age, lifelike images tormented her to the point that around age fourteen she experienced a dream of Judgment Day so vivid that she called it an "effectual call to my soul."[13] Even so, in her autobiography Elaw maintained, "I never experienced that terrific dread of hell by which some Christians appear to have been exercised; but I felt a godly sorrow for sin in having grieved my God by a course of disobedience to His commands."[14] However, after that dream she experienced bouts of depression and weeping spells that so much changed her disposition that her Quaker mistress attempted to console her, but to no avail, for the aftermath of the dream was an inner sense of conviction of her sinful state and a realization on her part that she was ill prepared to meet God's judgment.

During her teen years, Elaw began attending Methodist meetings, for Methodism had newly appeared in the area where she lived. Through her affiliation with this new group, she described her conversion as both "progressive and instantaneous." It began incrementally by a course in which "the darkness was gradually dispelled, the light dawned upon my mind, and I increased in knowledge daily."[15] Yet it culminated in a dramatic experience that provided her with what she described as the assurance of salvation. While she was milking a cow, she had a vision of "a tall figure . . . [in] long white robe down to the feet." She described the subject of that vision, whom she believed to be Jesus, as so real that even the "beast of the stall turned her head and bowed herself upon the ground." In this appearance, Jesus did not speak to Elaw. But through that vision she came to a state in which "the peace of God which passeth understanding was communicated to my heart; and joy in the Holy Ghost, to a degree, at the last, unutterable by my tongue and indescribable by my pen; . . . beyond my comprehension; but, from that happy hour, my soul was set at glorious liberty."[16]

Elaw proved to be very articulate in describing not only her salvation experience but also the fruit of her salvation. It brought about a change from a fearful and superstitious, yet insolent, girl to a fearless young woman able to withstand with God-given graciousness the derision of her peers and the often unwarranted rebukes of her employers.

> The love of God being now shed abroad in my heart by the Holy Spirit, and my soul transported with heavenly peace and joy in God, all the former hardships which pertained to my circumstances and situation vanished; the work and duties which had previously been hard and irksome were now become easy and pleasant; and the evil propensities of my disposition and temper were subdued beneath the softening and refining pressure of divine grace upon my heart.[17]

In 1817, at the age of twenty-seven, Elaw was sanctified at another Methodist camp meeting. She describes a supernatural encounter that occurred just as the meeting was about to disperse and while the attendees were singing a closing hymn and embracing each other to depart. In her words:

> It was at one of these meetings that God was pleased to separate my soul unto Himself, to sanctify me as a vessel designed for honour, made meet for the master's use. Whether I was in the body, or whether I was out of the body, on that auspicious day, I cannot say; but this I do know, that . . . I became so overpowered with the presence of God, that I sank down upon the ground, and laid there for a considerable time; and while I was thus prostrate on the earth, my spirit seemed to ascend up into the clear circle of the sun's disc; and, surrounded and engulphed [sic] in the glorious effulgence of his rays, I distinctly heard a voice speak unto me, which said, "Now thou art sanctified; and I will show thee what thou must do." . . . When I recovered from the trance or ecstasy into which I had fallen, . . . I clearly saw by the light of the Holy Ghost, that my heart and soul were rendered completely spotless—as clean as a sheet of white paper, and I felt . . . as if I had never sinned in all my life.[18]

Immediately after this experience, Elaw began to pray publicly with such fervor and clarity that she was often called upon to pray in public meetings. It was also during this meeting that she felt the "call" to begin her ministry of visiting the sick and witnessing to others about their need for salvation.

Julia Foote

Julia Foote, the first black woman to be ordained a deacon and the second to be ordained an elder in the African Methodist Episcopal Zion Church, was brought up by devout Methodist parents who were regular church attendees and held family devotion in the home. So, from early childhood, she was exposed to a Christian atmosphere and the religious ethos of Wesleyan Methodism. At age eight, she experienced a spiritual awakening that she was later to identify as a "first conversion," from which she determined she must have begun to backslide prior to her adolescence.[19] Once awakened, however, her spiritual sensibilities never died completely, for Foote also described an inward turmoil that began in her adolescent years. This tension caused her to fluctuate between her desire to "serve God whatever might happen" and a "faint desire to serve the Lord," mitigated by the draw of the "pomp and vanities of this world" that began to engage her attention as never before.[20]

When Foote was fifteen years old, she experienced actual conversion during a daylong experience that began in a Sunday evening quarterly Methodist meeting. That night she was "slain in the Spirit."[21] The conversion experience ended the next day in her home surrounded by a group of "saints" who had stayed with her through the night to pray her through. Her graphic account of that dramatic experience underscores what she perceived as the intense reality of the spiritual warfare in which she was involved:

> As the minister dwelt with great force and power on . . . the text, I beheld my lost condition as I never had done before. Something within me kept saying, "Such a sinner as you are can never sing that new song." No tongue can tell the agony I suffered. I fell to the floor, unconscious, and was carried home. Several remained with me all night, singing and praying. I did not recognize any one, but seemed to be walking in the dark, followed by some one who kept saying, "Such a sinner as you are can never sing that new song." Every converted man and woman can imagine what my feelings were. I thought God was driving me on to hell. In great terror I cried: "Lord, have mercy on me, a poor sinner!" The voice which had been cry-

> ing in my ears ceased at once, and a ray of light flashed across my eyes, accompanied by a sound of far distant singing; the light grew brighter and brighter, and the singing more distinct, and soon I caught the words: "This is the new song—redeemed! redeemed!" I at once sprang from the bed where I had been lying for twenty hours, without meat or drink, and commenced singing: "Redeemed! redeemed! glory! glory!" Such joy and peace as filled my heart, when I felt that I was redeemed and could sing the new song. Thus was I wonderfully saved from eternal burning.[22]

Foote experienced a six-month period of uninterrupted "peace and joy in Jesus, [her] love" in which she constantly prayed and read her Bible into late hours of the night.[23] But at the end of that period, following an unfortunate accident that led to a loss of sight in one eye, and succumbing to anger at the brother who had caused the loss, she was besieged by a spell of doubting: "Satan said: 'There! you see you never were converted.' . . . Though he could not make me believe that. . . ."[24] Repeatedly in prayer she sought relief from these feelings and attempted to apprehend what she called "the light of full salvation,"[25] for she desperately wanted to end her struggle with what she labeled "this inbeing monster."[26] Her prayers did not seem to avail quickly enough, for she continued in this condition for more than a year. She had heard about the Holiness doctrine of sanctification, and urgently sought more information about it, but neither her minister, her class leader, nor her parents were Holiness advocates. Each of them separately counseled her to give up her search and content herself to live with the struggle with sin all her life. They further counseled that release from sin and doubt came only with death. This was not a satisfying response for Foote, who continued to seek release from what she called "besetting sin" and the "up-and-down way" throughout this desperate time.[27] For, as she would relate it, "None but those who have passed up this way know how wretched every moment of my life was. I thought I must die."[28]

After hearing an elderly couple at a church meeting speak on sanctification, Foote began to seek instruction from them regarding the experience, against the wishes of her parents who were so vehemently opposed to it that her mother forbade her to pursue the matter. However, Foote deliberately disobeyed her mother and sought out the couple for greater enlightenment on the subject. After receiving their instruction concerning scriptural support for the sanctification, Foote sought the Lord more confidently for the experience in which she later said her "heart was emptied of sin," and within several days she received it in dramatic fashion.[29] "While waiting on the Lord, my large desire was granted. . . . The glory of God seemed almost to prostrate me to the floor. There was, indeed, a weight of glory resting upon me. . . . I no longer hoped for glory, but I had the full assurance of it."[30]

Foote's sanctification experience moved her into a spiritual state in which she "lost all fear." Though still considered a child by most within her hierarchical church and social contexts, she began to exhort others on the doctrines of Wesleyan Holiness and sanctification that she had come to love and understand and so dramatically experienced. And, though chided by some for her brashness at attempting to instruct some who considered themselves her spiritual seniors, she was buoyed by the fact that others actually were led by her instruction to seek and experience sanctification. This initial success launched her into a lifelong vocation of sharing God's Word.

Amanda Berry Smith

Amanda Berry Smith always considered herself a religious child. She writes: "I cannot remember the time from my earliest childhood that I did not want to be a Christian."[31] But she did not equate this childhood religiosity with conversion, for despite her early religious interest, her spiritual journey was not without its rocky places, which included a point in which she doubted the very existence of God.[32]

Her first memorable religious experience did not come until the age of thirteen, when she attended a series of meetings in a Methodist church. Though this experience resulted in her joining with the congregation and attending class meetings for a period of time, it was tainted by the racial constraints of the church and society in which she lived. Because she was a black girl in a predominantly white class meeting, she was always expected to be the last person in the class to be taught, forcing her to stay later than everyone else. At the same time, her employers expected her as a black servant to be available to serve their needs at the appointed time, which required her to leave the class early. When these two expectations inevitably came into conflict, she was forced to give up her attempts to attend class meetings, not returning regularly to church life for nearly six years.[33]

It was only after a near-death experience, in which she, at age nineteen, saw a vision of an angel telling her to "go back" and saw herself preaching the gospel, that she began earnestly seeking conversion.[34] First she attended a Baptist revival meeting, where she experienced a dramatic spiritual encounter.

> I sat there all at once,—I can't tell how,—I don't know how,—I never did know how, but when I found myself I was down the aisle and half way up to the altar. . . . So I rushed forward to the altar . . . with all my might: "O, Lord, have mercy on me! O, Lord, have mercy on me! O, Lord, save me," I shouted at the top of my voice, till I was hoarse. Finally I quieted down. There came a stillness over me so quiet. . . . The meeting closed. I went home.[35]

She went home, having been convicted of her need for salvation but seemingly lacking the faith to attain it. Since she did not consider that she had as yet experienced conversion, she "prayed incessantly, night and day" for what she called "light and peace."[36]

Through this prayer life she began her ongoing struggle with Satan over the state of her soul. During this period she prayed, fasted, and read her Bible, but this only seemed to invite Satan's relentless attack. In her autobiography, she writes:

> "You have prayed to be converted." I said "Yes."
> "You have been sincere."
> "Yes."
> "You have been in earnest."
> "Yes."
> "You have read your Bible, and you have fasted, and you really want to be converted."
> "Yes, Lord, Thou knowest it; Thou knowest my heart, I really want to be converted."

> Then Satan said, "Well, if God were going to convert you He would have done it long ago; He does His work quick, and with all your sincerity God has not converted you."
> "Yes, that is so."
> "You might as well give it up, then," said he, "it is no use, He won't hear you."
> "Well, I guess I will just give it up. I suppose I will be damned and I might as well submit to my fate." Just then a voice whispered to me clearly and said, "Pray once more." And in an instant I said, "I will." . . . And I felt it from the crown of my head clear through me, "I WILL," and I got on my feet and said, "I will pray once more, and if there is any such thing as salvation, I am determined to have it this afternoon or die."[37]

So Smith began to pray more earnestly, and she perceived that the struggle with Satan continued in earnest and even intensified.

> "O, Lord, have mercy on my soul, I don't know how else to pray."
> A voice said to me, "That is just what you said before."
> "O, Lord, if Thou wilt only please to have mercy on my soul I will serve Thee the longest day I live." "O, Lord, if Thou wilt only convert my soul and make me truly sensible of it, for I want to know surely that I am converted, I will serve Thee the longest day I live." "Yes," the Devil says, "you said that before and God has not done it, and you might as well stop."
> "O, what a conflict."[38]

This conflict ended in an experience she described as being flooded with "wild" joy and peace that continued from that time on. But she was again quickly accosted by Satan's challenge to show verifiable evidence of her salvation. This time, however, she did not despair and, though she answered Satan head-on that she was very sure of her salvation, she began to seek for this evidence. She prayed with earnestness but without any of the desperation of her previous prayers; and in a short time she reached the place of assurance and "never from that day . . . had a question in regard to [her] conversion."[39]

But even this evidence was not enough. She soon began her search for what she called "the blessing," or sanctification. Her search culminated in a dramatic experience in a Sunday morning Methodist service in which she and Satan were locked in a virtual battle over the logistics of how sanctification was to occur.

> How I lived through it I cannot tell, but the blessedness of the love and the peace and power I can never describe. O, what glory filled my soul! The great vacuum in my soul began to fill up. . . . I wanted to shout Glory to Jesus![40]

This battle continued for some moments with Smith locked in a mental struggle until, during the singing of a hymn, she finally stood to claim the witness of her conversion and to exclaim "Glory to Jesus!" As she put it: "I felt so wonderfully strange, yet I felt so glorious."[41]

Yet she still longed with an "indescribable want" for the "purity or sanctification," and she sought for it in prayer.[42] Twelve years after being converted, Smith experienced what she called full salvation. Immediately she began to witness to those around her that the Lord had sanctified her soul. She urged them to seek the blessing of sanctification. From there she went on to become a class leader, to hold prayer meetings in her home, and, finally, to become one of the most sought after evangelists on the camp-meeting circuit.

Conclusion

Four powerful women provide four dramatic stories of turning to God, being converted, and pursuing and receiving sanctification within the black Methodist and Holiness traditions. They were attracted to the special warmth of the people called Methodists and were converted within the young movement when it was considered scandalous to be a member of that sect. The strict moral and ethical code of the Methodism of their day that prohibited the usual youthful diversions—drinking, dancing, and going to parties—led to derision by their peers. But Lee, Foote, Elaw, and Smith gladly gave these up, as well as the usual comforts of home and family sought out by other young women of their day.[43] They traded it all to be part of "the fellowship of the saints" called Methodists, for something about these people made the women feel that this was where they belonged. According to Cornel West, "the major, primarily political appeal of Methodism [for blacks during the era of slavery] was its stress on individual experience and equality of every believer before God as well as its relatively non-hierarchical church polity and organization, uncomplicated membership requirements."[44] But this does not tell the whole story.

In one sense, to agree with West, these women were attracted to Methodism because, in spite of the strict moral and ethical requirements, there were relatively few social restraints and a relatively egalitarian atmosphere. But, further, the enthusiastic worship, deep spirituality, and emphasis on personal experience within black Methodist revivalism resonated with and closely mirrored the ecstatic religious practices of their more distant ancestors in African traditional religion, and of their more recent ancestors in the "invisible institution" of slave religion. Equally important, they found in Methodism a formula to help them steer through a journey to salvation, self-actualization, and liberation.

They speak of beginning the journey by being made aware of their sinfulness before God and by being brought under conviction of their spiritual neediness. From this followed an intermediate period of deliverance and spiritual respite. They then speak of the desperate struggle they faced to realize full salvation and to free themselves from the daily, debilitating warfare with the powers of sin and darkness. For in this sequence, conversion alone did not leave them satisfied but caused them to want more of God and to seek God fiercely with all their hearts. The spiritual ethos of their time and the cultural heritage of their community supported a belief in the reality of personal engagement with demonic powers, including Satan himself. They saw themselves locked in a battle for their very souls that took them on occasion "through the valley of the shadow of death" to the brink of despair. These battles caused them not only physical anguish but also a degree of mental and emotional distress that modern religionist and mental health professionals would possibly dismiss as neurotic. Only through appeal to God—and direct divine intervention on their behalf—could they possibly hope to win such a struggle.

Finally, they speak of the glorious victory attained by presevering in prayer to the one who they perceived was stronger than Satan. This victory brought with it not only assurance of eternal life in heaven and release from the engagement with earthbound evil powers, but also a new sense of personhood and identity. What West says about the conversion experience of slaves can be applied to these women:

> Conversion . . . not only created deep bonds of fellowship and a reference point for self-assurance during times of doubt and distress; it also democratized and equalized the status of all before God. The conversion experience initiated a profoundly personal relationship with God, which gave slaves a special self-identity and self-esteem in stark contrast with the roles imposed upon them by American society.[45]

With the new self-identity came a fearlessness that bordered on the supernatural. After their conversion and sanctification experiences, what these women feared most—indeed the only thing they feared—was not being obedient to the will and calling of God. They were loosed from the constraints of racism and sexism. They were liberated from the fear of white people, as a passage from Smith's autobiography so clearly illustrates.

> Somehow I always had a fear of white people—[not] in the sense of doing me harm . . . but . . . because they were white . . . and I was black and was here! But that morning on Green street, as I stood on my feet trembling, I heard these words distinctly . . . : "There is neither Jew nor Greek, there is neither bond nor free, there is neither male nor female, for ye are all one in Christ." . . . And as I looked at white people that I had always seemed to be afraid of, now they looked so small. The great mountain had become a mole-hill.[46]

In addition, Lee, Foote, Elaw, and Smith loosed themselves from the fear of men—white and black—who sought to maintain strict rules regarding the appropriate ministry for women in the church, and the appropriate place for them within the larger society. These women lost the fear of physical harm and of death. Because of this, they were ready to go into dangerous territories armed with the simple belief that it was God's will for them to do so. Elaw went back and forth from the safe North to dangerous slave territory in the South, while Foote ventured to the so-called "dark" continent of Africa as well as to Europe and Asia.

What Andrews said of the role of sanctification in the lives of Lee, Elaw, and Foote also applies to Smith:

> The experience of [conversion and] sanctification liberated [them] from the sense of personal inadequacy that their perception of their own sinfulness had placed upon them. Belief in the Wesleyan version of sanctification freed them to trust the promptings of their innermost selves because of their conviction that what came from within was of the Holy Spirit, not the corrupt ego. . . . Through [conversion and] sanctification, [they] believed that they had recovered their true, pristine identity in Christ. It was their religious duty, therefore, to be faithful to that renewed and purified self.[47]

Part Two

Biblical Perspectives

Chapter Six

"To Turn from Darkness to Light" (Acts 26:18): Conversion in the Narrative of Luke-Acts

Joel Green

From the ministry of John the Baptist to the ministry of Jesus in the Gospel of Luke, and from the ministry of Jesus to the ministry of his followers in the Acts of the Apostles, the Third Evangelist makes conversion a cornerstone of his narrative theology. Undoubtedly, this concern is grounded in the missional emphases of the Third Evangelist, since mission is both an expression of the ancient purpose and gracious initiative of God and expresses itself in calling persons on the basis of God's initiative to align themselves fully with God's will and purpose. For Luke, the concept of "conversion" thus draws together a number of ways in which one properly responds to the good news. These are oriented toward a transformation of beliefs and commitments and include related behaviors such as baptism and "fruits worthy of repentance."

As a concept, "conversion" has become associated above all with the Christian faith, but it is not a particularly biblical term, nor in the ancient world is the concept of conversion peculiar to early Christian proclamation and literature.[1] In Greek literature, including that of the New Testament, the concept is typically lexicalized with the terms *metanoia* ("repentance") and its verbal form *metanoeo* ("to repent"), or *epistrepho* ("to change one's beliefs or ways"). But the appearance of such terms in the literature helps us only a little, since on the basis of word usage alone a whole range of issues important to the interpreter remain ambiguous. Is "conversion" an event, a process, or both? Is conversion a cognitive or a moral category, or both? What is the relationship between "rejection of one way of life for another" and "embracing more fully the life one has chosen"—both easily illustrated connotations of *metanoia*? Is conversion a crossing of religious boundaries? It is true, of course, that the concept of conversion is often present where no such terms are used, but where relevant episodes are narrated.

What is the contribution of the narrative of Luke-Acts to our understanding of the concept and experience of conversion? This question focuses the agenda of this essay. In addressing it, I will first suggest that, though the Third Evangelist has no clearly delineated "technology" of conversion, he is nonetheless adamant regarding the necessity of conversion for Jew and Gentile alike. I will then sketch the narrative portrayal of conversion in the Lukan narrative, beginning with the ministry of John the Baptist and following Luke's portrayal of the disciples in his two volumes. Finally, I will underscore the important links that Luke draws between conversion and the nature of the Christian community, between conversion and hospitality, and between conversion and the Spirit. I hope to demonstrate that for the narrator of Luke-Acts conversion is the transference of one's orienting allegiances which (1) gives rise to and is confirmed in practices appropriate to those new allegiances, (2) opens the way to ongoing, sometimes profound transformations in one's theological and moral imagination, and (3) necessarily locates and immerses one in the multiethnic community of God's people.[2]

A "Technology" of Conversion?

On the basis of recent literature on conversion, which tends to focus on a crossing of religious boundaries, it might be helpful to distinguish between repentance and conversion in Luke-Acts. Accordingly, "repentance" would be expected of the Jewish people, conversion of Gentiles. Some evidence, especially within the speeches of Acts, initially supports such a distinction. Peter and

Paul call their Jewish audiences not to serve a new God but to return to the God of their ancestors.[3] As Odil Steck has shown, prophetic speeches calling Israel to repentance follow a well-established tradition in Israel's scriptures and the literature of Second Temple Judaism,[4] and the preaching of Peter and Paul among Jewish audiences in Acts conforms to this pattern.[5] In their preaching in the Temple and synagogues, then, Jesus' witnesses in Acts function less as "missionaries" and more as "prophets." Conversely, in those situations in which Paul addresses specifically Gentile audiences, he refers to "the living God" (as opposed to worthless idols—Acts 14:15) and proclaims that this God "commands all people everywhere to repent" (Acts 17:30). At Lystra and Athens, Paul builds a case for the nature of God, while among Jews Peter and Paul alike proclaim that Jesus is the Christ. For Jews, the needed response is a reorientation toward the God of Israel and his purposes, known in the advent of Jesus Christ. For Gentiles, the needed response is a departure from idolatry in order to join the people of the God who raised Jesus from the dead.

As helpful as such a distinction might be, in the end it is much too facile. First, many Gentiles within the narrative of Acts need no conversion to the God of Israel but, like the exemplary Cornelius (Acts 10:1-4), already worship this God; they are recipients of the gift of repentance in the same way that the Jews are (see Acts 5:31; 11:18). Second, in subtle but important ways, Luke underscores the idolatry of even the Jewish people; the Jerusalem temple itself has become a manifestation of Jewish idolatry, according to Stephen's speech (see 7:48; 17:24-25). Indeed, membership among the people of God cannot be assumed simply on the basis of Abrahamic ancestry (Luke 3:7-14), with the result that the privilege of God's grace is no presumption of the Jewish people.[6] Third, when Paul recounts before King Agrippa his commission, he proclaims that Jesus sent him "to open their eyes so that they may turn from darkness to light and from the power of Satan to God" (Acts 26:17-18). In this case, Luke draws on the familiar language of religious conversion,[7] but interprets it so as to situate the redemptive purpose of God within the cosmic battle of competing kingdoms. It is an important component of this text that Gentiles and Jews alike need deliverance from darkness (see Luke 1:78-79). As Paul goes on to observe, obedience to the heavenly vision entailed declaring "first to those in Damascus, then in Jerusalem and throughout the countryside of Judea, and also to the Gentiles, that they should repent and turn to God and do deeds consistent with repentance" (Acts 26:19-20). The same response is expected of Jew and Gentile alike.

The necessity of response is set forth programmatically in the narration of the Pentecost address where Peter is interrupted by his audience: "What should we do, brothers?" (Acts 2:37). Why some sort of response is necessary is also clear. According to Peter, the exaltation of Jesus and the consequent outpouring of the Holy Spirit have signaled a dramatic transformation in history. To put it somewhat differently, the message of Jesus' witnesses calls for a radically different understanding of the world than that held previously. Within the speeches of Acts, Jewish people might hear the familiar stories borrowed from their scriptures, but these stories have been cast in ways that advocate a reading of that history that underscores the fundamental continuity between the ancient story of Israel, the story of Jesus, and the story of the Way. Israel's past (and present) is understood correctly and embraced fully only in relation to the redemptive purpose of God, but this divine purpose can be understood only as articulated by authorized interpretive agents—first, Jesus of Nazareth, and then his witnesses. Thus, for example, Paul's question to King Agrippa, "Do you believe the prophets?" (Acts 26:27), concerns not simply a commitment to the prophets, but to the prophets as they have been expounded by Paul. The coming of Jesus as Savior may signal the fresh offer of repentance and forgiveness of sins to Israel (Acts 5:31; 13:38-39), but the acceptance of this offer by Jewish people is dependent on their embracing this interpretation of God's salvific activity. Greek audiences, too, are asked to adopt a new way of viewing the world. Note how, at Athens, Paul distinguishes between how God worked in the past (17:30*a*; see also 14:16) and how he will now operate (17:30*b*)—a distinction that calls for repentance.

In effect, the necessary response to the salvific message is initial and ongoing identification with God's purpose, manifest in the Way. Beyond this, the Lukan narrative supports no technique or pattern of conversion.[8] It is true that two texts in particular seem to present a paradigm of response, following as they do the direct questions, "What should we do?" (Acts 2:37-38) and "What must I do to be saved?" (Acts 16:30-34).[9] In the first case, though, Peter counsels his audience to repent and be baptized. In the second, the jailer is told (simply) to believe, though he and his household respond also with hospitality and baptism. If these texts were to be understood as establishing a pattern of response, then they do so poorly, since the instructions given in the one case may complement but certainly do not mimic the other. If one were able to discern an "order of salvation" in these accounts, it would appear on a much grander scale: God initiates, people hear the message of salvation, people respond. In fact, this is the heart of Peter's defense of the inclusion of Gentiles in the community of God's people in Acts 15:7-11: "God made a choice," "Gentiles would hear the message of the good news," they become "believers."

To deny that Luke presents a particular pattern of response is not to deny that some forms of response might be regarded as conventional in some sense, however. (1) *Baptism in the name of Jesus* is a characteristic response, as suggested by the Ethiopian's question, "Look, here is water! What is to prevent me from being baptized?" (Acts 8:36; see also 2:41; 8:12; 9:18; 10:47-48; 16:15; and so forth). (2) *Repentance* is often mentioned explicitly as an appropriate and expected response to God's salvific work (see 2:38; 3:19; 5:31; 11:18; 17:30; 20:21; 26:20). (3) That Christians are sometimes called "believers" signals the importance of *faith* in Luke's understanding of salvation (see 2:44; 3:16; 11:17; 13:39; 14:9; 15:7; 16:30-31; 18:8). Indeed, another name given Jesus' disciples in Acts, "those who call on the name" (9:14, 21; my translation), marks these disciples as those who *believe* in the name and have identified with the name of Jesus in *baptism* (2:38; 3:16; 8:12, 16; 9:48; 19:5; 22:16).

What is the appropriate response to the good news of salvation? Luke addresses this question with an array of possibilities—for example, believe, be baptized, turn to God, listen, see, repent, and so on—but singles out no particular pattern of response as paradigmatic. God has acted graciously in Christ to bring salvation to all humanity. All humanity are called to welcome the good news, to respond with receptivity, and thus to share in that salvation not only as recipients but also as those who serve God's redemptive aim.

Conversion in Luke-Acts

The importance of conversion in the Lukan narrative is signaled immediately in the opening chapter of the Gospel, in Gabriel's announcement to Zechariah that the son to be born to him, John, would have a prophetic role of effecting repentance in preparation of "a people prepared for the Lord" (Luke 1:16-17).[10] This summary of John's message is set in parallel to underscore the centrality of the call to repentance:

> *He will turn* many of the people of Israel to the Lord their God
> . . . he will go before him,
> *to turn* the hearts of [fathers] to their children, and
> *[to turn]* the disobedient to the wisdom of the righteous, to make ready a people prepared for the Lord. (Luke 1:16-17)

Why fathers? At one level, this fills out Luke's interest in portraying John in the guise of Elijah, as this phrase is spoken of the eschatological Elijah in Malachi 4:6 (see also Sir. 48:10). More to the present point, fathers within the Gospel of Luke are sometimes portrayed as having rejected God's ways and design (Luke 6:23, 26; 11:47-48); fathers in Roman antiquity were widely known as remote from their children, with reports of excessive disciplinary measures easily documented; and God himself is presented in the Gospel as a father to be emulated in his care for his children and redemptive activity on their behalf (for example, Luke 6:36; 11:2, 13; 12:30, 32). As will be characteristic of repentance in Luke-Acts, then, so here the call to repentance is aimed at specific practices and not theological abstraction. It is not for nothing that "fathers" are juxtaposed in Gabriel's words with "the disobedient," a reference to the people of Israel in need of a wisdom that entails obedience (cf. Isa. 30:9; Jer. 5:23). Importantly, Gabriel's sketch of John's vocation is profoundly *theo*centric: He will turn people to *the Lord*, go before *the Lord*, and prepare people for the advent of *the Lord*. Clearly, God is on the move, and this requires responses of repentance, entailing obedience and restored relationships.

What begins with the angelic message in Luke 1 continues throughout the Lukan narrative, where repentance, or conversion, is central to the expected and needed human response to the divine initiative. The significance of repentance is grounded in the ministry of John but continues in the work of Jesus and of his followers.

The Repentance-Baptism of John in Luke 3:1-20

In Luke's portrayal, the ingredients of John's ministry—proclamation, repentance, and forgiveness—come to expression centrally in the baptismal activity of John. The current lack of scholarly consensus concerning the immediate precedents of John's baptism within Judaism does not detract from a striking point of similarity. This is the metaphorical role of water as a human cleansing agent, leading to the correlation of washing and ethical comportment.[11]

What aspects of John's activity of repentance-baptism are of particular significance? First, perhaps most obviously, John's ministry ties together cleansing and moral uprightness. By submitting to baptism, persons symbolized their surrender to God's will—thus reorienting their lives around the divine aim and professing their renewed, fundamental allegiance to God's purpose. According to the model proposed by van Gennep,[12] people thus participated in a ritual of initiation, the result of which was identification within a new community marked by a transformed social network and group-sanctioned practices.

For John, repentance is a thoroughgoing realignment with God's purpose that blossoms in repentance-appropriate behavior—"fruits worthy of repentance," which demonstrate one's genuine kinship with Abraham (Luke 3:7-9). In the examples of response provided by Luke (Luke 3:10-14), repentance is evidenced especially in socioeconomic relations. Extra food and clothing, possessions that lift one beyond subsistence—these are to be deployed on behalf of those in need, as though they were members of one's extended family. Even toll collectors and soldiers are to demonstrate their alignment with God's aim in this way, by reflecting God's justice in their refusal to participate in economic misappropriation or to use their positions of power to manipulate others. On the one hand, we must recognize that orientation to God's purpose of necessity gives rise to new behaviors that reflect God's purpose; on the other, it is equally true that it is only those who have thus embraced God's purpose who are free to act with such self-abandonment.

Second, John's message had a prophetic edge, according to which he challenged persons to put aside competing loyalties and align themselves fully with God's salvific project and purpose, but he also held out the promise of deliverance and restoration in the forgiveness of sins. Inasmuch as forgiveness was the means by which persons excluded from the community of God's people might (re)gain entry into the community, the promise of forgiveness has an obvious social dimension. More important still is the centrality of divine forgiveness to the restoration of Israel in contemporary Jewish thought.

Third, this means that John's baptismal ministry was very much about the character and reformation of the people of God. Indeed, by addressing the Jewish crowds as he does (Luke 3:7-9), John clarifies his understanding that the definition of God's people would not be worked out along ethnic lines. That category of people known as "children of Abraham" was composed of those who demonstrated their full embrace of God's project through "fruits worthy of repentance"—even if this required God's raising up "stones," or the inclusion of soldiers, who quite likely would not have been Jewish (Luke 3:7-9, 13-14).

Calling People to Repentance

Calling people to repentance continues in the ministry of Jesus. In Luke 5:32, while sharing a meal with toll collectors and sinners, Jesus fashions his own mission statement as calling sinners to repentance. Later in the Gospel, likewise set against the backdrop of controversy related to Jesus' table companions, the centrality of repentance to Jesus' ministry is again highlighted. Jesus is in the dock for his table habits in Luke 15:1-2. This is because meals serve important religious and social functions. In Luke 13:22-31, for example, presence at the end-time meal spells participation in the kingdom of God; and in Luke 14:1-24, meals establish "in-group" boundaries and embody values pertaining to status and purity. In these texts, the table is an expression of kinship, and dining manifests concerns for honor and acceptance.

Given the social and religious importance of meals, it is not surprising that in Luke 15:1-2 Jesus attracts hostility for his table practices. Given the flow of the Gospel of Luke thus far, it is not surprising that the Pharisees and scribes are the sources of that hostility. Though Luke can speak more positively of the Pharisees, when they appear with the scribes they function as antagonistic monitors of Jesus' behavior. In this capacity, they repeatedly conclude that he has neglected the law of God. On the one hand, then, Jesus' disregard for the usual conventions regarding table companions helps to construct a people who, like these toll collectors and sinners, hear and heed his message. "Let anyone who has ears to hear listen!" Jesus has just proclaimed (14:35), and immediately these social outcasts are presented as those who "listen to him" (15:1). On the other hand, this new community of Jesus' followers raises by its very existence an unflattering and threatening voice against the attitudes and practices embraced by Jesus' adversaries.

Jesus has a lot to answer for, and the parables of Luke 15 are cast as his defense of the character of his entire ministry. What apology does he make for himself? He insists that repentance leads to celebration—joy in heaven, earthly feasting within God's family. That is, Jesus presents the disposition of his own ministry as the necessary complement to God's own character. In welcoming such persons as these social and religious outcasts to the table, Jesus is only giving expression to the expansive grace of God. By calling Jesus' behavior into question, these scribes and Pharisees are actually calling into question the character of God!

The Journey of Discipleship

If repentance plays such an important role in the ministries of John and Jesus, it is not surprising that the journey of discipleship is generally marked by repentance. When we recall that the experience of repentance is worked out with regard to the realities of day-to-day existence in Luke 3:10-14, we should also not be surprised to find those who follow Jesus leaving everything to do so (Luke 5:11, 28). At one point, Jesus even asserts, "None of you can become my disciple if you do not give up all your possessions" (Luke 14:33; see also 18:22, 28); such a response follows from the gift of the kingdom of God (Luke 12:32-34). Even family ties become forfeit in light of the unrelenting claims of God's kingdom (Luke 9:59-60; 12:52-53; 14:26). These are new times, Jesus proclaims, and they demand a fresh level of obedience to the ancient-and-present purpose of God.

If repentance marks the onset of the journey, however, the evidence of the Lukan narrative is that this beginning, as crucial as it is, may be far removed from the destination![13] Simon Peter, James, and John may recognize their sinfulness, they may receive Jesus' call to join him in "catching people," and they may leave everything to follow him (Luke 5:1-11), but in an important sense this act of conversion marks the beginning of a process of conversion. Jesus goes on to instruct these and other disciples in the dispositions and practices appropriate to the converted life (especially Luke 6:12-49), but they show little understanding of the character of his mission (for example, Luke 9). In fact, just before the beginning of the lengthy journey to Jerusalem (Luke 9:51–19:48), Luke says of the disciples, "They did not understand [what Jesus was] saying; its meaning was concealed from them, so that they could not perceive it" (Luke 9:45). This is not because God concealed from them Jesus' significance; after all, the disciples are those to whom the secrets of the kingdom have been revealed (Luke 8:10), and Jesus assumes that they should be able to understand his words (Luke 9:44*a*). Rather, in spite of their conversion and experience thus far with Jesus, they remain too much in the clutches of old ways of reckoning God's ways, old allegiances, and old values. What is more, even at the close of the lengthy period of instruction narrated in the central journey section of Luke's Gospel (9:51–19:48), in which the formation of the disciples is a paramount concern, Luke records again that "they understood nothing about all these things . . . , and they did not grasp what was said" (Luke 18:34). Discipleship, as Luke develops it, entails a reconstruction of one's self within a new web of relationships, a transfer of allegiances, and the embodiment of transformed dispositions and attitudes.[14] Such a conversion requires resocialization within the community being formed around Jesus, and this is a process that continues for these disciples even beyond the Gospel narrative itself.

Brief reference to two episodes will highlight the degree to which conversion is for Jesus' disciples a process and not only a single point of beginning. In Acts 6:1-7, Luke records a moment of crisis within the Christian community centered in Jerusalem: "Now during those days, when the disciples were increasing in number, the Hellenists complained against the Hebrews because their widows were being neglected in the daily distribution of food" (v. 1). Typically glossed over as a practical problem having to do with resource allocation, the dilemma Luke describes is fundamentally theological in character. This becomes clear when it is realized that lack of sufficient resources due to the exponential growth of the community has led to a segregation within the community, between "Hellenists" (that is, Jewish Christians more fully influenced by Greek culture) and "Hebrews" (that is, Jewish Christians who were less so). According to the missionary portfolio given to the disciples by Jesus, such distinctions were to be of no consequence; disciples were to cross all social and religious boundaries as they served as his Spirit-empowered witnesses "to the end of the earth" (Acts 1:8). However, not only had these believers not yet departed Jerusalem, but they had in fact allowed socioreligious distinctions to divide them within their own community in Jerusalem. That is, far from demonstrating their readiness to engage in missionary activity "to the end of the earth," the Jerusalem disciples are portrayed as initially unable even to secure unity within their own ranks of intercultural discourse—this in spite of the apostles' tutelage under Jesus' teaching and the larger community's formation under the apostles' teaching (Acts 2:42). Of course, this event leads to a happy conclusion, but here we find no unmitigated endorsement of the Jerusalem leadership, who still seem possessed by old allegiances and values.

A second illustration of the process of conversion is found in Acts 10:1–11:18, Luke's complex narration of the encounter between Peter and Cornelius and its aftermath in the Jerusalem church. Cornelius is introduced first, with the result that we may gain the mistaken impression that this narrative unit essentially concerns him and his household; in fact, however, Luke's focus is more fundamentally on Peter and the Jerusalem church, and especially on the issue of ethnocentric practices. The significance of what transpires here is accentuated by multiple evidences of the divine hand at work—for example, the presence of an angel and the complementary visions (10:3-16), the prayer motif (and consequent anticipation of divine revelation [10:3, 4, 9]), and the spontaneous outpouring of the Spirit (10:44-47). Why is this level of divine intervention necessary? This emphasis does not serve the legitimation of the communication of the good news to Gentiles, which has already been mandated by the risen Lord (Luke 24:47-48; Acts 1:8) and performed by Philip (Acts 8:26-40). Rather, the emphasis falls on the question of full fellowship between Jew and Gentile; indeed, hospitality, not preaching or baptism, was at stake in the protestations first of Peter (Acts 10:28*a*) and then of the circumcised in the Jerusalem church (Acts 11:2-3). Cornelius is converted, to be sure, but so are Peter and those of the Jerusalem community—Cornelius, in the sense that he moves from his position as a God-fearer on the margins of the Jewish religion to full membership within the community of God's people for whom Jesus is Lord; Peter and the Jerusalem community to a more full understanding and expression of their own confession that Jesus is indeed "Lord of all" (Acts 10:34-36).

The practice of the church in Acts was, finally, to welcome Gentiles into their communities with a status equal to that of existing members. Jesus' ministry had paved the way for such a practice, as had his missionary directives. However, it was only as Jesus' followers embraced more and more fully their own faith—that is, as the process of conversion continued—that this became so.

Summary

Although evidence for the experience of conversion in Luke-Acts is more pervasive and runs deeper than I can document here, I have at least begun to sketch Luke's portrayal of conversion, beginning with the ministry of John the Baptist and continuing into and beyond the ministry of Jesus in the Gospel. In doing so, I have demonstrated that conversion within the Lukan narrative is both event and process—or, better, an event leading to process. For both Jew and Gentile, conversion is the transference of allegiances that govern one's life; in the case of the Jew, this has to do especially with reformed conceptions of Yahweh's character and purpose, while for the Gentile it has to do with trusting the one true God, the living God. In either case, this is the God whose character and design are known through Jesus Christ. For Luke, conversion gives rise to and is confirmed in practices appropriate to these new allegiances, opens the way to ongoing profound transformations in one's theological and moral vision, and necessarily locates and immerses one in the multiethnic community of God's people. As Wayne Meeks has written of "turning" among early Christian groups more generally, converts acquire a new, primary reference group and are urged to act in a way worthy of what had happened to them and to their world;[15] theological transformation thus funds moral reform and the formation of a new community, *and* vice versa.

Conversion, the Spirit, and the Christian Community

Even if more can be made of Luke's presentation of conversion by following the unveiling of his narrative sequentially, it is also helpful to speak in terms of a more summary nature about important aspects of his portrayal. In particular, I want to highlight the important links that Luke draws between conversion, the Spirit, and the nature of the Christian community.

Within the narrative of Luke's second volume, Acts 2:42-47 has a special place. This is because it is the first of a series of summaries that dot the landscape of Acts which sketch the nature of the community of God's people. It reads as follows:

> (42) They held diligently to the teaching of the apostles and to the fellowship, to the breaking of bread and to the prayers. (43) Everyone had a sense of awe, and many wonders and signs were being done through the apostles. (44) Those who believed all joined in solidarity and held all things in common. (45) They would sell their property and possessions and distribute them to everyone according to each person's need. (46) Every day, while persisting in their unity in the temple, they were breaking bread in each other's homes—sharing food joyfully and unpretentiously, (47) praising God and having goodwill toward all the people. And the Lord was adding

> daily to the community those who were being saved. (my translation)

Following immediately on the heels of Peter's call to repentance and baptism, and the subsequent baptism of "those who welcomed his word" (Acts 2:38-41), this narrative summary serves two important and related functions. First, it exhibits the communal dimension of the consequences of the outpouring of the Spirit;[16] second, it demonstrates the quality of daily life among those who repent and are baptized in the name of the Jesus Christ. Luke thus amplifies the response urged by Peter in 2:38: "repent and be baptized."[17] In Luke 3:7-14, John the Baptist had amplified his call to repentance in response to questions from the crowds gathered around him by summarizing faithful response in down-to-earth, socioeconomic terms. Luke's summary in Acts 2 performs much the same role and serves to define the boundaries of the community being formed in the name of Jesus Christ with reference to its characteristic behaviors.

One of those characteristic behaviors, marked by the references to holding all things in common and "breaking bread in each other's homes—sharing food joyfully and unpretentiously," comes in for repeated development in the narrative of Acts. This is the practice of hospitality. The conversions of Peter and Cornelius are set within the context of hospitality (Acts 10:23, 48), for example, and hospitality figures prominently in two further conversion episodes. The conversion of Lydia and her household is denoted by their being baptized; immediately thereafter she urges Paul and his companions, "If you have judged me to be faithful to the Lord, come and stay at my home" (Acts 16:15). Similarly, the baptism of the Philippian jailer is set within the context of his washing the wounds of Paul and Silas and his bringing them into his home and setting food before them (Acts 16:25-34). This is consistent with Jesus' words to his disciples in the Gospel of Luke; sending them out in pairs to carry on the work of proclamation and healing, he observes the intimate association of reception of the good news and reception of those who share the good news (Luke 10:7-8). Luke's summary in Acts 2 situates this meal-sharing in the context of the larger experience of salvation ("joyfully") and speaks to the coherence between the gospel and the sharing of food ("unpretentiously"). Just as the gospel is offered without reference to concerns with religious purity and social position, so meals were to be shared freely, without the usual expectations of reciprocity and without concerns for purity and status. The community embodies in its common life the message of repentance.

A crucial point that the summary in Acts 2:42-47 does not mention explicitly, but that is evident from its location immediately after the outpouring of the Spirit and Peter's Pentecost address, is the basis for repentance and for the proclamation of repentance. Elsewhere, it is evident that repentance itself is a gift from God (Acts 5:31; 11:18), but Acts 2 clarifies why this gift is now available and why the moment for repentance, among Jew and Gentile alike, has come. This is because Jesus has been enthroned as Lord and Christ and has received and poured out the promise of God, the Holy Spirit; and this marks the decisive shift in the history of the actualization of God's promises to his people. These are "the last days." Salvation is available to all. Faced with the crisis of impending judgment, all people are called to repent and in this way join the community of God's people. The times have changed. Nothing can be the same. Repent.

Conclusion: From Darkness to Light

Let me now attempt to draw together some of the threads of Luke's presentation as this relates to conversion, both in relation to the overall theological drama in which conversion is embedded and with regard to the experience of conversion as this is developed in Luke-Acts. Luke grounds the call and experience of conversion most pointedly in his understanding of the purpose of God. This apparently simple statement is actually profound in its implications. First, it means that the sort of conversion sponsored by the narrative of Luke-Acts is deeply embedded in the ancient story of God's dealings with Israel; it is to this God, the God of Israel, that life must be directed. Second, it means that this conversion is to a particular reading of that ancient story—a reading that insists that the only genuine line tracing the actualization of God's purpose passes through the life, death, and exaltation of Jesus,

Messiah and Lord. For Jew and Gentile, alike, then, conversion is ultimately christological, and the community of the converted are known as those who call on the name of the Lord Jesus. Third, it means that this conversion is eschatologically driven, since it is the eschatological outpouring of the Spirit that marks the turn of the ages, that motivates the Christian call to conversion, and that makes conversion possible. All of this means that conversion is both gift and response. Luke's perspective on conversion thus takes seriously that the first and initiating act is God's.

Luke's contribution to our understanding of the concept and experience of conversion is to ground conversion in the grand narrative of God's ancient and ongoing purpose. Additionally, Luke's perspective refuses any facile distinctions between conversion as act and process, between cognitive and moral change, between movement from one religion to another and deepening commitment within one's religion, and between personal and community formation. To each of these possible emphases, Luke's narrative issues a resounding yes. This is because conversion is for Luke a radical allegiance to the Lord and, concomitant with this relationship, a fundamental orientation toward the vision of God and God's work expressed through the life, death, exaltation, and ongoing presence of the Lord Jesus. To embrace the Lord in this way—"to welcome the word," as Acts 2:41 has it (my translation)—is a transformative act that places all of life in a new light; that leads one inexorably into an intercultural, communal existence with others who "call on the name of the Lord" and who thus espouse and propagate this vision of God's restorative purpose; and that manifests itself necessarily in behaviors congruous with the way of Jesus Messiah.

Chapter Seven

New Creation or New Birth? Conversion in the Johannine and Pauline Literature

Ben Witherington III

Though it is certainly possible to talk about interpreting the Bible in a Wesleyan or Calvinistic manner, and it is of course true that no one comes to the text of the Bible without a point of view, when one speaks about interpreting the biblical text *according* to a certain tradition, one has already made certain assumptions about what should have priority in interpretation—namely the tradition rather than the Scripture itself. In his preface to the *Standard Sermons*, John Wesley professed to be a true son of the Reformation when he called himself *homo unius libri*. He, at least in principle, endorsed the hermeneutical approach of allowing the Scripture to have its own say, having the first and indeed the last word; and if that word is at odds with one's church tradition, so much the worse for that tradition. The Scripture was seen as the ultimate authority and the final arbiter of the truth about any given tradition, experience, or rational claim.[1]

In that spirit, I intend in this chapter not to examine purple passages or proof texts in the New Testament that have to do with conversion "from a Wesleyan point of view," but rather to simply examine those texts that were especially crucial to Wesley, those that most formed his views on the matter of the new creation, whether he understood those texts correctly or not. Without question, most of those texts come either from the Johannine or Pauline literature, and we will examine a sampling from each of these bodies of literature.

Conversion from the Eagle's Viewpoint—John and 1 John

Though this point is often overlooked, it is only in the Fourth Gospel that we actually have any discussion about being "born again" or "born from above," and that language is actually only featured in one passage—John 3. It is true, of course, that one cannot determine the theological importance of an idea by the frequency with which it is mentioned in the New Testament. Nonetheless, it needs to be said from the start that the concept of "being born again" is not frequently mentioned even in the Johannine corpus. In the heat of a revival, like the eighteenth-century Wesleyan revival, a few texts were used with great frequency because of the need for renewal or revival. It is this urgency that makes a text like John 3 especially important to someone who stands in the Wesleyan tradition. What then does Jesus' dialogue with Nicodemus actually suggest?

First, it is extremely important not to be anachronistic in one's reading of this much used text. The discussion here is not about baptism, or baptismal regeneration, but indeed about a spiritual transformation or about-face that we usually call conversion. Here we have a presentation of a discussion between two adult Jews, and one of them is saying to the other that a radical transformation of one's self is required in order to see the dominion of God. Such a conversation was not unknown amongst early Jews, but there is an unexpected element in the conversation here. Jesus is suggesting that those who are Jews, indeed even leading teachers among the Jews, must experience this transformation in order to see the dominion of God. Early Jews might discuss such a matter when the subject was what Gentiles or proselytes might need to do to join the people of God, or perhaps even if the subject turned to bad or apostate Jews, but Nicodemus fits neither of these categories. In this regard, Jesus' behavior may be compared to that of John the Baptist as he is portrayed in Matthew 3:1-12 (contrast Luke 3:7-17 where it is the crowd, tax collectors, and soldiers rather than

Pharisees and Sadducees who are addressed by John). The upshot of Jesus' dialogue with Nicodemus is surely that everyone needs to be born again, or born from above—even Jesus' fellow Jews, even his fellow Jewish teachers. It is not surprising that such a teaching produced a response of shock and bewilderment on the part of Nicodemus. Was God then treating his chosen people like pagans or proselytes as the eschatological reign of God broke in? Some of the details of the text need to be attended to at this juncture.

John 3:5 speaks of a birth "out of" or "from" water. As I have shown in many other works, water was the normal Jewish metaphor for various parts of the procreating process—insemination (with a drop of water), the water surrounding the child in the womb, the childbearing, and the actual birthing process (coming forth from water—see Prov. 3:15-18; Song of Sol. 4:12-15; m. Abot. 3:1; 3 Enoch 6:3; 1 QH 3:9-10).[2] The phrase "born out of water" in such an environment would normally be taken to refer to physical or natural human birth. Our text couples the reference to that sort of birth with a reference to birth out of or from Spirit. Water and Spirit are seen as the mediums or agencies through which birth happens. It is possible, since we have but one preposition before the phrase "water and Spirit" and neither of these nouns has the definite article, that the Evangelist is referring to one birth not two. But grammatically this conclusion is not required; and in verse 6 (NIV), "flesh gives birth to flesh, and Spirit gives birth to spirit" suggests two births are meant—hence the phrase "born again." The Gospel of John, of course, is laden with irony, and so Nicodemus assumes that Jesus is somehow referring to a second physical birth. Thus Jesus must distinguish the two births here, not identify them.

In the parallel text in 1 John 5:6-8 we have articleless references to water and blood, preceded by one preposition; and there it is rather clear that we are dealing with metaphors for two different events—namely the birth and death of Jesus, by which means he comes to us. Thus neither the Gospel context nor the larger Johannine corpus favors the view that water and Spirit refer to the same event, much less that the author means that one gets the Spirit through water baptism. The issue here is spiritual regeneration, not sacramental theology. But behind the discussion here lies also a robust theology of creation—both being physically born and being spiritually reborn are required if one is to see the dominion of God or enter it. John 3:7 indicates that Nicodemus is astounded by Jesus' teaching. The following verse draws an analogy between the wind and its work and that of the Spirit. The analogy is especially apt because in this Gospel *hearing*, not seeing, the Word is the necessary prerequisite to new birth and entering the dominion of God.

It may be said that John Wesley's instincts, in the way he chose to preach on this particular text, were generally consonant with the thrust of the passage itself. Though Wesley offers a notional assent to his Anglican tradition affirming baptismal regeneration in his sermon "The Marks of the New Birth," he says: "That these privileges . . . are *ordinarily* annexed to baptism (which is thence termed by our Lord in the preceding verse, the being 'born of water and of the Spirit') we know";[3] but he then immediately goes on to say that the first mark of the new birth is faith, by which he means true living faith, not mere notional assent to various propositions.

Indeed, drawing on John 1:12-13, he stresses that the new birth comes by no natural means, but rather only from God. That text does indeed contrast physical human birth (and human decisions and activities that lead to it) with birth from God.[4] Will Wesley then go on to repudiate his Anglican baptismal teaching? No, but he does say clearly enough that though a person may have been baptized, may have been made a child of God by that means, in terms of actual spiritual experience "how many are the baptized gluttons and drunkards, the baptized liars and common swearers, . . . the baptized whoremongers, thieves, extortioners?" He stresses that one can and must be born again outside of baptism if one does not manifest the marks of the new birth subsequent to baptism.[5]

He adds: "Lean no more on the staff of that broken reed, that you *were* born again in baptism. Who denies that ye were then made children of God, and heirs of the kingdom of heaven? But, notwithstanding this, ye are now children of the devil? Therefore, you must be born again."[6] Thus, while on exegetical grounds, one might fault Wesley for trying to have it both ways (baptismal regeneration and the new birth subsequent thereto in the case of most persons), his instincts throughout the revival to placing the emphasis on the *marks* of the new birth as proof of the condition, with the primary mark being living faith, were surely correct. Wesley chose wisely when he picked this text to preach on the marks of the new birth, to focus on spiritual experience gained through faith rather than on sacramental theology.[7]

Conversion, from a Johannine perspective, then is something brought about by the Holy Spirit and involving a real spiritual experience that in some ways is analogous to birth, an experience that results in a change in human character and behavior. It should be noted that the analogy with childbirth clearly places the emphasis not on the action of the one being born, but on the action or influence of outside forces. The unborn does not make a decision to be born. Notice that in John 1:12-13 the author specifically denies that human will is what *causes* or produces the new birth. Rather it is a divine action and initiative of God that creates this condition. This is not to deny that such actions of God require that one respond in faith, but the emphasis in John is placed squarely on the divine side of the equation, not on the voluntarist side of the ledger, as is so often the case in Wesleyan and Arminian discussions of conversion.

First John

It will be in order to consider briefly another Johannine text, 1 John 3:9, which also was the theme verse for Wesley's sermon "The Great Privilege of Those That Are Born of God." As is well known, the Elder (or "old man") who wrote these epistles makes a distinction between sin as a condition and sins as activities. The verse in question would seem to be referring to activities in view of the verb "to do" here, which is in the present tense. Some have attempted to argue that we should translate this as "does not continue to/in sin," or even "does not continually sin," on the basis that this verb is seen as in the present continual tense. This is probably overpressing the grammar at this point, for the author of this material is not famous for his nuanced use of the language's capacity. Is, then, our author an early advocate of the Wesleyan view that, if one defines sin as a willful violation of a known law, a person who is born again can avoid such an act?

Some consideration must be given to the possibility that the author is deliberately putting things dramatically or with use of rhetorical hyperbole, a point supported by the observation of many scholars that 1 John is more of a homily than a letter. What we know is that because the Elder is operating in a situation that is spiritually dangerous for his converts, he feels a need to use strong language involving polar opposites in order to persuasively warn his converts not to sin. I. H. Marshall puts the matter succinctly: "John makes his statements in absolute terms: the way in which he can interchange subjects and predicates indicates that there is a one-to-one correspondence between those who are born of God and those who do what is right, love one another, believe in Jesus, overcome the world, and refrain from sin. There are no shades of grey here: it is a case of belonging to the light or the darkness, to God or to the devil, to righteousness and love or to sin."[8] When one is faced with real spiritual danger, even the prospect of apostasy, strong and polemical language is in order. Such language is meant to be taken seriously, but it is usually not intended absolutely literally.

What, then, should one conclude from 1 John 3:9 when considered in its own original literary and rhetorical context? It is probably *not* true that the Elder defines sin so narrowly that it only refers to willful acts, for when he speaks about "having sin" in 1 John 1:8 it appears not to be the same thing as "doing sin." When in 1:7 he speaks of the blood of Jesus cleansing one from all sin, he is speaking not of deeds but of cleansing from the inward effects of sin such as guilt, yet this can be called sin as well. It is true, however, that our author believes Christ's blood will cleanse the believer from all the effects of sin, and it is also true that he believes that a person born of God need not "do sin" (that is, willfully and willingly commit sinful acts). The bottom line is that our author believes wholeheartedly the theology of the new birth enunciated in texts like John 3; it involves a radical transformation of individuals which cleanses their hearts and empowers them to walk in light and so avoid conscious acts of darkness.

It would be hard to overplay the importance for Wesley of the insights about sin and human nature, including the Christian's nature, found in 1 John. In his sermon on 1 John 3:9, he stresses several points that were crucial for his own theology of conversion: first, he did not concur with those of the Reformed faith who tended to equate justification by faith with the new birth. Justification has to do with one's position in relationship to God, the new birth has to do with one's actual spiritual condition. "The former changes our outward relation to God, so that . . . we become children; by the latter our inmost souls are changed, so that . . . we become saints."[9] Second, "the being born of God . . . implies not barely the being baptized, or any outward change whatever; but a vast inward change, a change wrought in the soul, by . . . the Holy Ghost."[10] Third, if one abides in God, in love, in faith, in the spirit of prayer and thanksgiving, in such a state and in such a condition of relationship with God focusing wholeheartedly on God, one does not commit, indeed cannot commit sin—one is too busy doing other godly things.[11] Fourth, but so dependent is the believer on God in this matter that he requires the continual spiritual respiration of God into his soul so that he may keep his soul from sin. The believer must fight an ongoing battle with temptation, and if the believer remains in living dependency on God, reliant on God's daily supply of aid and grace, he or she can overcome temptation and avoid conscious sin.[12] These are the sort of conclusions Wesley draws from the material in 1 John. He welds a Pauline conception of justification with a Johannine conception of sin and the new birth, or what it means to be born of God.

Yet it must be said that even for the author of 1 John the definition of sin as "a willful violation of a known law" is surely too narrow. As Marshall says, the issue of law does not come up in 1 John, and accordingly there is not a focus in 1 John on sin being a matter of violating or breaking a known law.[13] There is more to be said for the view that the Elder is focusing on rebellion against God (and so apostasy), as the essence of what is meant by sin. And such rebellion involves both a condition and the actions that manifest that condition. It is a violation of a relationship, not a violation of code or a commandment that the Elder is chiefly thinking of when he speaks of sin. The Elder, however, seems to agree with Wesley that victory over willful sin is possible if one abides in God.

Conversion from the Groundling's Point of View—the Pauline Corpus

One cannot help but be struck by how very dependent Wesley was on Paul for the essence of his message about justification, salvation by faith, and the work of the Spirit in the believer's life. Of the first seventeen of the Standard Sermons, no fewer than twelve of them have as their theme text some passage from either Romans, Ephesians, or 2 Corinthians. It follows, of course, from this that, as with the case of the Johannine corpus, if Wesley badly misunderstood the thrust of the apostle to the Gentiles, this must mean he badly misunderstood matters at the heart of the *ordo salutis*. We must consider now several Pauline texts in their original context, and afterward ask how Wesley's understanding of them fares by comparison.

Romans 7

Perhaps it would be well to start with one of the most difficult of Pauline texts, Romans 7:7-25, which has been a battleground in the fight to determine just what is the spiritual state of the unbeliever and of the believer. To put it another way, what does conversion actually accomplish in the one who comes to faith in Christ? Does Romans 7 in essence describe some sort of believer in Christ, or some sort of unbeliever outside of Christ? If it describes the believer, one may ask: What is it that God hath wrought in the human soul that is converted? Is *simul justus et peccator* really the most Paul wants to say about the state of the converted person?

A good deal of the problem in properly understanding Romans 7:7-25 comes from not recognizing two important factors: (1) the nature of Paul's rhetoric here, and in particular the multiple use of the devices of impersonation and also personification; and (2) the narrative thought world and storyline that undergirds the text. I have dealt with this matter at greater length elsewhere,[14] and here will be able only to summarize what I see as the drift of the text. First, Romans 7 is not an isolated excursus, but a continuation of the discussion of the Law, and of the thread of discussion in Romans 1–6. The text also flows quite naturally into Romans 8.

Romans 7:5-6 should probably be seen as a preview of the argument that follows. Paul here states what the believers *were* (imperfect tense verb) in the flesh, and in verse 6 there is reference to what "we" (believers) now have been made. Notice that Romans 8:8-9 is quite emphatic that being "in the flesh" is a condition that for the Christian is in the past. Believers have been released from the Law, which does not simply mean set loose from the Law's condemnation. The analogy with the death of the husbands surely suggests a total release from this Law. It is natural then to assume that Paul is going to go on and contrast the believer's condition before and after conversion, before and after the point of release from bondage.

Careful attention must be paid to the shift in verb tenses that occurs in this passage. In Romans 7:7-13 we have past tenses, whereas in verses 14-25 we have present tenses. This suggests to most commentators that Paul is changing the subject somewhat in the second half of this passage, or at least he is changing the time frame with which he is viewing the subject. In my view, Adam is the subject of verses 7-13, while verses 14-25 are about those who are in Adam. Adam is portrayed as the prime example of what happens when humans submit to temptation. Paul will then explain how Adam's legacy has been continued, how the effect of his sin has caused bondage for all. Thus, all fallen creatures inevitably perpetrate Adam's error again and again.

Perhaps the major question about Romans 7:14-25 is Who is the "I"? The two major categories of opinions with many lesser permutations and combinations is either that the "I" is autobiographical or that it is non-autobiographical. Even if it is autobiographical the question becomes whether it is Paul speaking as the Christian apostle, or Paul speaking about his life before his conversion to Christ. We may break down the autobigraphical possibilities as follows: (1) it is Paul painfully speaking about his current Christian experience; (2) it is Paul speaking about his past, pre-Christian experience as he viewed it *then*; (3) it is Paul speaking of his pre-Christian experience as he views it since becoming a Christian.

A second set of options in regard to the "ego" is that Paul is using the rhetorical device of impersonation for dramatic effect. On this showing, the "I" could be Paul referring to the Jewish experience as Jews view it, or the "I" could refer to how Christians view the Jewish experience.

A third set of options suggests that the "I" is indeed Paul speaking, but he is speaking as a representative of all Christians, describing their experience in general. A variant of this suggests that Paul is speaking of the experience of carnal Christians, Christians living at a substandard level and trying to fight the battle against sin with their own might or will power.

Finally, it is possible that the "I" in the latter half of Romans 7 refers to a person at a particular juncture in his or her life, namely at the point of but just prior to conversion. This person is under conviction of sin and feels the weight of guilt from the Law's condemnation of sin. This person is spiritually alive enough to know and want to do what is right, but has not yet been converted and so is fighting and losing the battle against temptation and sin. This last option suggests that there is a subtext to Romans 7:14-25, and that the story climaxes at verse 25*a* ("I thank God through Jesus Christ" [my translation]) and with the pronouncement of God in Romans 8:1 about Christians: "There is therefore now no condemnation."

New Testament scholars have in general concluded in light of the study of early Jewish literature that Paul could not possibly be referring to the actual experience of early Jews in relationship to Torah, or put a different way, he could not be referring to how early Jews themselves actually *felt* about their experience under the Law.[15] Bolstering this conclusion, and applying it to Paul himself when he was Saul the Pharisee, is a text like Philippians 3:6, where Paul says that in regard to the righteousness that the Law requires he be blameless. One may take literally the term *amemtos,* in which case Paul likely means that there was nothing the Law could accuse him of, which is different from saying he was faultless or had perfect character. Nevertheless, it is a claim that rules out the suggestion that Paul was like Luther when Luther was an Augustinian monk—full of angst and guilt about his sin, and continually frustrated at his inability to avoid breaking God's commandments or laws. As K. Stendahl has shown, it is a mistake to retroject the "introspective consciousness of the West" as embodied in a person like Luther, into the experience of a first-century

Jew like Saul of Tarsus.[16] Notice that Paul almost never speaks of repentance or forgiveness in a Christian context, manifesting a robust rather than a sin-laden conscience as a Christian. To the contrary, Philippians 3:12-16 indicates that he believes he is making progress in his Christian life, working out his salvation with fear and trembling because God is indeed making progress in and with his soul. His anxieties in life are basically about his converts and about his fellow non-Christian Jews, not about himself or his own spiritual condition. One would be hard-pressed to find anywhere in Paul's letters an apology for or a confession of sins he had committed as a Christian, though he certainly admits to some weaknesses, including physical weaknesses, and to his vulnerability. When he speaks with regret, he speaks of his horrible behavior while a Pharisee in regard to his persecution of Christians (1 Cor. 15:9; Gal. 1:13). But Paul is equally clear in Galatians 1:13 that this was his "former" way of life; he is not describing current sins.

I would suggest that the most viable and profitable way to read Romans 7 is not through the grid of the Augustinian and later Protestant foreground, but rather, as Paul did, with the Genesis story of creation, human fall, and redemption in the background. Romans 7, then, is a reflection primarily on Genesis 3 and its sequel, a reflection on what it means (1) to have been Adam, and (2) to be Adam's children. This explains neatly the change in tenses between 7:7-13 and 7:14-25. Adam is dead and gone, and even when the device of impersonation is used, past tense verbs are required to make the point. But, of course, Adam's progeny are still very much alive and still struggling with his legacy.

It will be noted that throughout the Pauline corpus Paul contrasts the state of those who are in Adam and those who are in Christ (see 1 Cor. 15:21-22; Rom. 5:12-15). Redemption or conversion for Paul means a great deal more than just a change of position in relationship to God, or even a change of opinions about God. It is not just a matter of justification by grace through faith, though that is very important for Paul, as it would later be for Wesley. For Paul, there is a real change or transformation involving a new creation (2 Cor. 5:17; see also Rom. 8:2-9; 12:2). This change affects the human will, mind, or heart, and the emotions. It is only the physical human body and the inclinations or desires stimulated by that body that is largely untouched by redemption and will not be set right until the resurrection. Thus Paul can say, "Though the body is dead because of sin, the Spirit is life because of righteousness" (Rom. 8:10). By the power of the Spirit, the believer can indeed put to death the fallen deeds prompted by the body (8:13). This was certainly not true of the person described in Romans 7:14-25 who can only cry out in dismay, "Who will deliver me from this body of death." That person has not experienced the deliverance that the person described in Romans 8:1-13 knows and depends upon.

The present tenses of Romans 7:14-25 must be taken seriously—Paul is describing the condition of some current group. It is important that one relate the last eleven verses of Romans 7 back to Romans 7:5-6. There is a group of people, namely Christians, who *were* in the flesh, but the group described in 7:14-25 are in that condition now. About his Christian audience Paul says in Romans 8:9, "You are not in the flesh," and the law or rule of sin and death in a person's life has been vanquished by the law or rule of the Spirit of life. The verb *freed* in Romans 8:2 is in the aorist tense and refers to a punctiliar event of past conversion. In short, in light of what is on both sides of Romans 7:14-25, namely Romans 7:5-6 and Romans 8:1-9, it is highly unlikely that Paul thinks he is describing the normal or even the abnormal Christian life in that most controverted of all Pauline texts.

It is thus far more likely that in Romans 7:14-25 Paul is presenting a Christian view of the state of non-Christians, perhaps even non-Christians on the verge of conversion. He describes the plight of those who are in Adam. This argument is bolstered by the following considerations about Romans 7:6-13 which show that those verses are indeed likely about Adam: (1) the Genesis story was introduced in a preparatory way in Romans 5:12-21; (2) Romans 6:17-20 makes evident that sin reigns in death and that those outside Christ are "slaves to sin," unable to avoid sinning or to free themselves from sin's bondage; (3) Romans 7:7-13 retells the story of the Fall in the midst of the discussion of the Law and its effects on fallen human beings (they are death-dealing rather than life-giving); (4) believing that Moses wrote the Pentateuch, Paul believes that the commandment originally given to Adam is part of the

Mosaic Law; (5) Paul seems to have understood original sin as violation of the tenth commandment, the one about not coveting—desiring something other or more than one ought to desire; (6) Romans 7:7-13 deals with the paradox that though God's commandments are certainly good, yet human beings would not know what sin is had there not been commandments: "I would not have known what it is to covet had the Law not said, 'You shall not covet' "; (7) Paul retells the tale of Adam with a personification of sin and with impersonation, through the "I" of Adam; and (8) the story as told in verses 8-11 is as follows: "But sin [the serpent], seizing an opportunity in the commandment, produced in me all kinds of covetousness. . . . [But] I [Adam] was once alive apart from the law, but when the commandment came, sin revived and I died, and the very commandment that promised life proved to be death to me. For sin [the serpent], seizing an opportunity in the commandment, deceived me and through it killed me." Here indeed is the familiar primeval tale of life apart from sin, a single commandment given, deception, disobedience, and finally spiritual and then physical death. Only Adam and Eve experienced life before the commandment or the Law was given and only Adam and Eve were given just the one commandment. The same verb for *deception* is used here as in 2 Corinthians 11:3, where the deception in the Garden of Eden is clearly in view.

With this preface to Romans 7:14-25, it is hard not to read those latter verses as a description of all those who are outside of Christ but in Adam, but Paul speaks of them not just in the abstract but concretely as those who have a story, and can be led to the point of conversion to Christ and released from the bondage to the Law and sin and death. This narrative of a conversion in Romans 7:14–8:2 is a compelling one, and it is a major mistake to isolate 7:14-25 from either the Adamic background in 7:6-13 or the Christian foreground in Romans 8.

How then did John Wesley view Romans 7?[17] First, Wesley rightly stresses that Romans 7 is a continuation of Romans 6, and the subject is the comparison between the former and present state of a person who has become a Christian. He adds that Paul is trying also to wean Jewish believers from their fondness for the Mosaic Law. Of Romans 7:5 he says Paul speaks of the state of nature, before a person believed in Christ. It is interesting that from a rhetorical point of view, Wesley takes verses 7-25 of Romans 7 as a digression. Here is how he describes Paul's rhetorical tactics in these verses:

> The apostle, in order to show, in the most lively manner, the weakness and inefficacy of the law, changes the person and speaks as of himself, concerning the misery of one under the law. This St. Paul frequently does when he is not speaking of his own person, but only assuming another character, Rom. iii, 6, 1 Cor. x,30; chap. iv.6. The character here assumed, is that of a man, first, ignorant of the law, then under it, and sincerely, but ineffectually striving to serve God. *To have spoken this of himself, or any true believer, would have been foreign to the whole scope of his discourse; nay; utterly contrary thereto; as well as to what is expressly asserted, [Rom.] viii,2.*[18]

At the end of this exposition Wesley reminds the reader that Paul was not referring to himself or Christians ("the person whom I am personating, till his deliverance is wrought"). When Wesley comes to Romans 8:1, he says that Paul picks up again the thread of his discourse that he had interrupted at 7:7.

What can be said about Wesley's exegesis of this difficult text? First, it will be noted how he insists on reading the text in its larger literary context, and thus avoiding a certain kind of "proof-texting." Second, Wesley rightly attributes to Paul a certain degree of rhetorical finesse and flexibility. He believes that Paul not infrequently uses the device of impersonation—taking the point of view or playing the role of someone other than himself. He profitably points to Romans 3:5 as another example of this practice, and he refers to 1 Corinthians 4:6 as demonstrating that Paul is perfectly capable of using rhetorical figures of various sorts. There are, however, some difficulties with Wesley's general assumptions in dealing with Romans 7. He rightly recognizes that Paul believes in the bondage to sin of those outside of Christ, but this admission sits somewhat awkwardly with Wesley's theology of prevenient grace. Furthermore, the person in Romans 7:14-25 is specifically denying he has the power of contrary choice to avoid sin. He would like to do so but is unable to do so, for there is a power at work in him so great that the will of his mind is constantly overcome by the rule of sin and death in members. Yet perhaps one could argue that prevenient grace does not give one the power of contrary choice, but rather does something less than that for the non-believer (illuminate him about the will of God and about his own spiritual condition?). Thus, while Wesley's instincts are right on target in regard to seeing Romans 7 as a description of those outside of Christ, as seen from a Christian point of view, his theology of prevenient grace seems to cause him to somewhat underplay the radical nature of conversion. In fact, he uses a threefold paradigm of natural man, legal man (man under the Law), and evangelical man, and sees Romans 7:14-25 as describing a conversion from the second to the third of these states. But Paul knows no such threefold paradigm. All those who are in Adam are already in one sense under the Law, whether that Law is only written on their hearts or known through study of Torah (see Rom. 2:14-15). The Law was first given to Adam, and it was part of the Mosaic Law. Thus, while Wesley is quite right that Paul is offering an anatomy or story of conversion in Romans 7–8, it does not have quite the nuances Wesley wishes to find there in regard to particulars such as prevenient grace or the distinction between natural and legal "man."

Ephesians

At this juncture I wish to turn to a few of the Pauline texts Wesley used repeatedly during the revival to speak about the nature of conversion, asking first what Paul meant in these verses. The first of these texts is Ephesians 2:8, which speaks about salvation by grace through faith. The first thing to be said about the larger context of this verse is that the subject under discussion in the main is Gentiles. There is in this entire epideictic homily which we call the letter to the Ephesians a toggling back and forth between what Paul wants to say is true about Jews, and in particular Jews in Christ, and what he wants to say about Gentiles, both outside and within Christ.

Careful attention must be paid to the personal pronouns in this sermon whether the term is "we," or "you" (most often used to refer specifically to Gentile converts; see 2:11 and 4:17), or "I" to refer to the apostle himself. A case can be made that in Ephesians 1, for example, the discussion is entirely about Jewish Christians in 1:3-12 who are called the saints in 1:1, while at 1:13-14 Paul is referring to Gentiles, those who are called the faithful in 1:1. Again, we may notice how in 2:1-2 Paul refers specifically to the case of Gentiles, though he goes on to add that their condition outside Christ is not greatly different to anyone else who is also a child of Adam (see 2:3). The emphasis at 2:8, however, is that the Gentiles he is addressing have been saved by grace through faith, not by works, a point that needs to be emphasized, since the heart of Greco-Roman religion was works of piety such as prayers and sacrifices. Paul stresses that the Gentiles were far off (2:13), as opposed to God's first chosen people, the Jews, who were near (2:17).

Notice the language in 2:19, especially addressed to Gentile converts: "You are no longer foreigners and aliens, but fellow citizens with God's people and members of God's household" (NIV). The statement stresses that the Jews have always been God's people, and it is a matter of including Gentiles into that fold. But more particularly Paul means that God has made one new humanity of first Jews in Christ, to which has been added Gentiles in Christ, reconciling both not only to God but to each other as well (2:15-17). This is the "one body" referred to in 2:16. The argument then recognizes the priority of Jews and of Israel but sees the current people of God as Jew and Gentile united in Christ. This is even more apparent in Ephesians 3:6, where the distinction between the Gentiles and Jews, the former becoming heirs of God with the latter, is stressed. Again, at 3:18, the distinction is made between "you" and all the saints, with the latter appearing to be a reference to the Jewish Christians whom the Gentiles have been joined together with in Christ.

Paul is the apostle to the Gentiles, and the latter is the "you" he addresses in this homily. He must exhort them to turn their backs on the way they lived as pagans (4:17-20) and to turn their backs on darkness and embrace the light (5:8-13). The language used through this letter is typical Jewish language used when speaking about non-Jews who need to be converted. This is the especial topic of this letter, but Paul also admits that Jews who are now in Christ were in need of redemption as well (see 2:3).

How does Wesley use Ephesians 2:8? There is first of all the strong emphasis that salvation is not a matter of human works of any kind. Wesley does not appear to be cognizant that the discussion is particularly about the works, in particular the religious works of Gentiles, as he thinks more broadly of human efforts in general. Rather, Wesley stresses that salvation is a matter of mere grace, undeserved benefit from God. It is in order to point out that while the argument in Ephesians stresses that Gentiles have been included by grace through faith in the body of Christ, the language of predestination is used in Ephesians 1 of God's dealings with the saints (that is, the Jews, and more particularly the Jewish Christians). A distinction is made between those who are far off and are simply brought in by faith, and those who are near who are said to have been chosen in Christ, destined in advance and the like, and are finally said to have been the first to hope in Christ (see Eph. 1:11-12). Paul speaks of the burden of his own gospel to the Gentiles as being a mystery, an apocalyptic revelation that was given to him. This mystery is that God had decided as his purpose to bring together in Christ all things on heaven and earth and indeed all peoples both Jew and Gentile (1:9-10). It is in particular the inclusion of Gentiles into the fellowship with the saints that is said to be the mystery revealed to Paul and proclaimed by him as the apostle to the Gentiles (3:3-8).

Of these nuances in the Pauline argument, Wesley seems to be ignorant. He studiously avoids the subject of election broached in Ephesians 1 and sticks with what Paul says is true about Gentiles. He concentrates instead on the discussion of the sort of faith that could be called saving faith, by which he means a true and sincere faith and trust in Christ for salvation, not a mere notion assent to a list of religious propositions or dogmas. He goes on to stress that the salvation referred to in the Ephesian text is a present salvation, not merely a promise of salvation. Emphasis is placed on the particular grammar—"you have been saved." Wesley then expands and expounds of this to stress that this means salvation from all guilt and fear for past sin, indeed salvation from all original and actual, past and present sin. Notice that nothing is said about salvation from sin committed in the future by the Christian.[19] What Wesley also says is that this means salvation from habitual sin and from willful sin. The point is that sin no longer reigns in the believer's life.

It should be clear that Wesley goes well beyond what Paul says in the text, though one could argue that the pith or essence of Wesley's case is indeed grounded in the text here. Paul is indeed talking about real present salvation that changes a person's life, affecting his or her will, emotions, mind, heart, but Paul is addressing his particular audience, the Gentiles, when he does so. Paul does not make the distinctions Wesley would between habitual and occasional sin, or between willful or accidental sin. The latter is one of the greatest difficulties in dealing with Wesley. If one defines sin narrowly enough, then of course one can talk about Christians being entirely sanctified and so avoiding sin or not sinning, and having clean hearts; but it would appear that Paul has a broader and more comprehensive concept of sin, even though it is true to say that the emphasis in Ephesians is placed on willful trespasses or sinful deeds.

Romans 4 and 8

It will be possible to deal with Romans 4:5 and 8:1 together, since Wesley uses these texts to preach on the nature of justification by grace through faith, and the first fruits of that faith. It is fair to say that for the Wesleyan revival, like the Lutheran and Swiss revivals before it, justification by grace through faith was the theological dynamite that produced the most noise and effect throughout the church and the culture when the notion was promulgated. The first question, however, must be What is the Pauline thrust in these Romans texts that were so crucial to the Wesleyan revival?

We must begin with the observation that the term *dikaiosune* is used outside the New Testament mainly in forensic contexts and sense. Aristotle, for instance, says *dikaiosune* is that moral disposition that renders people apt to do just things and act justly, by which is meant to do things that are legal (*Nic. Ethics* 5.1129[a]). *Dikaiosune* involves doing what is due, what is owed. While in the Old Testament there is a regular distinction made between the righteous and the wicked, with God being on the side of the former (see Gen. 18:25; Ps. 24:5), Paul stresses that there are none righteous, all have sinned and fallen short of God's glory. This means that for Paul, God counts or reckons as "righteous" those who are not in fact intrinsically righteous. It is true to say that Paul emphasizes salvation by grace more than is done in early Judaism, and of course he stresses that Christ is the agent and means of this salvation, something non-Christian Jews would not agree with. The classic question of how God can be both just and the justifier of sinful persons was a live issue for Paul.

Often salvation and righteousness were linked in the Old Testament, as they are in Paul's letters (see Isa. 46:13; Pss. 98:2; 103:6), which explains in part why some Judaizing Jewish Christians were incensed over Paul's idea of justifying the sinner by or through faith. But Paul's point is that God relates to sinners on a different basis and in a different manner than he did in the Mosaic era. God now pardons the wicked or the sinner. Since all receive salvation while still sinners, this shows that God justifies the ungodly. It would appear that Paul believes that there are two standards of righteousness, one which the Law demands, about which Paul says he was blameless in regard to violations (Phil. 3:4-9), and then the righteousness of God himself, by which standard no one is righteous, for here the standard is not just a matter of avoiding illegal behavior but of being positively just and righteous. Yet when Paul uses the phrase "righteousness of God" in Romans 1:17, he appears to mean by it the same thing as what he means by the phrase the righteousness of faith (see Phil. 3:9). In other words, Paul is talking about God's eschatological redemptive activity. Yet clearly enough at Romans 3:25-26 it seems obvious that the phrase refers to God's character rather than his saving activity.[20] Christ's death proves that God is indeed righteous and could not overlook sin forever. His justice had to be served at some point.

When righteousness is predicated of God, it refers in part to God's activity at the final judgment when he will play the role of the just judge. However, Paul believes that God was manifesting that judgment already on the cross, with Christ bearing the brunt of it. Divine righteousness was firmly vindicated at Calvary, and it is vindicated again when God accepts only those who have faith in the Christ who atoned for sins on the cross. In what sense, then, are believers righteous through faith?

Is righteousness through faith a position or a condition, a status before God or a standing? Is this righteousness a legal fiction? Is God deceived about believers, so that when God looks on them he only sees the perfectly righteous Christ? No, rather what the term means is that such people are acquitted in God's court, justified, reconciled to God, in right standing with him. This means that God has pardoned their offenses, but not without those offenses being atoned for first by Christ. Notice that in 2 Corinthians 5:17 the new creation and righteousness are not synonymous. It is the right-standing with God that is the basis of the transformation of the person and his or her moral life.

In a key text, Romans 4:3ff., Paul uses the ledger language "to reckon." Abraham is seen as the prototype of Christian faith. Yet notice that Abraham's faith in God was not righteousness in itself but was counted as righteousness. The same is said to be true of Christians in Romans 4:3—faith in Christ's death is credited or reckoned to believers as acquittal, leaving them in right standing with God. This is not merely a legal fiction, because someone has actually already paid the price for the sin that separates the believing person from God. Notice, however, that Paul goes beyond a forensic sense in Romans 5:9-10, where we are told that the believer is righted or made righteous by the blood of Christ, which is seen as involving the believer being reconciled to God. Not merely are negative obstacles removed from the divine-human encounter, but there is the positive reestablishing of a living relationship and fellowship between the two parties. Being reckoned as righteous means also in part being saved from the wrath to come on Judgment Day. It has an eschatological reference. Christ makes things right between the sinner and God.

The conclusion of this discussion must be that when Paul uses the *dikaiosune* language of human beings, he is referring primarily to the status or standing they have before a righteous God. When Paul wants to speak of moral purification and sanctification, Paul uses an entirely different set of terms. Paul neither fuses nor confuses the ideas of justification or objective righteousness and sanctification or subjective righteousness. As Romans 8:33-34 says, to make righteous is the opposite of to condemn (see Rom. 8:1). Second Corinthians 5:19 means that Jesus was reckoned to be sinner, so that we might be reckoned to be righteous. *Dikaiosune* has to do with one's legal guilt and position as a result. Thus, while it is true that Paul primarily only uses this language in Romans and Galatians, one cannot determine the importance of the idea by mere word count. This is the language Paul chooses to refer to how one is incorporated into Christ, or how right relationship with God is reestablished.

One of the two sermons Wesley preached most often during the revival was "Justification by Faith," based on Romans 4:5. In this sermon Wesley stresses that actual righteousness is not what is meant by this language. It is not a matter of being made just—that is what is meant by sanctification. Justification is the clearing of the sinner from the accusations against him or her, the pardoning of his or her offenses.[21] God's Son has made propitiation and expiation on the cross, and the result is reconciliation with God of the ungodly. Wesley insists that of course it is the ungodly whom God justifies, for if there were those who were perfectly righteous, they would not need to be justified by God. Christ was not in a condition that he required to be justified before God. The sinner was in a condition where he had to be justified by God, and the objective means of that justification was the death of Christ, while the subjective means was by faith alone. In this presentation, Wesley does not differ significantly from the classical presentation of Luther or Calvin, though he disagreed with both about the scope of the atonement (for example, Christ died for all sinners, not just the elect). The fruit or results of justification are discussed in Wesley's sermon "The First Fruits of the Spirit." When one is justified through faith, one has right standing with God and is no longer condemned by God. To put this in a positive manner, one is at peace with God and is capable of walking in or by the Spirit.

It must be said that while Wesley puts more emphasis on the concept of justification than does Paul, it does not appear that he deviates in any serious way from the Pauline sense of the concept. Wesley clearly sees the forensic thrust of the language and does not confuse justification with sanctification, or even justification with the new creation. The language of legal reckoning or crediting is familiar to Wesley, and he understands the point of the Pauline analogy between Abraham and the believer in regard to the matter of faith. However, one could quarrel with Wesley about the lack of clarity about the issue of final justification and its basis on Judgment Day. Wesley, in other contexts, insisted that final justification is based on faith plus works, if there is time and opportunity to perform them. It is not clear that this is wholly congenial to what Paul says about justification, but the matter could be debated.

Conclusions

The author of the Johannine literature presents conversion and salvation from a divine point of view, from the top down (born from above, born of God, born again). Paul on the other hand presents conversion from a more mundane and human point of view, from the bottom up (new creature, new creation; formerly in Adam, now in Christ). Both use dramatic metaphors to describe a dynamic event, an event like a human birth, an event like the beginning of the human race. Both sense the drama and the necessity of human conversion if persons are to cease being sinners and become saints, move from darkness to light, abandon Adam for Christ, who is the eschatological Adam. Both believe that conversion results in a change not just of opinions or orientation, or even of relationship with God and humans, but a real inward change, a change of heart and will and mind and emotions, though the new creature, the reborn, still awaits a new body. It is this reality that involves both relational and real change that these writers use a variety of metaphors to describe. What makes this especially amazing is that in the Greco-Roman world of the first century, not many believed that human character could be changed. Most felt that character was determined at birth by generation, gender, or geography, and only revealed, not developed or changed, over time. Against this flow of widespread cultural assumptions comes the Jewish and Christian theology of conversion. As it turns out, early Jews and Christians were saying you can teach old dogs new tricks, as Nicodemus learned, to his surprise, from Jesus.

All interpreters of the Bible have their own urgencies when they approach the text, and John Wesley was certainly no different. Some of the concerns and emphases of the Elder or of Paul are absent in Wesley. Sometimes Wesley overlooks or distorts the real thrust of a biblical text, but on the whole his exegetical instincts and his concern for context are commendable. On the central question of this essay, Wesley was surely correct to conclude that conversion is a major thrust of both the Johannine and Pauline literature. However, on the one hand, there are issues the Johannine and Pauline texts raises that Wesley does not address; and, on the other hand, there are concepts Wesley adds or brings to the text that are probably not part of the original author's intended meaning. A few examples will suffice.

For example, Wesley's handling of Romans 7 is remarkably deft and nuanced. Wesley recognizes that Paul is involved in rhetorical role-playing by his use of the first person singular in this text. He rightly stresses that the earlier portion of Romans 7 and the material that follows in Romans 8 must rule against identifying the "I" with a Christian. Yet he also brings his tripartite schema of natural, legal, and evangelical man to the text; this is foreign to Paul, who knows only two categories—those in Adam or those in Christ, those freed from the Law or those in its thrall. Nor does Wesley really grapple with the issue of the "I" exclaiming that he is unable to do what his mind wishes to do. This surely has implications for theology of prevenient grace. Still, his overall handling of this crucial text is consonant with Paul's theology of lostness and of salvation.

Again, Wesley's instincts in his treatment of John 3 are good. The real thrust of the material has to do with spiritual experience, not sacramental practice. He is right that Jesus is suggesting that all persons must be born again in order to see the dominion of God. Wesley does not recognize that the word *water* in this text is a metaphor for natural birth, as it is in 1 John 5, but still he understands the essence of the dialogue with Nicodemus. While not denying his Anglican heritage of baptismal regeneration, he minimizes its importance by saying that the vast majority of people can and do need to be born again after infant baptism, having sinned away the blessing of baptism by their adult years.

The discussion of the material in 1 John led to the conclusion that a definition of *sin* as lawlessness or lawbreaking was inadequate. Though it appears the Elder would agree that a Christian can avoid a willful violation of a known law, he would not agree that this is the full scope of sin which he is discussing. He speaks of both having and doing sin, of both sin as condition and sin as behavior. Wesley seems to understand some of this complexity, but he wishes to place the emphasis on the real positive change that happens in conversion enabling a Christian to have victory over temptation and sin.

There is not a great deal to quibble with when it comes to Wesley's handling of justification in Romans, although he places more stress on the idea than does Paul. This is perhaps because Paul is largely addressing those who are already Christians. More exception can be taken to Wesley's treatment of Ephesians 2 in this respect: on the one hand, he fails to read the signals in the text that suggest Paul is discussing almost entirely the plight of the Gentiles; and on the other hand, he generalizes the text to make it refer to all sorts of human works. Yet Wesley is surely right that Paul wanted to stress the present nature of salvation, and that it is experienced through or by means of saving faith. The relationship of Jews and Gentiles in Christ falls outside Wesley's purview because it is not the burning issue that it is for Paul.

Clearly the texts Wesley regularly used in the revival address matters of conversion and salvation. The Pauline and Johannine writers placed great stress on the need for the new birth or the new creation, and indeed stressed that all need to experience it. The issue is not just one's position before God—God's declaration that, though a sinner, a person will not be condemned—but one's actual spiritual condition. Salvation amounts to more than justification, even for Paul. The difficulties cited above in the way Wesley handles some of these texts should not be allowed to deflect us from the conclusion that essentially he was well-grounded in the Word when it came to his theology of conversion. Indeed, one could only wish that his progeny of today were equally well-grounded in such texts.

Part Three

Theological Perspectives

Chapter Eight

A Mutuality Model of Conversion

Barry L. Callen

To reach a desired goal, one must begin in the right place and proceed in the right direction. When seeking decisive theological perspectives, I begin with the nature and ways of God revealed in Scripture, and especially in the person of Jesus Christ. In relation to the specific question of this essay, Christian conversion, the Bible reveals a God who is voluntarily open to suffering (Gen. 6:6)[1] and demonstrates the divine self as loving grace.[2] Here is the appropriate place to begin to explore the subject of Christian conversion. Here, conversion is acknowledged to be rooted in a context in which God judges sin and provides grace despite sin. Those who undergo conversion, in turn, recognize God's judgment, accept joyously God's grace, and remain prayerfully open to whatever God chooses to do to eliminate sin and redeem sinners. A mutuality model of Christian conversion features the biblical God reaching lovingly to all persons and enabling them with the ability to respond in ways that can activate the salvation that is God's intention—and an ability that also includes the possibility that some will choose to reject salvation, which is God's willingly chosen risk.

In what follows, I seek to identify and explore five ways a mutuality model of human redemption reflects the biblically illumined nature, will, and redemptive initiatives of God. First, I identify a pivotal paradox that requires recognition and vigilance if it is to remain in essential balance. Conversion is both the initiative of God and the grace-enabled "work" of the one being converted. Second, I affirm that true Christianity by definition is *transformed* life in *transformed* community. Something less than new life in Christ and in Christ's community is something substantially less than God's intention. Third, I express a key concern about much of the contemporary evangelical world that long has been rooted in a subtle rationalism and limited by an excessive individualism. John Wesley and Clark Pinnock in differing centuries have come to agree that the will of God is seen less in believers holding to cold, even if correct, theology, and more in the divine provision for sinners being released to a liberated freedom that truly responds and loves. Fourth, using Clark Pinnock's recent theological journey as a guide, I enumerate benefits that follow from taking seriously the concept of reciprocity. Sinners cannot be converted without God; God will not act to convert without the reciprocity of sincere human response. Finally, recalling the content of the apostolic kerygma of the early Christian church, I note the eschatological context for an adequate perspective on new life in Christ. True Christian conversion is God's future in the present tense! It is the fruit of the person and work of Jesus Christ that defies final articulation and inspires unspeakable joy. It is the new-creation reality of the church where selfish individualism is overcome by a marvelous mutuality of believers who share new life in Christ's Spirit and together constitute the church at worship and on mission.

A Pivotal Paradox

In our now fallen state, we humans walk in reverse, traveling away from God and our own true selves and intended destinies. The urgent need is a radical reversal that turns around, converts, and redirects us toward our Life-giver. If humans are in bondage to sin, and we are, then how can we respond to God's loving Christ-initiative on our behalf? The only answer is an enabling grace that is divinely given. There lies at the heart of Christian conversion a pivotal paradox that often becomes a troubling dilemma when allowed to go out of balance. Saving faith in God's redeeming work is *both* the work of God *and* the responding work of receiving and believing humans. God alone initiates and provides the potential of a redeemed divine-human relationship. However, by divine choice, this true redeeming love is not coercive; saving grace is not received irresistibly.

In reflecting on the soteriological teaching of 2 Peter, for instance, Gilbert Stafford correctly identifies the pivotal paradox:

> Throughout the epistle we are made aware that the power of God does not abrogate free will, nor does free will abrogate the necessity of the power of God. Rather, the power of God is the prerequisite for the exercise of free will, and the exercise of free will is the concomitant of the power of God. In 2 Peter, we find that in the Christly phenomenon of salvation the divine initiative, sustenance, and consummation is inextricably linked together with human response, decision, and willingness.[3]

In the mystery of divine love and grace, God chooses to make the completion of human redemption contingent on human response to the divine offer of justification, regeneration, and sanctification—an offer that is accompanied by the sheer gift of response-enabling ("prevenient") grace. This divine choosing and enabling brings the concept of the conversion of sinners into the arena of the very nature of the divine. Who God is directs how God chooses to relate to a fallen creation. John Sanders observes that the debate surrounding Arminius, John Wesley, and their Calvinistic counterparts is "not primarily about salvation but about the nature of God." The crux of the debate is "whether God ever *responds* to us and does things *because* of us (not merely through us)."[4]

Affirmation of the possibility and necessity of human response to divine initiative requires a model of conversion in which divine-human reciprocity is central. A mutuality model differs significantly from a more mechanical and manipulative model that features the premises of absolute divine sovereignty, election, predestination, and irresistible divine grace. A mutuality model focuses, instead, on the divine intent of producing redeemed people who reflect the trinitarian love in all of their relationships. The general trajectory of a divinely predetermined and fully controlled conversion model derives from the "I-it" style of assumptions typical of a scholasticized Calvinism, in considerable contrast with the kind of "I-thou" assumptions of what is sometimes called "freewill theism."[5] The recent conservative Christian scene in North America has been dominated theologically by a Reformed theological mindset that tends to resist real mutuality in the divine-human saving process. Even Norman Geisler, a committed Calvinist, now has come to see the need for a more balanced view of divine election and has set forth the biblical argument against what he calls "Hyper-Calvinism."[6] I affirm the direction of his recent movement and call for even more.

When Christian theology is based on the assumption of divine sovereignty, defined as God necessarily standing unaffected and unconditioned by human sin and response, it remains captured by a nonbiblical philosophy of the divine nature. Such a Greek assumption drove Arius long ago to separate the human Jesus from the ontological being of God. It must not now be allowed to drive a wedge between divine grace and human response in the conversion process. Even so, a renewed recognition of divine-human mutuality should not misrepresent the necessary human participation by seeing it in any moralistic way, "as if an increase in education, virtue, or even the employment of the means of grace was all that was entailed in this glorious work of God."[7] Believers do participate in the redemption process, but the process nonetheless is divinely generated and graciously enabled.

Rebirth and Radical Discipleship

Christian conversion is both a freedom-from and a freedom-to reality. It is justification, the forgiveness of sin, the freedom-from-guilt release that God does *for us*; it also is spiritual rebirth, an inward renewal and freedom-to-life that God does *in us*. John Wesley says that "justification precedes the new birth" regeneration as "that great work which God [through Christ] does *for us*, in forgiving our sins"; this new birth is "the great work which God [through the Spirit] does *in us*, in renewing our fallen nature."[8] Such new birth inaugurates and is part of the larger and ongoing process of sanctification. The Christian faith, then, is not simply about *knowing* the truth about God in Jesus Christ; it also is about being *transformed* by that truth and becoming part of a *transformed community*.[9] Obedience to Christ, spiritual discipline, and voluntary participation are to be characteristics of this new-creation community, the church.

The human free choice element basic to a mutuality model of salvation has several dimensions. God allows free choice through the gift of prevenient grace. Once a positive choice is made, it then is important that no secular power be allowed to impose its defining will on the church, or that any leader within the church impose a rigid system of structures or beliefs on other believers. To be in Christ begins as and must remain a free choice that leads to voluntary communities of genuine believers. These believers, while mutually accountable as the faithful church, are to remain open to the ministry of the Spirit of Christ who alone is Lord of the church and the architect of the new creation. Renewal in Christ and a radical discipleship are at the core.[10]

Lutheranism is a tradition that originated primarily as the search for a merciful God despite the ugly face of human sin (how can we humans be saved?). In some contrast, even though accepting Luther's central faith concern, Anabaptism or the "radical reformation" developed around "the central idea of a righteous walk with the Lord after the experiences of repentance and rebirth—(how should we humans live once having been converted?)."[11] Menno Simons stubbornly insisted that the new birth in Christ is more than a private experience of sins being forgiven. There is a necessary link between the *new birth* and the *life* of a newborn Christian. If Christian faith is to be considered authentic, discipleship must give tangible evidence of the gift of saving grace. Menno challenges the temptation to preach any gospel of grace that fails to declare the necessity of joining and living faithfully in community.[12] Put another way, any true reformation of individuals and the church must include the quest for and fruit of holiness.

True Christian faith is not merely what church members believe, although that is very important. True faith also and significantly is *who believers are* and *how they live*, especially as a committed faith community in contrast to "the world." Howard Snyder paraphrases the thought of John Wesley: "Men and women do not truly *believe* the gospel without a moral change which enables them to *live* the gospel. Faith not only believes; it *works*—in both senses."[13] The fundamental work of God's Spirit at Pentecost was the formation of a new community of the Spirit. This Christ community of the Spirit, when faithful, acts like the Spirit and thus itself becomes an extension of the incarnation drama.

The necessary visibility of effectual converting grace should be affirmed consistently in relation both to individual disciples and to the integrity of the life of the church itself. For example, in 1939 church historian Charles Brown wrote *The Church Beyond Division*, an exposition of the biblical picture of Christ's people united and visible in the world as intended by the Spirit. This book puts into prose the vision of the church that Charles Naylor and Andrew Byers earlier had shared poetically and musically in a beloved hymn of the Church of God (Anderson, Indiana):

> The church of God one body is,
> One Spirit dwells within;
> And all her members are redeemed,
> And triumph over sin.
>
> O church of God! I love thy courts,
> Thou mother of the free;
> Thou blessed home of all the saved,
> I dwell content in thee.[14]

Believers need the inspiration of such a vision that "sees the church" in a way that fits the grace-filled idealism of the New Testament and leads to a visible expression that encourages the world to believe. All members of the church, by definition, "are redeemed" and "dwell content" in divine courts that function as the "mother of the free." The "triumph over sin" is a commitment to holiness, that is, being like God as God's people through the Spirit, in the church, and in the world. This is a multidimensional view of Christian conversion that is both biblical and timely.

According to Menno Simons: "The true evangelical faith sees and considers only the doctrine, ceremonies, commands, prohibitions, and the perfect example of Christ, and strives to conform thereto with all its power."[15] This view differs sharply from an institution based ecclesiology in which participation in rites and acquiescence to the doctrines of the church is all that is required (a tendency exhibited by some strains of Roman Catholicism) as much as it does from Protestant scholasticisms that tend to be rationalistic, propositional, and individualistic at heart. Properly central should be the transformed lives of individual Christians and the distinctive life of the whole church together, a life focused on Christ that exceeds structural considerations, transcends rational and creedal barriers, and is in contrast with and thus potentially a real witness to the world. Clark Pinnock puts it well:

> The effectiveness of the church is due not to human competency or programming but to the power of God at work. The church rides the wind of God's Spirit like a hawk endlessly and effortlessly circling and gliding in the summer sky. It ever pauses to wait for impulses of power to carry it forward to the nations. . . . The main rationale of the church is to actualize all the implications of baptism in the Spirit.[16]

The central need is rebirth, regeneration, reconstitution by the Spirit into the ongoing life of Christ in the new-creation community of the Spirit. The Western tendency, however, too often has been to harden the faith into the articulation of right beliefs and the practice of right liturgical and lifestyle actions. Two prominent theologians, one from the eighteenth century and one contemporary, have sought to show the way out of this negative tendency.

Escaping Scholastic Strangleholds

In recent years, significant similarities between the theological work of John Wesley in the eighteenth century and the current work of Clark Pinnock have become apparent.[17] Both have strong ties to England and a significant impact in the "new world." In their different historical contexts, both grieve over the unchurched masses and yearn for renewal in the church by the power of the Spirit of God. Both write extensively without being "systematic" theologians in a technical and rationalistic sense. Both affirm the basic tenets of the Reformed tradition, but struggle against hardened scholasticisms within the Protestant ranks with an appreciative eye on select emphases of Eastern traditions. Wesley unlocked "the scholastic doors to allow the vibrant 'Word of God' to illuminate and vitalize the cold, correct Reformation theologies."[18] Philip R. Meadows explains that Wesley was

> struggling to find a more acceptable balance between the freedom of nature and the sovereignty of grace that can satisfy a truly biblical life of faith. . . . [For Wesley] the idea of divine justice involves a limitation of God's sovereignty in respect of and response to the genuine creaturely freedom of choice between good and evil.[19]

Wesley, echoed now by Pinnock, concluded that God is a "loving personal agent whose gracious power is exercised not at the expense of human agency but in order to set persons free to love."[20] The issue of human freedom is key and, as we have seen, requires an understanding of salvation based upon a mutuality between divine initiative and human response. Traditional Protestant teaching has understood "original sin" to mean that the image of God in humans has been completely corrupted, and, consequently, that apart from grace humanity has no freedom to respond to God. Such teaching has led a deterministic logic in which God alone is able to choose who will be graced with the ability to respond and those so graced will respond irresistibly. But Wesley, now joined by Pinnock and many others, came to believe that the loving God of the Bible "preveniently" graces *all people,* hoping that all will respond and be saved by uncoerced choice. Such a position is dependent on Eastern understandings of sin and grace, ones that include real freedom for humans, and, therefore, requires the joint functioning of divine grace and human free will—a mutuality that is God's intent, provision, and risk. Randy Maddox has concluded that the closest resemblance between Orthodoxy (early Eastern) and Wesley likely lies in "their respective doctrines of deification and sanctification."[21] Similarly, Pinnock has come to embrace the centrality of relational theological categories that focus on the transformation into Christlikeness, which implies that Christians come to walk closely and voluntarily with the Spirit.[22]

Wesley and Pinnock are active theological innovators, men with literary skill and sincere passion for a faith that truly transforms life. Their prophetic voices focus on questions of the present without losing deep roots in the classic Christian tradition. They both are men of "one book" who defend the revelational nature and central authority of the Bible for Christians; they also focus more on the role of Scripture in leading readers to the salvation intended by God and less on preoccupation with rational arguments about a necessary errorless perfection of the biblical text itself. Maddox, in reviewing Pinnock's 1984 *The Scripture Principle,* observes that this "highly nuanced articulation of a constructive position" is the most "critically aware exposition of biblical inerrancy available." Perhaps most significant, reports Maddox, is Pinnock's view that the dictation approach to biblical inspiration (said to be implicit in the claims of many inerrancy advocates) is an "outgrowth of the tendency of Calvinistic orthodoxy to construe all God's actions in terms of total divine control."[23] Here, at a key point of authority for Christians, one sees the emergence of a sense of mutuality between God and humanity that necessarily questions the presumption of total divine control of human history. The Bible is of divine origin by way of human participation.

Pinnock asserts that when one recognizes that God has allowed for the possibility that human beings can resist divine grace, one can appreciate positively the human side of the Bible.[24] Such a view has a comfortable home in the Wesleyan tradition. As early as 1978, Pinnock observed that U.S. evangelicals were gaining greater sophistication in understanding Scripture from various historical perspectives, finally reaching beyond the relatively recent and narrowing perspective of fundamentalism. He saw within the English Puritan, Wesleyan, and American revivalism streams less preoccupation with "precise inerrancy" and "a healthier concern for the spiritual power and authenticity of Scripture instead."[25] As in the Eastern Christian tradition, salvation history is more a journey to renewal, the actual transformation or sanctification of Christians by divine grace, and less an almost singular focus on being justified of past sin as an escape from damnation and the promised bliss in the next life. Wesley believed that divine grace effects more than pardon; it is not a legal transaction to remove the guilt of sin.

Grace also and especially is the transforming power of God in human life. It is a power associated closely with the presence of God as believers experience decisive renewal in the Spirit (conversion) and persistent maturation of this renewal (sanctification). Pinnock's book *Flame of Love* (1996) radiates the same belief and hopes to set the reader on a journey with the Spirit, a journey of true transformation.[26]

The passion that has driven the theological work of Wesley and Pinnock has hardly been for intellectual elitism, although their education certainly allowed for that. Pinnock has joined Wesley in being a genuine churchman and a "practical" theologian who is deeply concerned about church renewal.[27] This renewal is related closely to the sanctifying work of the Spirit of God through both established "means of grace" and the sometimes unexpected manifestations of the Spirit that are uncontrolled by rigid definitions, structures, and traditions. In fact:

> As Christ's body, the church is filled with the Holy Spirit and can experience the presence of Christ in both sacramental and charismatic life. Often we are required to choose between sacramental and charismatic modes of the real presence of Christ, which is unfortunate because both are valid and should be integrated. . . . As if to mimic the secular rejection of mystery, we [Protestants] have often turned away from the means of grace in which the Spirit renders material things and actions graciously efficacious to faith.[28]

Both men experienced a theological journey that led away from a scholasticized Reformed determinism that eschews the very imagery for God that Jesus utilized, portraying the Father as loving, gracious, sacrificial, wounded by human transgressions, nonmanipulative in the use of available power, and prepared to risk on behalf of all who are lost. For Pinnock, the tight Calvinistic logic had unraveled in the 1970s. Two centuries earlier, Wesley "broke the chain of logical necessity by which the Calvinist doctrine of predestination seems to flow from the doctrine of original sin, by this doctrine of prevenient grace."[29]

In contrast to tight theological logic, the work of Wesley and Pinnock has an open, humble, and generous spirit. They share a "catholic spirit," an intense love for God and all humankind that drives out bigotry and sectarianism. While certainly not indifferent to matters of truth, this spirit respects those who disagree and prods all sincere seekers after God to love, to pursue truth, and to build community, rather than to remain frozen in propositional faith, to berate others, and to tear down. William Abraham puts it this way:

> Wesley's emphasis expressed itself historically in ways that are exasperating to many evangelicals down to this day. Thus it led Wesley to set no theological standards for membership in the Methodist societies. The only condition required was that one desired to flee from the wrath to come. Even where Wesley did impose standards, they were deliberately imprecise. He did not . . . impose a system of formal or speculative theology but . . . set up standards of preaching and belief that would secure loyalty to the fundamental truths of the gospel and ensure the continued witness of the church to the realities of the Christian experience of salvation. This is a far cry from the five points of Calvinism or of fundamentalism.[30]

The regeneration of individuals and of the church itself is the goal of the Spirit. When seen in a model of mutuality, new life in Christ is a grace-filled possibility infused by the principle of reciprocity. From this principle flow significant salvific results.

The Salvific Results of Reciprocity

The significant theological changes in Clark Pinnock's thinking during the 1970s were enabled primarily by having "the insight of reciprocity in hand."[31] Although not at first consciously aware or intentionally motivated by particular Christian traditions that utilized a notion of reciprocity, Pinnock soon realized that this insight that grew out of his exploration of Scripture was shared by significant streams of Christian tradition. His insights were both very old and quite fresh. For example, the Eastern churches tend to view both Roman Catholicism and Protestantism as deadeningly rationalistic, at odds with true spiritual life in Christ. The Eastern tradition does not hold that the human fall into sin deprived persons of all divine grace or responsibility for responding to

God's offer of restored relationship with Christ. Salvation, instead, necessarily involves reciprocity in divine-human relations.

While Western theologians have shied from such reciprocity, because of their fear of falling into a works-righteousness heresy, Eastern theologians have insisted that, while certainly never *meriting* God's acceptance because of human action, it nonetheless is the case that God's freely bestowed grace empowers humans for responsible cooperation.[32] A key verse for the Eastern tradition is 2 Peter 1:4, which speaks of participating in the divine life as the goal of Christian believers. In other words, Christianity is the story of the gracious descent of God that opens a path for human ascent to God. The Western emphasis on the legal and forensic stands in sharp contrast to the Eastern view that healing and renewal come about through the mystical union of the divine and the human. It is important to note again that to representatives of the East both Roman Catholicism and Protestantism share the unfortunate emphasis on legalism and rationalism. The solution, however, is not to reject Western notions of divine sovereignty for Eastern emphases on divinization, but rather to strike a balance between them.

Wesley affirmed the universal gift of "prevenient grace," reflecting early Greek theology (especially Macarius).[33] Pinnock more recently has adopted the vocabulary of this ancient church tradition, freshly championing a divine-human mutuality that is stimulating a wave of theological innovation, by which I mean a reconsideration of positions that are truly biblical and long-held but neglected. Wesley united "pardon" and "participation" motifs, resulting in what some judge his greatest contribution to ecumenical dialogue.[34] Pinnock offers a similar gift to us today. One might say Pinnock has reclaimed an Arminian paradigm that first appeared in his work on the nature of Scripture and now filters its way into all of his theological reflections.

The first link in the Calvinistic chain to break for Pinnock was the doctrine of the perseverance of the saints. Why, he wondered, are Christians warned not to fall away from Christ (for example, Heb. 10:26) and exhorted to persevere (for example, Heb. 3:12) if they enjoy the absolute security taught by Calvinism?[35] In fact, he concluded, human responses to God *are* taken seriously by God—

there is a dialectic of divine and human interaction, a relationship of reciprocity. With this, the garment of Calvinism started coming apart. A believer's security in God is linked to the faith relationship with God that must be intentionally maintained and never forsaken. There is, in other words, a "profound mutuality" between God and believers.[36] God's will can be frustrated by human intransigence. A believer's continuance in the saving grace of God depends, at least in part, on the human partner in the divine-human relationship.[37] Pinnock began to understand that, once the factors of reciprocity and conditionality are introduced, the landscape of theology is altered significantly. He could begin to regard people "not as the product of a timeless decree but as God's covenant partners and real players in the flow and the tapestry of history."[38]

The Future in the Present Tense

In the very beginning, the divine Spirit swept across formlessness and a beautiful creation came to be (Genesis 1). At the very end, the same Spirit will invite a redeemed creation to come and take the water of eternal life as a gift (Rev. 22:17). Between this beginning and this ending, there is God's converted people who are called to be faithful. In this crucial interim, new creation is still the work of the Spirit. In fact, the church is seen best as "a continuation of the Spirit-anointed event that was Jesus Christ," a community of the faithful created by the Spirit on the day of Pentecost "to carry on the kingdom ministry of Jesus and be firstfruits of the new humanity he represented."[39] John Wesley said it well:

> No, it cannot be; none shall live with God, but he that now lives to God; none shall enjoy the glory of God in heaven, but he that bears the image of God on earth; none that is not saved from sin here can be saved from hell hereafter; none can see the kingdom of God above, unless the kingdom of God be in him below. Whosoever will reign with Christ in heaven, must have Christ reigning in him on earth. He must have "that mind in him which was in Christ," enabling him "to walk as Christ also walked."[40]

Salvation involves the potential of a destiny with God premised on the chosen reality of life with God in the present. It involves a current bearing of the image of God, a grace-enabled reigning of God within one's life that reflects both the mind and the mission of Christ. True conversion is more than turning away from sin and toward God. It is turning toward a new creation that is far more than an individualistic avoidance of hell. Conversion is being turned to God and God's church, the new-creation community in which the Spirit dwells, through which the Spirit ministers, and into which the Spirit places each new believer with Spirit-gifts designed to build up the body of Christ. Here is another key aspect of the mutuality model of conversion. Beyond participating responsively with God in the conversion process, we also are to participate fully with other believers in the ongoing process of God's converting mission in the world.

In other words, in Jesus Christ the time is *now*. God's primary promises have been fulfilled. God's Son now reigns and is coming again. God's Spirit now is available as a gift of grace to form and empower the church for its mission in the world. The call is to repent, receive, and become part of the new creation that now functions through the ministry of the Spirit as an advance taste of the Age to Come, that Age of God already here in the crucified and risen Jesus and soon to come in the return of the victorious Jesus. Turn around. Repent. Receive. Be converted!

While we, like Wesley, affirm a variety of metaphors to describe the work of salvation, the operative dynamic in the salvation process is divine grace that leads away from subjectivism and self-deification and into grateful cooperation with the enabling and redeeming work of God's Spirit. God in loving grace is a covenant maker. The central paradigm of the divine-human saving relationship is the covenant motif. Being brought back to right relationship with God is an interpersonal issue not to be hindered by vain attempts to finally "explain." Indeed, we should "stress the covenant relationship between God and His people while minimizing the insertion of theological constructs which are external to the canonical text or which are *occasional* rather than *universal* paradigms for atonement."[41]

The Christian teaching on atonement comes in the form of a

story, not a *theory*. A beloved gospel song speaks about "an old, old story" of Jesus and his love. The point is that God, in the life, death, and resurrection of Jesus, loves, suffers from our sin, provides opportunity for new life, and expects that we will move in faith from being *observers* of the cross of Jesus to being *receivers* and *participants* in his resurrected life! To fully and finally explain the *how* of the atonement accomplished by God in Jesus Christ is beyond human knowledge and human language; but to celebrate and participate in the atonement is our privilege and calling. God graciously provides all that is necessary. We respond as God's grace enables us to by our own genuine choice. God's provision and our response are the two essential and inseparable elements of a mutuality model of conversion.

The familiar hymn "Joy to the World" reflects the triple office of Christ by announcing that "He rules the world with truth and grace." He *rules* as God's appointed king over all things. He rules *with truth* as the dependable prophet of God. He rules with truth *and grace* as the divinely anointed priest who brings mediation between loving Creator and fallen creation. It is no wonder that, given the comprehensiveness of this mission of Christ on our behalf, this hymn calls on us to "repeat the sounding joy."

Chapter Nine

Conversion and Baptism in Wesleyan Spirituality

Ted A. Campbell

Very truly, I tell you, no one can enter the kingdom of God without being born of water and Spirit. (John 3:5)

But when the goodness and loving kindness of God our Savior appeared, he saved us, not because of any works of righteousness that we had done, but according to his mercy, through the water of rebirth and renewal by the Holy Spirit. (Titus 3:4-5)

Introduction

The spirituality of the Wesleyan movement and of historic Methodist churches can be described as a *sacramental Evangelicalism*.[1] By this expression, I mean that Wesleyan spirituality shares both (1) the conviction of the broad "catholic" tradition[2] that the sacraments are divinely appointed, indispensable signs and means of grace, and (2) the conviction of the Pietistic and Evangelical movements that normative experiences of affective, personal repentance and conversion lie at the heart of the Christian life. It is customary for Wesleyans to plead that in this balance of sacramental and Evangelical spiritual traditions lies the genius of the Wesleyan movement. In practice, however, the juxtaposition of these two strands of Christian spirituality has posed very difficult issues for the interpretation of Wesleyan theology and spirituality.

Nowhere are these difficult issues of reconciling catholic and Evangelical spiritual traditions more apparent than in the Wesleyan tradition's attempts to deal with the role of baptism in relation to conversion in the spiritual life. The question can be placed rather sharply in the following apparently contradictory claims:

- The catholic spiritual tradition maintains that baptism is the instrumental means of our regeneration or new birth in Christ.
- The Evangelical spiritual tradition maintains that a personal and affective experience of conversion to Christ is the means of our regeneration or new birth in Christ.

The juxtaposition of both of these claims in John Wesley's works poses what Bernard Holland called "The Riddle of Wesley's Baptismal Beliefs."[3] When are we born again? At baptism, or in the moment of a personal conversion experience?

The temptation to an easy resolution of this "riddle" must be avoided as being unfair to the complexity of Wesley's own beliefs on the matter, and unfaithful to the balance of historic Wesleyan spirituality. John Baillie, for example, claimed that "Wesley altogether dissociated regeneration from baptism, being the first clearly to do so. Unlike the Anabaptists, he held to baptism in infancy, yet would not allow that infants could be regenerated. Regeneration for him must be a conscious experience."[4] As we shall see, this claim involves a fairly clear contradiction of Wesley's own stated views of baptism in relation to the new birth, but it reflects the desire for a straightforward resolution. This chapter will attempt to reckon with the complexity of Wesley's own views, and will offer a suggestion of three historical contexts that help to explain the logic of Wesley's views of conversion and baptism.

The Sacramental Understanding of Baptismal Regeneration

As a base point for an understanding of conversion and baptism in Wesleyan spirituality, we should consider the understanding of baptism and the new birth in the broad catholic tradition of spirituality that had preceded Wesley. In this spiritual tradition, baptism was consistently understood as the means by which a person was incorporated into Christ and the Christian community, bringing the fruits of justification (forgiveness of past sins) and regeneration (new birth in Christ). In the precise language of the Council of Trent, baptism was the "instrumental cause" of justification and regeneration.[5] On this understanding, Christian spirituality amounts to the outworking of the grace received in baptism, and the memory of one's baptism is the grounds of Christian renewal.

This spiritual tradition was reflected not only by Roman Catholic and Eastern Orthodox Christians but by Lutherans as well, and it was incorporated into Anglican liturgy. Luther's assault on historic catholic sacramental teachings, his treatise on "The Babylonian Captivity of the Church" (1520), offers thanks to God that baptism, alone among the sacraments, had been preserved untainted in the church. The opinion expressed early in the work that penance was a third sacrament is rejected by the end of the book, with Luther's recognition that penance simply amounted to the renewal of baptismal grace, and therefore did not have the character of an independent sacrament. Baptism for Luther was simply the means by which a person is justified and born again, and the memory of baptism is the grounds of Christian hope.[6] Although Anglicanism reflected the Reformed understanding of the sacraments at many points (especially in the Articles of Religion), the ritual for baptism in the *Book of Common Prayer* reflected this older spiritual tradition, especially in the prayer of thanksgiving following infant baptism, where the celebrant offers thanks to God: "Seeing now, dearly beloved brethren, that this child is regenerate, and grafted into the body of Christ's Church, let us give thanks."[7] This particular prayer, with its presupposition of infant baptismal regeneration, was a consistent target of Puritan attack and of attempts at liturgical reform within Anglican circles.

That John Wesley believed in infant baptismal regeneration is clear from Wesley's own published works, and has been acknowledged by all but a handful of serious Wesleyan scholars (see the comments in the next section on the view of James H. Rigg). Thus, Wesley's account of his Aldersgate conversion experience begins: "I believe, till I was about ten years old I had not sinned away that 'washing of the Holy Ghost' which was given me in baptism."[8]

Consistent with this, Wesley's sermon "The New Birth" (1760) cautions against the presumption that because one is baptized one must be currently in a state of regeneration. It acknowledges, however, that the grace of regeneration does accompany infant baptism.[9] Such passages about infant regeneration are consistent in Wesley's writings, and a train of Wesley interpreters has acknowledged Wesley's teaching in this regard.[10]

Given Wesley's commitment to infant regeneration in baptism, many Anglican and Methodist interpreters of John Wesley have taken his views to be quite straightforwardly those of the broader catholic tradition. Thus, a nineteenth-century Anglican concluded:

> Here then we have Wesley's uniform Teaching on this subject throughout his life. He proclaims that "in the waters of Baptism" as a means we are regenerated or born again—infants absolutely so, adults "where the outward sign is duly received." That in Baptism, "original sin is washed away," and the baptized "engrafted into Christ." That Baptism "is the ordinary instrument of our justification," and that "there is no other means in the ordinary way of entering Heaven," inasmuch as John iii.5. is spoken of nothing more or less than Baptism.[11]

This particular account bears the animus of religious polemic (its author sincerely believed that if Methodists were truly Wesleyan, they would be Anglicans), but less polemical interpreters, influenced by Tractarianism or by twentieth-century liturgical renewal, have made similar claims about Wesley's commitment to baptismal regeneration. Thus, contemporary United Methodist author William H. Willimon offers a spirituality of baptism according to which the Christian life itself is the remembrance and the outworking of the gift of new birth given in the sacrament.[12]

Nuanced scholarship that takes a more sacramental or catholic view of Wesley's understanding of baptismal regeneration must acknowledge Wesley's repeated warnings against relying on the fact of one's baptism as a surety of salvation. Charles R. Hohenstein, writing in response to an earlier article of my own, points out that Wesley's warnings were consistent with the older spiritual traditions that had maintained that baptism is effective so long as an individual does not contradict the grace given in baptism by disbelief.[13] This view is suggested by the author of the previously cited paragraph in stating that baptism effects the new birth for adults "where the outward sign is duly received." On this understanding, conversion is interpreted as "conversion of life" in the catholic spiritual tradition. It is the ongoing process of repentance and turning to God that is empowered by the grace given in baptism and renewed in participation in the Eucharist (and perhaps in the sacramental rite of reconciliation).[14]

The Evangelical Understanding of Regeneration

The Evangelical understanding of conversion is quite distinct. Consistent with a range of spiritual movements in the seventeenth and eighteenth centuries that stressed the centrality of the affections, including true repentance and love for God, the Pietist and Evangelical traditions in spirituality insisted on a distinct, affective experience of conversion.[15] One of the consistent notes of this spirituality was that no outward act (including baptism) could suffice in the place of personal conversion to Christ. In the words of Lutheran Pietist August Hermann Francke: "Thus you ought not to say: 'I am baptized, I go to church, I am a Christian.' The hypocrites do the same. There is many a person baptized who yet went back on his oath and was faithless and fell out of his baptismal covenant."[16] This was not—as sometimes alleged—to deny the objective power of God in salvation. It understood the locus of that objective power in a different place: rather than (or perhaps in addition to) the sacraments, the power of God was located in the personal religious experience of transformation.[17]

One of the reasons Wesley's commitment to regeneration in infant baptism sometimes strikes Evangelicals as anomalous is that Wesley is taken as a preeminent exemplar of the Evangelical spirituality. And indeed, the passionate force of much of the corpus of Wesley's sermons lies in their affective appeal for just the sort of conversion experience valued by Evangelicals. Wesley's sermon "The New Birth" draws these inferences: "And, first, it follows that baptism is not the new birth . . . ," and second, the new birth "does not always accompany baptism."[18] At this point, Wesley cited the distinction between the outward rite and the inward grace in the *Prayer Book* definition of a sacrament.[19] Yet it was also in this sermon that Wesley allowed that baptism does confer regeneration in the case of infants.

But in other places, Wesley speaks at length about regeneration, scarcely mentioning baptism. For example, his sermon "The Great Privilege of Those that are Born of God" defines regeneration, contrasts it with justification, and describes its relationship to sanctification, with only the barest mention of the sacrament of Christian initiation.[20] His sermon "The Original, Nature, Properties, and Use of the Law" makes the point that the second use of the Law is to bring believers to life in Christ (the language is the same as Wesley regularly uses to describe the new birth), but does not mention baptism.[21] Two of his sermons describe the way in which believers can know they are regenerate—both by the testimony of God's Spirit and the testimony of human conscience—but only one of them makes a passing mention of baptism in relation to the new birth.[22] These loci (and more could be cited) strike me as the strongest evidence of Wesley's departure from the historic sacramental spirituality of remembering one's baptism as the grounds of Christian hope. To speak of regeneration with only a nominal mention of baptism, as Wesley so often did, would have been incongruous with (perhaps inconceivable in) the older catholic sacramental tradition.

In fact, Wesley's insistence on the necessity of conversion led James H. Rigg to conclude that Wesley had in fact abandoned the doctrine of baptismal regeneration altogether by the end of his life. Rigg's study entitled *The Churchmanship of John Wesley* (1878) argued against Anglican claims that Wesley had maintained baptismal regeneration throughout his career. The principal evidence Rigg cited, beyond Wesley's frequent appeals for the conversion of the baptized, was Wesley's revision of the *Prayer Book* as *The Sunday Service of the Methodists in North America* (1784), in which the controversial thanksgiving prayer in the rite of baptism for infants was revised in such a way as to omit the overt reference to baptismal regeneration.[23] Although Rigg's thesis was widely accepted in late nineteenth-century Methodist circles, the bare omission of the reference to infant regeneration does not prove Wesley's repudiation of the doctrine. It may simply indicate Wesley's desire to avoid controversy in the newly founded Methodist church. The same prayer had occasioned appeals from some American Anglicans (soon to become Episcopalians) for its revision or deletion.[24]

Nuanced interpretations of John Wesley's thought from the perspective of those who advocate an Evangelical spirituality of conversion have acknowledged the difficulty presented by Wesley's commitment to infant baptismal regeneration. Most typically, they understand this to be an indication of Wesley's loyalty to the Church of England, but not part of his own distinctive theological or spiritual contribution. Thus William R. Cannon wrote: "It must be understood, it seems to me, that Wesley's acceptance of the efficacy of infant baptism is just an acceptance, and nothing more. He affirms it as a teaching of the Church. Nowhere does he stress it as a fundamental tenet of his own doctrine."[25] On the Evangelical understanding, then, the tension between Wesley's sacramental and Evangelical views is to be resolved by granting a primacy to the Evangelical as being at least the distinctive contribution that Wesley made.

Contexts for Understanding Wesley's Views of Conversion and Baptism

The sacramental and Evangelical elements of Wesleyan spirituality have often stood in an uneasy tension with each other. If it is tempting to defend either one of the previously described views as an easy solution to the "riddle" of Wesley's views of baptism and conversion, it is also tempting to dismiss Wesley on this issue as simply confused or inconsistent. Thus Holland's impressive study concludes: "Here is a treasure of the Church's sacramental devotion which it was not given to Wesley to grasp."[26]

I am not satisfied with this conclusion. It is true that Wesley could be confused or inconsistent, but is also true that the very material that led to accusations of inconsistency will appear, on closer examination or by closer attention to context, to reveal greater depths of understanding. One of the contributions of Kenneth J. Collins's *Scripture Way of Salvation* has been to show how often accusations of inconsistency have failed to comprehend nuances in Wesley's uses of terms and theological concepts. I shall make a similar claim with regard to the contexts in which we understand Wesley's views of conversion and baptism, but first I want to caution against one particular form of "nuanced" interpretation.

One of the temptations in dealing with these difficult issues of conversion and baptism in Wesley's thought has been the temptation to conclude that Wesley used the term *regeneration* in two discrete senses. Both Colin Williams (1960) and Bernard Holland (1970) argued that Wesley used it in distinct senses in reference to infants and to adults.[27] But although Wesley did use terms in different senses (he would sometimes write "in the sense that" in explaining a term), I do not find him distinguishing senses of *regeneration.* And although he did speak of regeneration both as a result of infant baptism and as a result of adult conversion, it is not necessary to see these as different things. The opening sentence of the account of Aldersgate seems to imply that what was recovered in the conversion experience was precisely the grace that had been given to Wesley in his baptism and subsequently lost by sin. Thus, although regeneration, or new birth, may come by means of baptism or of adult conversion, the effect of new life in Christ is the same. In this regard, we may consider Wesley's note on John 3:5 in his *Explanatory Notes upon the New Testament*: "*Except a man be born of water and of the Spirit*—Except he experience that great inward change by the Spirit, and be baptized (wherever baptism can be had) as the outward sign and means of it."[28]

Reformed Sacramental Spirituality

Rather than finding the logic of Wesley's views of baptism and conversion in an unnatural division of the term *regeneration,* I propose to examine three specific aspects of Wesley's historical situation that illuminate the ways in which sacramental and Evangelical spiritualities came together in his understanding. The first has to do with the broader history of Christian doctrine against which Wesley's thought is understood. Holland noted that the nineteenth-century debate about Wesley's understanding of baptism and conversion was shaped in reaction to the Tractarian movement. But Holland's own account, including his eventual judgment on Wesley's failure to comprehend the sacramental significance of baptism, was strongly formed by Lutheran sources, with little reference to the Reformed tradition proper.[29] What was not accounted for is the fact that the Reformed tradition had deeply influenced Anglicanism, as it was seen not only in Puritan divines but also in the broader doctrinal and liturgical inheritance of the Church of England.[30] Wesley's citation of the critical distinction between the outward sign and the inward grace (most immediately, from the *Prayer Book* catechism) reflects a consistent hallmark of Reformed sacramental theology and spirituality.

This distinction between inward grace and outward sign enabled the Reformed tradition to claim that although regeneration was normally "annexed" to baptism, it was not "invariably" so. Thus the Westminster Confession claimed with respect to baptism that

> V. Although it be a great sin to contemn or neglect this ordinance, yet grace and salvation are not so inseparably annexed unto it, as that no person can be regenerated or saved without it, or that all that are baptized are undoubtedly regenerated.
>
> VI. The efficacy of baptism is not tied to that moment of time wherein it is administered.[31]

That is to say, in the Reformed understanding, the grace of regeneration normally accompanied baptism, but divine freedom required that this could not be "invariably" claimed, and required further that the moment of regeneration might not be the same moment as when the water of baptism was applied.

Wesley's revision of the rite of infant baptism, by omitting the prayer of thanksgiving which announced that the newly baptized infant was (invariably) regenerate, was consistent with this Reformed understanding of regeneration and baptism. Moreover, the revision of the Articles of Religion that accompanied the *Sunday Service* of 1784 omitted a key phrase from the Anglican Article on baptism that asserted: "As by an instrument, they that receive Baptism rightly are grafted into the Church; the promises of the forgiveness of sin, and of our adoption to be the sons of God by the Holy Ghost, are visibly signed and sealed; Faith is confirmed, and Grace increased by virtue of prayer unto God."[32] The deletion of this phrase from the Article allows for a more liberal understanding of the relationship between regeneration and baptism, since this phrase demanded a very specific "instrumental" understanding of this relationship.[33]

My point here is that although Wesley's conjunction of baptismal regeneration, and regeneration by conversion experience makes little sense against the background of Catholic or Lutheran spirituality (hence Holland's conclusion), they do bear a kind of logic when understood against the background of the Reformed tradition, where the sacrament is normatively understood as bearing divine grace and serves as a testimony of grace revealed. It is crucial to note in this regard that the Reformed tradition must not be identified uniformly with Zwinglianism, either with respect to baptism or the Eucharist. The main stream of Reformed tradition had maintained a strong sense of the connection between baptism and regeneration (and between Eucharist and the "virtual" presence of Christ). In maintaining the regeneration of infants in baptism, Wesley took the logic of Reformed sacramental spirituality in a different direction than the Reformed tradition had done, but the revision of the baptismal service may indicate that even on this point he wanted to allow for a range of options within the Methodist community. His insistence that the baptism of adults does not invariably result in regeneration is quite consistent with historic Reformed teaching.

The Intersection of Anglicanism and the "Religion of the Heart"

A second context for understanding Wesley's beliefs about baptism and conversion has to do with his placement at the intersection of historic Anglicanism and contemporary movements for a "religion of the heart," that is, the Pietist and Evangelical movements of the seventeenth and eighteenth centuries. F. Ernest Stoeffler has shown that the Pietist movement had roots in Reformed theology and spirituality, so there is in fact an integral connection between this context and the previously discussed context of the Reformed tradition for Wesley.[34] For Lutheran Pietists, an emphasis on personal repentance and faith stood in a very uneasy tension with the historic Lutheran spirituality of the memory of baptism as the grounds of Christian hope. Consider the quotation from August Hermann Francke given above. Francke does not deny baptismal regeneration, but his rhetorical emphasis lies in the possibility that a person could "fall out of his baptismal covenant" by disbelief.

By way of the Moravians and Lutheran Pietists he met in Georgia, his continued interaction with Moravians in London, and his travel to Germany in the summer of 1738, John Wesley had come directly into contact with movements for a "religion of the heart." He also knew much of the Puritan literature that had shaped these movements. Take an eighteenth-century Anglican, mix with him a double portion of "religion of the heart," and what you get is something very much like John Wesley. And, I think, you get Wesley's dilemma with respect to baptismal teaching, for the inheritance of Anglican thought and spirituality grounded him in the catholic and sacramental understanding of the power of God available in the sacrament, and the Pietist and nascent Evangelical movements inspired his passionate insistence that a baptized person could stand in need of repentance and conversion.[35]

The tradition of Reformed sacramental spirituality, then, helps to explain Wesley's clear distinction between baptism and regeneration, with the implication that baptism (at least for adults) does not invariably produce regeneration. The Pietist and Evangelical movements brought the further clarification that this "variability" in the effect of baptism (its bringing about regeneration) was related to the divine grace that offered the possibility of affective repentance and conversion in the recipient. Following this logic, human disbelief nullifies the effect of sacramental grace, so that a sinner stands in need not of rebaptism, but of a fresh repentance and affective, heartfelt conversion to Christ. The catholic tradition had always maintained that the effect of the sacrament was conditioned upon the person's mature faith. Where Wesley departs from this tradition, in my reckoning, is that the older teaching had maintained that "regeneration" itself was a unique, onetime event (associated with the unrepeatable rite of baptism), whereas Wesley speaks of the need for a fresh "regeneration" even for those who were once regenerate in baptism. But why should the consistent stress in Wesley's sermons and other writings fall on the need for a fresh regeneration rather than the grace of regeneration available in the sacrament? The next consideration of context may help to explain this.

Conversion and the "Extraordinary" Vocation of the Methodist Movement

A third context that may illuminate Wesley's beliefs about baptism and conversion lies in his understanding of the "extraordinary" vocation or calling of the Methodist movement. This I offer as a more tentative suggestion that may explain Wesley's rhetorical emphasis on the need for conversion, overshadowing his commitment to rebirth in baptism. Wesley's later sermons, such as "On the Lord's Vineyard" and "Prophets and Priests" (in some published editions called "The Ministerial Office") reveal his sense of a distinct mission or apostolate for the Methodist movement. This sense is foreshadowed in such earlier documents as his open letter to Vincent Perronet entitled "A Plain Account of the People Called Methodists" (1748). In this earlier work, Wesley justifies the development of the distinct institutions of Methodism, showing how each had responded to particular needs or concerns that arose in the decade preceding. In the later sermons Wesley has a more comprehensive vision of the role of Methodism alongside the Church of England. The Church has its "ordinary" ministers who administer the sacraments and "institute" means of grace; the Methodists have such "extraordinary" ministers as lay preachers who proclaim the distinct message of repentance and conversion.[36] The Church is bound to proclaim the eternal gospel; the Methodists have a particular doctrinal mission to proclaim the balance of justification and sanctification together.[37] The distinct Methodist institutions and teachings are justified by the "extraordinary" calling of the movement.[38] One senses that in the proper nature of things, the sacraments and the "ordinary" ministries of the Church should suffice, but the Methodists had been called by God to address the specific situation of Wesley's time and place.

If this is true, then it might go a long way toward explaining the logic of Wesley's views of conversion and baptism. It might explain the consistent, rhetorical passion for conversion in Wesley's ministry. If my understanding is correct on this point,

John Wesley assigned the sacrament of baptism to some category like that of the "ordinary" ministries of the church. The Methodist movement was not to deprecate these, but its distinctive mission or apostolate lay elsewhere. In the normal course of things intended by God, baptism followed by regular repentance should have been sufficient. But as Wesley saw the church in his age, something had gone terribly wrong in the normal course of things, and God called for an extraordinary response. That response was to preach the necessity of the new birth, especially to the baptized pagans of Georgian Britain.

Conclusion

I would like to say that Wesley held together sacramental grace and Evangelical conversion in a careful balance that Methodists subsequently lost; however, such a conclusion is not justified. The sacramental and Evangelical strands of piety stand in a rather uneasy tension at many points in Wesley's own thought and experience. Wesley was accused of inconsistency on these issues within his lifetime, and decades after his death Methodists labored to explain his (and their) views. An article by "T.J." (almost certainly Thomas Jackson), published in 1824 in the *Wesleyan-Methodist Magazine,* offers the following fine summary of Wesley's views:

> [Wesley] not only acknowledged that a gracious communication is made to the minds of children in baptism, but to the effect of that communication he gave the name of the New Birth. . . . Mr. Wesley, nevertheless, denied that the same effect is invariably produced in cases of adult baptism; and believed that those children who receive that blessing in their infancy, generally lose it as they grow in years, and mix with the world. He also believed that when they are brought under the power of sinful affections and habits, the renewal of their minds in righteousness and true holiness, after the image of God, becomes again a matter of indispensable necessity; and to that renewal, whenever it is effected, and how often soever it may be repeated, he used to give the name of regeneration, or of the new birth.[39]

As we have seen, most serious Wesleyan scholarship has made these basic points, whether they come from an Evangelical or a sacramental perspective. What has been disputed has been not the basic points of Wesley's views, but rather the logic or sense of them.

I have tried to show that the Reformed tradition of spirituality (even as it influenced Anglicanism) illuminates Wesley's tendency to make a logical, and sometimes temporal, distinction between regeneration and baptism (especially in the case of adult recipients). The context of Pietism and the nascent Evangelical movement further illuminates Wesley's concern that adults could not rely on baptism alone, because they needed the divinely offered gifts of repentance and heartfelt faith in Christ. I have suggested, further, that Wesley's understanding of the particular or "extraordinary" mission of the Methodist movement—to proclaim repentance, faith, and holiness in the context of eighteenth-century Britain—allowed him to see baptism as part of the "ordinary" ministry of the church which, however important, was not part of the distinctive vocation of the Methodist movement as it existed within the Church of England.

Whether or not one accepts the particular conjunction of sacramental and Evangelical piety in Wesley's spirituality, a case must be made for such a conjunction. A variety of "Prophets and Priests" appear in the religion of the Hebrew Bible, and early Christian experience embraced both sacramental and experiential/affective forms of religious life.[40] One could make the case that a truly incarnational religion must embrace both, for both are deeply interwoven in human experience. But it is not easy to hold the two together, and the church through the centuries has been drawn back and forth between a reliance on the sacramental rite and on unmediated religious experience. This has been shown to be the case repeatedly in Protestant movements (such as Pentecostalism) that begin with an emphasis on personal religious experience and, after a few generations, begin to be reintegrated back into the broader Christian tradition. Contemporary Methodism is not in Wesley's place. As churches, we have to take responsibility for the "ordinary" as well as the "extraordinary" means by which divine grace comes to us. What is more, the debate between advocates of Evangelical and catholic spiritualities is overshadowed in contemporary experience by the experience of nominal Christians who have little sense of the divine presence, either in sacramental celebration or in the call to personal conversion. The poverty of our worship is revealed in its dearth of the sacramental and Evangelical senses of divine power. The Wesleyan tradition calls us to a renewed commitment to the divine power that enables conversion and to that grace that is given in the holy sacrament of baptism. It calls us to address the sad plight of the casually baptized pagans of our own age and of our own congregations.

Chapter Ten

The Epistemology of Conversion: Is There Something New?

William J. Abraham

It is commonplace to look upon John Wesley and his heirs as long on experience and mission and short on theology and reflection. When Methodists produce a collection of essays such as this book on the subject of conversion this assessment seems to have all the more credence. Since the time of the appearance of William James's *Varieties of Religious Experience*,[1] the scholarly community has tended to think of conversion in exclusively psychological terms. Moreover, Methodism is often linked with Pietism as essentially emotional in character; indeed Methodism is often seen as the quintessential form of Pietism. Do not look here, then, it is suggested, for serious engagement with Christian doctrine, philosophical investigation, sacramental practice, or Christian community. Everything is reduced, it would appear, to unmediated emotions unrelated to the life of the mind and divorced from what really matters in the life of faith.[2]

My own experience of conversion within Methodism belies this characterization. I first read Wesley precisely because I was in search of intellectual bearings for what was happening in my tangled and confusing spiritual journey. I found his canonical sermons astonishingly helpful. His clarity, good sense, forthrightness, and honesty were not in the least archaic; he unpacked the language of justification, new birth, the witness of the Holy Spirit, sanctification, and the like, with consummate skill.[3] His grasp of the temptations, the queries, the feelings, the intuitions, and the puzzles of the fresh convert were, for me, strikingly accurate and penetrating. The sermons spoke directly to my experience and remain landmarks in my intellectual development.[4] As I have explored the life and work of Wesley down through the years, I continue to be surprised at how versatile Wesley can be both theologically and philosophically.[5]

In this paper my aim is to sketch a contemporary and constructive account of knowledge of God that is in continuity with, yet significantly different from, that offered by Wesley. In the nature of the case my essay will be schematic and programmatic. Filling it out with care would require a major work in religious epistemology. Here, instead, I shall simply identify this deep problem that has been overlooked in the received account of Wesley's epistemology of theology.

A Dilemma at the Core of Wesley's Vision

By far the most interesting feature of current treatments of Wesley's epistemology is the radical diversity of interpretation it has evoked. One line of inquiry focuses on Wesley's conception and use of Scripture,[6] the other on his deployment of the spiritual senses tradition.[7] The first of these really takes us into the arena of special divine revelation and Scripture, the second into the validity of religious experience and anthropology. It is fascinating that both can stand as a substantial review of the Wesleyan corpus; it is disconcerting that they move in radically different directions. In appealing to Scripture and special divine revelation, Wesley is directing our gaze backward into history. We are invited to review what God has said and done in the past and to discern in that the true nature of the divine. In appealing to religious experience and to the change wrought in our spiritual senses by the Holy Spirit in the new birth, Wesley is directing our gaze upwards to the being of God to discern God's love for us in the present as something we can actually feel here and now. The natural question that arises is this: How can these two radically different perspectives be held in one single vision of knowledge of God?

There is no doubt that Wesley tried valiantly to blend them together. He takes this task up on various occasions in his efforts to explain the nature of faith. The tension can be discerned in the following representative quotations.

> Seeing our ideas are not innate, but must all originally come from our senses, it is certainly necessary that you have senses capable of discerning objects of this kind [that is, spiritual objects]—not those only which are called "natural senses," which in this respect profit nothing, as being altogether incapable of discerning objects of a spiritual kind, but *spiritual* senses, exercised to discern spiritual good and evil. It is necessary that you have the *hearing* ear and the *seeing* eye, emphatically so called; that you have a new class of senses opened up in your soul, . . . to be "the *evidence* of things not seen," as your bodily senses are of visible things, to be the avenues to the invisible world, to discern spiritual objects, and to furnish you with ideas of what the outward "eye hath not seen, neither the ear heard."[8]

> The Son of God begins his work in man by enabling us to begin to believe in him. He both opens and enlightens the eyes of our understanding. Out of the darkness he commands light to shine, and takes away the veil which the "god of this world" has spread over our hearts. And we see then not by a chain of reasoning, but by a kind of intuition, by a direct view, that "God was in Christ reconciling the world to himself, not imputing to them their former trespasses"; not imputing them to me.[9]

The primary modes of the senses identified here by Wesley are perception and hearing. Note, however, that one does not hear or see what has happened in the past; one hears various sounds or sees various objects in the present. Yet critical to Wesley's exposition of the operation of the spiritual senses is not just what we see or hear here and now but that we see or hear what has happened in the past, namely, that God was in Christ reconciling the world to himself, not imputing to us our trespasses. This historical component surely cannot be secured by the spiritual senses; it requires memory and testimony. There is simply no direct view of the past, as

Wesley would appear to suggest here. We do not intuit the past, not even the past action of God, without having to rely on witnesses from the past; the dependence is necessarily indirect. What we might see, of course, in the present is God's love for us now, or more precisely, that God does not impute our trespasses to us now. However, if this is linked to the death of Jesus Christ, the Son of God, Wesley has much more on his hands than information of the kind suggested by the appeal to seeing and hearing. He is relying on crucial information about the work of the second person of the Trinity in his great acts of salvation that took place two thousand years ago. It is hard to discern how this could be secured by mere seeing and hearing spiritual objects in the present. At a stretch, Wesley's concern to appeal to perception of the divine does fit his interest in experiences of the Trinity, but he never really goes into this in any detail, and even if he did, it would be precarious in the extreme to rest the case for the Trinity on religious experience alone.

Is there any way in which these two apparently competing proposals can be brought together in a minimally coherent manner?[10] One might try to get around the problem by saying that we are pressing Wesley's analogy of the spiritual senses too literally. This is a lame leg on which to stand. Wesley is very clear that he really means business about the spiritual senses, so much so that it is deeply integrated into his anthropological, theological, and epistemological commitments. Thus he is committed to a dualism of mind and body, he sees the provision of the spiritual senses as a current work of the Holy Spirit, and he wraps both of these in a hardheaded form of empiricism where nothing is present in the mind that is not first present to the senses. So talk of the spiritual senses is not some vague gesture with minimal content; it is a thick description of the way things really are.

The standard way to try and bring coherence to Wesley's proposals in the last generation of scholarship was by means of the famous Methodist Quadrilateral. The solution canvassed is to argue that revelation and spiritual sensation are folded into a fourfold appeal to Scripture, tradition, reason, and experience. Elsewhere I have called attention to the historical and normative difficulties in this proposal.[11] Recent attempts to keep the

Quadrilateral in place have repeated the standard line of the last thirty years and simply failed to reckon with the serious objections raised against it.[12]

Yet the very existence of the Quadrilateral indicates that the matter of integrating all that Wesley has to say on knowledge of God deserves our attention. The Quadrilateral represents a concerted effort to provide a unified vision of Wesley's epistemology of theology. There is a problem of unity and coherence in his views to be identified and solved as best we can. It is assumed in this effort that it is worthwhile exploring whether we can find some measure of reflective equilibrium in Wesley's scattered comments and proposals. As we pursue this, we shall see how the problem identified in a preliminary way above surfaces afresh as a very serious issue in the epistemologies of later generations.

It is natural in pursing our query to focus on revelation, reason, and experience. These are the relevant epistemological categories that need attention in making sense of Wesley's suggestions regarding the spiritual senses. Special revelation as found in Scripture is initially operating in the background when Wesley deploys the idea of the spiritual senses. Through the work of the Holy Spirit one comes to discern the truth about what God has done in the past and sees how it now applies in the present to oneself. It is information about the past, information about God's saving work, rather than objects of sense that constitute the data supplied through the spiritual senses. With this information and its reception in place, reason can then do its work, for it now has relevant data on which to work.

What is genuinely fresh, though not original to Wesley, is the appeal to personal religious experience of the kind associated with conversion. The appeal to special revelation in Scripture and reason had, of course, already surfaced within Anglicanism in the post-Reformation period. Tradition, as we find it in Hooker, for example, was really an appeal to reason; it was essentially the outworking of the best reason of the church reflecting on the meaning of revelation. For Wesley, revelation as found in divinely inspired Scripture was the foundation of theology. He was a determined classical foundationalist at this point.[13] He started with Scripture as given, even dictated by God, as the one sure foundation of our claims about God. In this he was thoroughly medieval, if not Thomistic, in orientation. Once Wesley found out what Scripture said, then the issue was settled. The only point left unresolved was whether Scripture is inerrant and infallible on matters related to salvation or whether it is inerrant and infallible *simpliciter*. Like many in the modern period, Wesley was ambivalent on this issue, never really resolving it satisfactorily. Thus in his endorsing the relevant Anglican Article of Religion on Scripture he restricts the authority of Scripture to matters of salvation, but elsewhere he sounds like a stout fundamentalist, worried that if he admits one error in Scripture, then there may as well be a thousand errors. Suffice it for now to say that the Wesley of the Anglican Articles was the wiser Wesley.

The appeal to divine revelation did not mean that Wesley eschewed the use of apologetic arguments for the truths derived from divine revelation. In the manner of Aquinas and in contrast to the approaches adopted more recently by Kierkegaard and Barth, Wesley engaged in a whirlwind of apologetic arguments appealing to reason and experience. He insisted that there be arguments for the proper identification of divine revelation, so he offered various proofs for the divine inspiration of Scripture.[14] What this means is that beneath his theological foundationalism he was forced to appeal to inference and experience to get the whole operation off the ground. Hence there was the constant danger that revelation would be displaced by reason and experience. After all, revelation now rested on inference and experience, hence it was essentially secondary. Moreover, once revelation was allowed to be confirmed by reason and experience, there was the constant danger that revelation would be displaced all over again from a different direction. It was as if revelation was being eaten away both from below and from above at the same time; divine revelation was like a mountain being undermined from the bottom and eroded from the top.

This was precisely the worry identified by Calvin in his search for adequate grounding for the canon of Scripture as the Word of God. Calvin was prepared to allow a vast array of arguments in favor of Scripture as the Word of God, but he was very clear that the true warrant for this move is the experience of the inner witness of the Holy Spirit.[15] Calvin was uneasy with merely human arguments or evidence as a warrant for the identification of the Word of God. Hence in Calvin the testimony or witness of the Holy Spirit worked as the primary warrant for Scripture as the locus of divine revelation.[16] In Wesley, who is much closer to Paul in his account of the inner witness, the testimony of the Holy Spirit worked as a warrant for the claim that one is now a child of God and has received the forgiveness of one's sins. Both Calvin and Wesley ran the risk of the radical erosion of divine revelation. This arose because both of them posited a new foundation beneath divine revelation in religious experience without which the appeal to divine revelation is left dangling in the air.[17]

The matter in Wesley's case is succinctly captured in technical terms by Matthews: "It seems clear, then, that the *particular* understanding of faith as one's personal spiritual experience of God's grace and mercy becomes the *foundation* for faith as *fiducia*, one's 'sure trust and confidence' of salvation, and for faith as *fides*, one's rational assent to the truth of divine revelation."[18]

This problem of experience replacing revelation as the foundation of theology has haunted the Reformed tradition right down to the present day. Happily, we need not pursue here how it has played itself out in Calvin and his disciples; the water is murky and the river banks are treacherous for even the most seasoned swimmer. In Wesley the difficulties are readily transparent. Effectively, as we have already seen, what Wesley did was develop virtually a full-blown form of spiritual empiricism. God was known through the spiritual senses in a manner analogous to the way the material world is made known through the five senses. While this is nothing new in itself, for it has a long history in Greek and Christian thought, it had repercussions and normative effects that Wesley never addressed. Thus it created a whole new foundation for Christian theology. This new foundation was most brilliantly developed in Schleiermacher's appeal to the affections or to religious feeling. In Schleiermacher, special revelation is not just left dangling in empty epistemological space, it has effectively been eliminated. Pressures to drop special revelation have grown apace over the last two centuries, most especially from the rise and practice of historical criticism.

The upshot of our discussion is this. At one level in his religious epistemology, Wesley was a classical Protestant, confident that he could ground all his claims on Scripture. Through academic training and intellectual self-cultivation, he was a vigorous apologist, using every argument and evidence at his disposal to make his case for the truths of revelation and to dispatch his critics. In the course of this operation he committed himself to a radical form of empiricism that put the senses at the foundation of all knowledge, including knowledge of God. This led him to mine the resources of religious experience, most brilliantly represented by his treatment of the inner witness of the Holy Spirit. However, he never really worked out how this was to be integrated into his classical Protestant sensibility. When the doctrine of special revelation came under fire in the tradition he founded and initiated, it was natural that this new, empirical foundation be asked to carry the load previously shared with divine revelation. Thus, unwittingly, Wesley paved the way for his followers take to liberal Protestantism with ease and enthusiasm. It is surely no accident that his heirs have been sorely tempted again and again to bet the store on appeal to religious experience. By this time, of course, the whole paraphernalia of spiritual senses have disappeared from the scene, but the original roots are still visible in the historical record.

Also especially interesting in all these later developments is that any appeal to conversion has dropped entirely from sight. The appeal to conversion can, in fact, take two forms. It can be an appeal to perception in which one comes to perceive the love of God for oneself, or it can be a causal argument deploying an appeal to the best explanation for conspicuous moral change in the human agent. Both are visible in the biblical accounts of Paul's conversion. Thus Paul perceives the person of the risen Lord, and this is then explained in terms of divine action and intention. Neither of these sorts of arguments appear in any shape or form within contemporary Wesleyanism. Yet they are entirely in keeping with Wesley's general theological orientation. Indeed, as we have seen, Wesley was fascinated by the reality of religious experience in part because he thought that it implicitly supplied the crucial evidence for the truth of the Christian faith.

Conversion and the Quest for God

The question that naturally arises is this: Can we develop a vision of knowledge of God that takes seriously the evidence of conversion but does so without eroding the place of divine revelation in the epistemology of theology? I think we can, but before we get to this, we need to say something more about conversion. In the exposition that follows I shall illustrate a network of descriptive comments about conversion by drawing attention to general developments in early Methodism.[19] My main concern is to explore in a phenomenological vein how conversion fits into a complex journey of faith as a prelude to providing a complex vision of knowledge of God into which the data of conversion fits naturally.

Many individuals first contemplate the existence of God when they sense the reality of God in their conscience and in creation, or when they reflect informally on the natural order. No doubt these two factors generally work in tandem. In neither case need there be dependence on formal argument or propositional evidence. Evidence comes in at a later reflective or second-order stage. Hence most of the people who were converted in Methodism were initially nominal theists. They were not Buddhists or agnostics. They were cultural Christians embedded in the life and thought of eighteenth-century England. Moreover, they were not argued into their initial convictions; they inherited them or formed them naturally with the help of the community.

Furthermore, belief in God itself is embedded in a wider theological vision that is supplied by cultural and ecclesial formation. Belief in God is not just belief in some divine will-o'-the-wisp deity; however vague or ill-formed, it is belief in some specific deity. Thus for Wesley, as for most people of his day in the Western world, belief in God was profoundly shaped by the Christian tradition. The God discerned in nature was effectively the God of the Christian tradition; the God of creation was the God of divine revelation. Hence, from the outset Wesley and his converts were dependent on the prior beliefs, doctrinal development, and epistemic practices of Christianity. They were rooted, grounded, and formed in the womb of the western Christian tradition.

Conversion in these circumstances is not simply some emotional exercise or event; it is turning in repentance and faith to the God of Jesus Christ announced in the gospel. Thus conversion to Christ is radically different from conversion to, say, Hinduism. Whatever the shared psychological or phenomenological features, Christian conversion involves the appropriation of a whole network of concepts, virtues, dispositions, doctrines, and practices that are derived from that form of the Christian faith into which one is initiated. Thus, those converted through Wesley and the early Methodists were from the outset planted in the soil of the western Christian tradition.[20] They were informally introduced to a host of materials and practices that became in time characteristic of Methodism. Virtually all of these were taken on trust; they were accepted not because of proof or formal evidence but because of testimony, because of social formation, and because of fit with their background beliefs and experience.

We might say that early Methodism was a sensitive and carefully constructed spiritual machine for the production of conversion. It was so effective that at one point in the nineteenth century Methodism became the largest Protestant denomination in North America. Outsiders naturally thought of conversion within or to Methodism in terms of manipulation, chicanery, emotional conditioning, and the like.[21] This is not how Wesley saw it. For Wesley to be born again, to receive the witness of the Holy Spirit, to be justified, to be sanctified, and the like, was to be subject to divine action. Primarily this action was directed to the healing of the human condition; it was divine salvation brought about by the Holy Spirit. However, salvation was also a matter of coming to know the truth about oneself and about God. Through salvation one found the truth about the love of God for the world. This was no mere formal notion; it was something one experienced in one's heart as it was shed within by the Holy Spirit. One came in this process to know God by acquaintance.

Experience of God, concept formation, and intellectual development are a seamless whole. Throughout, one is dependent on the community. Personal experience, while it may well incubate in the solitude of one's own soul, is inextricably meshed with the spiritual and intellectual resources supplied in the fellowship of the church. Spiritual direction by leaders and those further on in the journey of faith are indispensable. We can see this in the work of Wesley and his cohorts in evangelism. Through their good auspices one learned within Methodism to appropriate the Scriptures, to make good use of the sacraments, to take on board the doctrinal treasures of patristic and Reformed Christianity, and to learn the Christian moral tradition. In short, one was initiated into a complex web of belief, emotion, and practice.

In this pilgrimage one generally comes to know God without knowing how one knows that one knows God. Thus, in the case of Methodism, thousands of "simple" believers could sing the great hymns of the tradition and assent to their content without having a clue how to provide a reasoned argument in their favor, much less a theory of knowledge that would articulate the relevant arguments or reasons. They knew nothing of the virtues or vices of natural theology, of the credentials of divine revelation, or of criteria to test the validity of religious experience. They did not to speak of the difference between a correspondence or coherentist theory of truth, or the epistemic significance of the proper cognitive functioning of our various faculties.

At some stage, however, profound intellectual questions do arise for converts. It fell in his day to Wesley to deal with these as best he could, although he readily ransacked anything at hand to help out; and he encouraged others, like Joseph Fletcher, to join in the work. This pastoral and apologetic intention of Wesley explains the scattered and occasional nature of his proposals. He worked at two distinct levels.

At one level he provided various arguments for the beliefs and practices he handed over to his converts. The former are radically varied in nature, depending on the particular case before him. On this score Wesley comes across as an inveterate rationalist, constantly marshalling arguments for his views. As to the practices, he built a vast array of spiritual disciplines that were indispensable in nurturing and disciplining new believers.

At another level Wesley sought to supply a network of epistemic concepts that explored why the various reasons and arguments he deployed were pertinent to the issues at hand. Here, as we have seen above, Wesley does the best he can to work out a robust form of empiricism that ultimately stakes everything on the creation or re-creation of the spiritual senses as directed to God's past action in Jesus Christ. In this he sought to supply his own inimitable account of knowledge of God.

A Fresh Look at Knowledge of God

How might we proceed today to provide an account of knowledge of God that avoids the dilemma we posed above but that arises out of conversation with Wesley's work? I suggest the following eight fundamental theses.

First, no single theory of knowledge does justice to the great variety of things we know about ourselves, the world, and God. All general theories fail either by leaving out something we do actually know, or, to succeed, they have to be supplemented by bringing in elements not covered by the theory of knowledge in hand. This applies as much to the empiricism of the eighteenth century to which Wesley was indebted as to any other theory before or since.[22] What we can rightly hope to develop is a modest network of suggestions that provide an illuminating overview of our varied epistemic moves.

Second, our everyday knowledge of the world of persons and things is derived by various cognitive or doxastic practices like perception, intuition, conscience, memory, inference, judgment, testimony, and the like. These practices are bedrock in the sense that anything we provide by way of argument in their favor already depends on these practices. There is nothing deeper or more basic that is more reliable; either we take these practices as *prima facie* reliable or we do not.[23] If we do, then we take ourselves to have access to reality; if we do not, then we are doomed to a barren skepticism nobody can put into practice.[24]

Third, a theistic vision of the universe provides a natural home or setting for the embrace of these practices. In a theistic vision these practices are seen as designed by God, so that when they are functioning properly they do not deceive us.[25] Hence for the theist, they are embedded in a rich ontological perspective that provides additional warrant for taking them seriously. Thus while the secularist may be skeptical of, say, conscience, seeing it perhaps merely as childhood initiation into social mores, the theist will treat it with appropriate qualification as the voice of God, lending it an authority that might otherwise be ignored. More generally, the theist will look upon perception, judgment, inference, and the like, as underwritten by the goodness and power of God.

Fourth, in our knowledge of God these practices naturally come into play. How they do so is a matter of intense debate and discussion that has never been resolved across the years. Different believers gravitate toward different proposals, and they develop radically diverse accounts of our epistemic obligations and duties. Thus those drawn to classical natural theology stress the role of inference;[26] those drawn to religious experience stress perception;[27] those taken by the cumulative nature of the evidence stress the role of judgment;[28] those impressed by the crucial role of the proper functioning of our cognitive faculties stress the propriety of properly basic beliefs.[29] Theists differ greatly in this arena, yet they can still agree on the eventual outcome. Indeed it is astonishing how far theists can agree on what they think they know, all the while disagreeing on how they know what they know.

Fifth, inside the Christian theistic universe, divine revelation plays a pivotal role. Thus the proclamation of the gospel is at once a matter of salvation and a matter of divine revelation, for the multiple acts through which God has come to reclaim the world from sin and to restore human dignity are equally acts through which his intentions and nature are made manifest. Once acknowledged, divine revelation has a privileged position. It has a role analogous to testimony in the law courts, or experiment in science, or perception in our knowledge of material objects. Such an appeal does not override memory, inference, judgment, conscience, and the like. Rather it extends the range of doxastic practices to include the testimony of God mediated in complex ways through divinely inspired means of grace. Hence, once written and canonized, Scripture has always been pivotal in our knowledge of God, even though the primary purpose is to make us wise unto salvation.

Six, despite disclaimers to the contrary, Scripture is both created by the church and mediated to us within the church. It is received within a network of canonical materials, persons, and practices that work together through spiritual formation to introduce us to the great truths of the gospel that liberate us from darkness and error.[30] Here tradition is an inescapable form of social knowledge where trust is essential.[31] We are inextricably dependent on communities of faith that, with varying degrees of success and reliability, build up and hand over their intellectual treasures. We are indebted to interpretive communities that sift and ponder the deposit of divine revelation by the aid of the Spirit.

Seventh, in the reception of these treasures we are healed by the Holy Spirit to perceive the truth as it is in Christ Jesus. Given that sin and evil have corrupted and harmed our cognitive faculties, and given the adverse effects of our passions and self-interests, we need the healing activity of God to recover our spiritual sight and rightly discern the truth. Grace comes to us to enable us to repent and make progress in virtue, thus curbing the effects of sin on our vision. Our cognitive faculties for discerning the divine in the world and in special revelation are restored so that they function properly, and so that we see for ourselves the way things are.

Eighth, within this healing process the measure of our assurance and confidence is dependent on the overflowing presence and testimony of the Holy Spirit in our hearts. Hence the whole process of genuine conversion brings with it over time an awareness of God's love and mercy not otherwise possible. This awareness is not something divorced from other avenues to our knowledge of God. On the contrary, this awareness or perception is precisely the deep, personal awareness that the love of God manifest in Jesus Christ and displayed before the world, as on a placard, though his cross extends not just to the world as a whole but to oneself personally. Moreover, it is this love shed abroad in our hearts by the Holy Spirit that is the wellspring of moral and spiritual transformation that makes possible commitment, self-sacrifice, and love of others. This love is the source of all virtue and goodness in the convert, so that the whole endeavor is seen from beginning to end as radically dependent on the overflowing generosity and grace of God. It is also the source of undying hope for oneself and for creation, for the resurrection of Jesus Christ from the dead is perceived as the first fruit of the world to come, promised in the gospel of the kingdom.

Taken in the round, then, knowledge of God is progressive,

complex, multilayered, and informal. It is not merely a matter of propositional evidence, yet evidence and argument have a place. It is not merely a matter of personal experience, yet the experience of turning to God in conversion has its own indispensable role in the overall process. It is not merely a matter of appeal to community and tradition, yet communal practices have a necessary function in the production of knowledge. It is not merely a matter of divine revelation, yet special divine revelation has a pivotal role, so much so that in time what we know of God in creation is read through the lens of Scripture in an entirely natural and fitting way. It is not merely a matter of our cognitive faculties working properly, yet the healing of these faculties is indispensable in perception and discernment of the signs of the divine in creation, conscience, history, Scripture, and religious experience. The whole process is so intricate in its web of judgment and data that it lends itself less to a linear, inferential progression and more to an ongoing conversation where ample use is made of creative suggestion, poignant testimony, extended explanation, and illuminating disclosure. In short, it is naturally displayed in a network of homily, expansive essay, polemical rebuttal, tract, and personal epistle, such as we find abundantly represented in the works of Wesley.

Conclusion

We have traveled a long way from Wesley, of course, but the proposal outlined has deep roots in many of his scattered epistemological suggestions. Thus it appeals to the notion of cognitive faculties, to the general reliability of reason and perception, to the idea of special divine revelation, to the epistemic effects of sin and evil and their antidote in the healing activity of the Holy Spirit, and, most especially, to the inner witness of the Holy Spirit in providing certainty and assurance. It differs from Wesley in eschewing any general theory of knowledge as represented by his empiricism, in rejecting any and every form of classical foundationalism, in expanding the boundaries of the canonical commitments of the church, in lifting up the social dimensions of knowledge, in stressing the place of virtue in gaining knowledge of God, and in refusing to privilege religious experience over divine revelation.

Matthews's assessment of Wesley's efforts strikes me as exactly right.

> A part of Wesley's lack of clarity and precision . . . is due to the fact that he certainly had not the leisure, and probably had not the ability, to press theological and philosophical questions or issues to these depths. Despite his broad general familiarity with the concerns of such 18th-century philosophical and theological figures as Locke, Browne, Malebranche, Norris, Butler, Hutcheson, and Edwards, Wesley's mind was of a less systematic and inquiring turn. He had an acute intellect and was certainly capable of being a fierce disputant; he had formidable skills in logic and debate which he used in controversy with critics of his message or his movement. But, in general, he was much more concerned to defend his general theological, and epistemological, position against such critics than to attempt to trace out the conclusions and implications of his analogical and metaphorical language concerning such matters as the "spiritual senses" of faith and the "direct experience" of the divine realm which he claimed to be possible through them.[32]

If this is a correct assessment, then we best serve the tradition not simply by repeating Wesley but by going beyond him in order to salvage his best insights for the future. The extraordinary advances that have been made in epistemology over the last generation make such a development possible. In recent years philosophers in the Reformed tradition have provided a rich contemporary account of how we might think of knowledge of God from within the Reformed tradition. My efforts in this short essay are a gesture toward supplying a different vision of knowledge of God from within the Wesleyan tradition. However that account is played out, it must, if it is to be recognizably Wesleyan, exploit the epistemic significance of conversion, taking that in a rounded sense as the work of God in the human heart and soul. It must also find room for a robust account of special divine revelation that is intimately related to Scripture. Bringing these together is indeed a daunting challenge that awaits a full-scale elaboration as an exercise in the epistemology of theology.

Such a venture must not be seen as divorced from the rich and manifold ministry of the church in evangelism and ongoing Christian nurture. No doubt Wesley had many things in mind when he inaugurated Methodism as a movement and then as a denomination. He was seeking a wider vision of the church than is available in Congregationalism, and he was engaged in a complex experiment in spiritual formation and evangelism. Our current recovery of nerve in embracing conversion, together with the lively drive to implement those complex ministries that, under the Spirit, make conversion possible, have enormous promise for the future. One delightful byproduct of this development is that in the very process of engaging in this work we gain genuine knowledge of God here and now.

Part Four

Pastoral Perspectives

Chapter Eleven

Conversion: Possibility and Expectation

Sondra Higgins Matthaei

In my first year of seminary teaching, one of my students was preoccupied with the interrelationship of conversion and nurture, as well as the role of church leaders in Christian formation. My student's questions are not new. For centuries, the church has sought to articulate how persons become Christian, and the church's role in passing on the faith. The relationship of these two elements of Christian faith formation continues to be debated in the Wesleyan tradition today. We ask, "Is conversion an expectation for which evidence must be presented, or a possibility that the church must cultivate in its members?"

We live in a time when we can no longer assume persons have grown up knowing themselves to be Christian. So churches and their leaders need to take a new look at Christian formation. The church's responsibility in "making disciples" has been the focus of my most recent research on Christian formation in the context of the early Methodist movement. The term "making disciples" itself expresses the need for a new intentionality about participating in God's work of transformation in the world. As a result of this research, I have proposed in several works that Methodists need to create a Wesleyan ecology of faith formation composed of relationships, structures, and practices that are grounded in the theology of the Wesleyan tradition, particularly John Wesley's understanding of the Trinity, the Way of Salvation, and the church.[1]

One of John Wesley's strongest convictions was that God's grace radically transforms persons for a holy life in which they are empowered and enabled to love God and neighbor fully. Over time, as John Wesley developed his understanding and articulation of justification, assurance, and sanctification, he asserted that we are able to know we have been justified through the witness of God's Spirit in our own spirit. He writes:

> The testimony of the Spirit is an inward impression on the soul, whereby the Spirit of God directly "witnesses to my spirit that I am a child of God"; that Jesus Christ hath loved me, and given himself for me; that all my sins are blotted out, and I, even I, am reconciled to God.[2]

In other words, conversion is both an *experience* of God's transforming work and an *interpretation* as persons seek to understand, articulate, and share that religious experience with others.

The goal of Christian faith formation in the Wesleyan tradition is to share the good news of God's grace in Jesus Christ in order to help people recognize their need for the transforming power of God's grace while learning what it means to be faithful in everyday life.[3] The church provides instruction and nurture in light of the expectation that God, through the work of the Holy Spirit, will transform those who seek a new life in Christ. As a result, the question of the interrelationship of nurture and conversion is central to the church's educational ministry of Christian faith formation.

Since Horace Bushnell first wrote *Christian Nurture* in 1847,[4] more attention has been given to Christian nurture and less to conversion in mainline Protestant denominations. Nurture has to do with cultivating growth in faith through a variety of approaches such as "religious instruction," enculturation, faith development, and "educating for social transformation."[5] These approaches all include the hope for and expectation of lives transformed by God's Spirit, but they do not anticipate a particular type of religious experience. In recent years, the hunger for deeper religious experience has led Christian educators to make creative proposals about spirituality, spiritual direction, and spiritual disciplines for those who would be disciples.[6] In this chapter, I will argue that both nurture and conversion are important for a Wesleyan ecology of faith formation, and I will discuss ways that the faith community participates in God's transforming work.

Conversion is understood here as a transformative experience through which lives are radically changed as persons come to know God's forgiveness and salvation through Jesus Christ and experience their adoption as children of God. Conversion encompasses both an experience of transformation *and* a lifelong endeavor of responding to God's redeeming grace through faithful discipleship. This is why Wesley could assert that God's work in us is not complete with an experience of new birth. The Holy Spirit's perfecting work continues in us so that we might become more Christlike in our daily lives with the support and accountability provided by participation in Christian community.

The occasion of John Wesley's own conversion is a matter of some contention. As Richard Heitzenrater noted, proponents of the argument that the May 1738 Aldersgate experience was a conversion "point to Wesley's own comments at the time, his claim that he was *now* a Christian whereas previously he was not."[7] Yet opponents of this argument also use Wesley's reflections "that before 1738 Wesley claimed to be a Christian" and occasions after 1738 when he reported "he was not now a true believer."[8] Clifford Towlson observed that Maximin Piette, writing in 1937, argued that if the word *conversion* is to be used at all, it should be in connection with John Wesley's entry into orders in 1725, and not with the "heart-warming" at Aldersgate.[9] It is clear that 1725 marks the time when Wesley's deeper attention to his spiritual life was evident in correspondence with his parents and in the activities of the Holy Club. In addition, Piette argued, along with Umphrey Lee, that Wesley's ongoing spiritual struggles following Aldersgate and his lack of later reference to that experience supported this position. On the other hand, Towlson reported that Wesley's contemporaries such as Adam Clarke and John Whitehead[10] agree, as does later historian Luke Tyerman,[11] that the Aldersgate experience was vital. And J. Ernest Rattenbury concluded that the uniqueness of Aldersgate was John Wesley's experience of assurance of salvation that shaped his formulation of doctrine from that time on.[12] Heitzenrater concurs that "the primary issue in 1738 for Wesley (both in terms of anticipation and experience) was that of *assurance*."[13]

Each of these perspectives not only tells us something about John Wesley's religious experience, but also points to different understandings of the nature of conversion that Towlson attempts to reconcile. He writes: "The consensus of opinion is that, whatever were the influences leading up to the experience, and whatever name is given to it—conversion, decision, or rededication—it was the experience itself which changed the direction and impact of John Wesley's life, and which may therefore be said to have given birth to the Methodist revival."[14] Heitzenrater provides another perspective in his interpretation of the Aldersgate experience by offering a helpful distinction "between Wesley's spiritual pilgrimage and his theological development," noting that theological reflection on a doctrinal issue can take years.[15]

Our challenge as twenty-first-century observers of the experience and interpretation of John Wesley's conversion in the eighteenth century is twofold. The first challenge is theological: What is the nature of conversion? The second challenge could be described as psychosocial: How does this religious experience have an impact on relationships with God and others? These two challenges result in further questions: By what criteria do we judge whether a conversion has taken place? Are we judging the experience or the interpretation?

These questions were also at the heart of John Wesley's spiritual pilgrimage.[16] In his reply to Josiah Tucker's "A Brief History of the Principles of a Methodist," which accused Wesley of inconsistency in his theological interpretation, Wesley wrote "The Principles of a Methodist" in 1742. In this post-Aldersgate account, Wesley is already articulating his theological view of God's initiative of grace through Christ and human response through living faith. "I believe three things must go together in our justification: upon God's part, [God's] great mercy and grace; upon Christ's part, the satisfaction of God's justice by the offering his body and shedding his blood, 'and fulfilling the law of God perfectly'; and upon our part, true and living faith in the merits of Jesus Christ."[17] In discussing his understanding of assurance and the aftermath of justification, Wesley reflected his conviction that conversion is an instantaneous act of God's grace "and that the moment a [person] has living faith in Christ he [or she] is converted or justified.' . . . 'Which faith he [or she] cannot have without knowing that he [or she] has it.' "[18] But how did Wesley come to such an understanding?

We turn now to examine the four months prior to John Wesley's Aldersgate experience upon his return from the colonies. With the complete failure of John Wesley's rational approach to faith and salvation on his mission to Georgia, the person who receives the most credit for bringing him to the point of seeing himself as a sinner in need of salvation is the Moravian Peter Böhler.[19] But John Wesley's spiritual pilgrimage was also shaped by Böhler's influence on Charles Wesley's search for spiritual and physical health during the same time. And ever in the background were Susanna Wesley's teachings that had already shaped the Wesleys' ministries. Keeping with our Wesleyan tradition, we turn now to see what we can learn about conversion and faith formation from observing the experiences of others.

Case Study: In Search of a Living Faith

Shortly after his return from the devastating mission trip to Georgia, John Wesley met Moravian Peter Böhler on February 7, 1738, "a day much to be remembered."[20] Wesley found lodging for Böhler and his companions, and "from this time [Wesley] did not willingly lose any opportunity of conversing with them while [he] stayed in London."[21] Böhler was five years younger than Wesley, but they had much in common, particularly since Wesley had just returned from the colonies and Böhler was on his way there as a missionary. Wesley's previous contact with the Moravians on board a ship to Georgia, as well as his relationship with August Spangenberg, provided motivation for cultivating this relationship.

Both John and Charles Wesley seemed to be drawn to Böhler because of his spiritual state and the model of piety he provided. After an instantaneous conversion in Jena, Böhler was received into the Moravian Church in Herrnhut in 1737 and ordained by

Moravian leader Count Zinzendorf.[22] For Böhler's part, he assessed the Wesleys' spiritual state on February 17 in a letter to Zinzendorf after walking to Oxford with the Wesley brothers: "The elder, John, is an amiable man; he acknowledges that he does not yet rightly know the Saviour and suffers himself to be instructed. He loves us sincerely. His brother, with whom you conversed frequently in London a year ago, is greatly troubled in spirit and knows not how he shall begin to know the Saviour."[23]

In late February 1738, Charles Wesley suffered a period of serious physical illness during which Böhler stayed by his side, praying and speaking of salvation with him.[24] By March 4, when John Wesley visited Charles who was recovering, John declared that he was "clearly convinced of unbelief, of the want of 'that faith whereby alone we are saved,' with the full, Christian salvation."[25] It was at this point that John Wesley asked Böhler if he should stop preaching because of his lack of faith. And Böhler replied, "By no means."[26] By March 6, John Wesley reported that he began preaching "this new doctrine" of "salvation by faith alone" to a prisoner named Clifford. Wesley wrote, "Peter Böhler had many times desired me to speak to him before. But I could not prevail on myself so to do, being still (as I had been many years) a zealous asserter of *the impossibility of a death-bed repentance*."[27]

After two months of discussion about the nature of salvation, particularly the issue of God's initiative and human responsibility in salvation, both Wesleys had come to recognize their need of forgiveness and justification. John Wesley had begun preaching on justification by faith alone when Böhler wrote to Zinzendorf on March 23, 1738:

> I had a very full conversation with the two Wesleys, in order to impress upon their minds the Gospel, and in order to entreat them to proclaim the same to others as they had opportunity, at Oxford and elsewhere. Thereupon they confessed their doubts respecting the truth of the doctrine of free grace, through the merits of Jesus, whereby poor sinners receive forgiveness, and are set free from the dominion of sin. The Saviour, however, granted me grace to convince them from the Scriptures; and they had no way of escape, except to ask to see and converse with persons who had made the experiences of

> which I spoke. I told them that in London I hoped to be able to show them such Christians.[28]

John Wesley's record of this conversation noted that Böhler "amazed me more and more, by the account he gave of the fruits of living faith—the holiness and happiness which he affirmed to attend it."[29] But Böhler's next step was clear. He would bring living witnesses of God's work of grace through instantaneous conversion to speak to the Wesleys.

The meeting with the four witnesses took place on April 22, 1738. Böhler described the encounter in a letter to Zinzendorf: "I asked Wesley what he now believed? He said, four examples did not settle the matter and could not convince him. I replied that I would bring him eight more here in London. After a short time he arose and said: 'We will sing the hymn, *My soul before Thee prostrate lies.*' "[30] But after the hymn Wesley took Böhler into his bedroom and indicated that he was convinced by Böhler's argument and asked "how could he now help himself and how should he attain to faith?"[31] We can only imagine what Böhler thought when he reported that John Wesley said "he was a man who had not sinned as grossly as other people," but Böhler replied simply that "not to believe in the Saviour was sinning enough."[32]

John Wesley's account of this experience provides his perspective:

> I met Peter Böhler once more. I had now no objection to what he said of the nature of faith, viz., that it is (to use the words of our Church), "A sure trust and confidence which a man hath in God, that through the merits of Christ *his* sins are forgiven, and *he* reconciled to the favour of God." Neither could I deny either the happiness or holiness which he described as fruits of this living faith.[33]

But John Wesley still could not comprehend or accept justification as instantaneous. So Wesley turned to searching the Scriptures for evidence and, to his amazement, he "found scarce any instances there of other than *instantaneous* conversions—scarce any other so slow as that of St. Paul, who was three days in the pangs of the new birth."[34] But Wesley was still looking for a way out: "*Thus,* I grant, God wrought in the *first* ages of Christianity; but the times are changed. What reasons have I to believe [God] works in the same manner now?"[35] By the next day, additional witnesses convinced Wesley.[36] Wesley wrote that his disputing ended here, and after talking with Peter Böhler once more, he began speaking to others about "the nature and fruits of faith."[37]

By the end of April, Charles Wesley had also come to desire assurance of salvation. In Böhler's words: "The younger Wesley now also believes that he is a poor sinner and seeks grace in the bloody wounds of the Redeemer."[38] Early in May, Böhler left for the colonies and Charles was left in the care of Mr. Bray and Mr. Holland, who introduced him to Luther's commentary on Galatians on May 17, 1738.[39] Charles Wesley's conversion came on May 21 when he heard a woman's voice say, "In the name of Jesus of Nazareth, arise, and believe, and thou shalt be healed of all thy infirmities."[40] Even when Mr. Bray came and prayed with him, Charles resisted. "Still I felt a violent opposition and reluctance to believe; yet still the Spirit of God strove with my own and the evil spirit, till by degrees he chased away the darkness of my unbelief. I found myself convinced, I knew not how, nor when; and immediately fell to intercession."[41] Charles reported that he found himself to be at peace and able to resist temptation through the "protection of Christ."[42]

Before embarking for the colonies, Böhler had sent a letter to John Wesley admonishing him to continually trust in God. "Beware of the sin of unbelief; and if you have not conquered it yet, see that you conquer it this very day, through the blood of Jesus Christ."[43] And Böhler closed his letter with "Abide in faith, love, teaching, the communion of saints."[44] Two weeks later, Wesley's readiness for God's transforming grace is revealed in his letter of May 24 to John Gambold:

> I feel what you say (though not enough), for I am under the same condemnation. I see that the whole law of God is holy and just and good. I know every thought, every temper of my soul ought to bear God's image and superscription. But how am I fallen from the glory of God! I feel that "I am sold under sin." I know that I too deserve nothing but wrath, being full of all abominations; and having no good thing in me to atone for

> them, or to remove the wrath of God. All my works, my righteousness, my prayers, need an atonement for themselves. So that my mouth is stopped, I have nothing to plead. God is holy; I am unholy. God is a consuming fire; I am altogether a sinner, meet to be consumed.[45]

On the evening this letter was written, John Wesley went to Aldersgate Chapel and reported that his heart was "strangely warmed." Wesley's description of his experience reflects expectations of "new birth." "I felt I did trust in Christ, Christ alone for salvation, and an assurance was given me that he had taken away *my* sins, even *mine*, and saved *me* from the law of sin and death."[46] According to Kenneth J. Collins, John Wesley found "freedom from the guilt *and* the power of sin" through this experience.[47]

Reflection: Transformed for a Holy Life

This case study provides insight for our consideration of faith formation in the Wesleyan tradition, particularly the readiness for conversion, the interpretation and witness that follows, and the role of the Christian community in nurturing faith. We will examine this case study through the lens of faith formation and ask, What have we learned about conversion and nurture? What clues do we have for the role of the church in a Wesleyan ecology of faith formation that takes both conversion and nurture seriously?

Readiness for Conversion

Readiness for conversion came for both Wesleys through the work of God's prevenient grace in a time of spiritual and physical vulnerability. By 1738 both John and Charles Wesley were seeking salvation. Not as much is known about Charles Wesley's spiritual journey to this point, but it is clear that his serious physical illness generated questions about salvation. For John Wesley, the question of salvation and the kind of faith needed were apparent as early as 1725. The failure of his rational, well-disciplined piety led to spiritual distress when John learned he could never do enough to merit salvation. What John Wesley came to experience through his spiritual struggles and the guidance of Peter Böhler is that humans are totally dependent on God for salvation. In the sermon "Salvation by Faith," John Wesley wrote: "All the blessings which God hath bestowed upon [humanity] are of [God's] mere grace, bounty, or favour: his free, undeserved favour, favour altogether undeserved, [humanity] having no claim to the least of [God's] mercies."[48]

But Böhler was not the first to tell Wesley that he needed to trust God more. In August 1725, for example, Susanna Wesley wrote, "Divine faith is an assent to whatever God has revealed to us, because [God] has revealed it."[49] Susanna knew from their discussion that John needed to trust God more. And in a letter to Miss Bolton in 1789, John Wesley provided evidence that William Law, who preceded Peter Böhler as his spiritual guide, had also told him to trust God. " 'Sir, you are troubled,' said Mr. Law to me, 'because you do not understand how God is dealing with you. Perhaps if you did, it would not so well answer his design. He is teaching you to trust Him farther than you can see Him.' "[50] It could be argued that what John Wesley knew in his mind he did not yet know in his heart. And we can clearly see God's prevenient grace at work in Wesley's search for a deeper faith.

Interpretation and Witness

This search began early in John Wesley's life when he asked, "What must I do to be saved?"[51] What resulted was an experience of God's transforming grace for John just days after his brother's conversion. What followed their experiences in May 1738 was ongoing self-examination and further questioning in true Wesley fashion as the Wesleys sought to interpret their experience in light of their expectations for evidence of new birth. Heitzenrater wrote that both Wesleys were looking for evidence of the "authenticity" of their experience such as the "necessary fruits of faith and assurance . . . freedom from sin, doubt, and fear, and the fullness of peace, confidence, and joy in the Holy Ghost (otherwise called 'holiness and happiness')."[52] John Wesley almost immediately began noting his continuing struggle with temptations and lack of joy in comparison with the religious experience of others.[53] Through searching the Scriptures and praying, John Wesley finally indicated that he had reached some degree of peace by June 6.

A letter disrupted this peaceful state and revealed Wesley's expectation for full assurance of faith: "It was asserted therein that no doubting could consist with the least degree of true faith; that whoever at any time felt any doubt or fear was not *weak in faith,* but had *no faith* at all; and that none hath any faith till the law of the Spirit of life has made him *wholly* free from the law of sin and death."[54] In response to the letter, John Wesley once again found consolation in Scripture "where St. Paul speaks of those whom he terms 'babes in Christ' "—and concludes "surely, then these men had *some degree* of faith, though it is plain their faith was but *weak.*"[55]

On June 8, 1738, prior to leaving for Germany to spend time in the Moravian community, John Wesley read the spiritual pilgrimage account of May 24 to his mother.[56] Wesley records her response a year later after Samuel Wesley Jr. sent a copy of the account to Susanna with his own interpretation. In John's words: "He sent an account of it to my mother, whom I now found under strange fears concerning me, being convinced by 'an account taken from one of my own papers' that I had greatly erred from the faith."[57] John found his mother's distress to be puzzling, since she had affirmed his thinking only one year earlier, writing that "she greatly approved it and said she heartily blessed God, who had brought me to so just a way of thinking."[58] John concludes that his mother's distress results from Samuel's interference: "How hard is it to form a true judgment of any person or thing from the account of a prejudiced relater!"[59]

In October 1738, Charles Wesley shared his conversion with his mother, who responded, " 'Tis with much pleasure I find your mind is somewhat easier than formerly, and heartily thank God for it."[60] Susanna concludes by asking Charles how he understands justifying faith. This discussion continues in her letter of December 6 when Susanna writes: "I do not judge it necessary for us to know the precise time of our conversion. 'Tis sufficient if we have a reasonable hope that we are passed from death to life by the fruits of the Holy Spirit wrought in our hearts. Such are repentance, faith, hope, love, etc. Our Lord acts in various ways and by various means on different tempers, nor is the work of regeneration begun and perfected at once."[61] Susanna also admonishes him to be thankful for the peace he has received: "You say you have peace but not joy in believing. Blessed be God for peace. May his peace rest within you. Joy will follow, perhaps not very close, but it will follow faith and love. *God's promises are sealed to us but not dated.* Therefore, patiently attend his pleasure. He will give you joy in believing."[62] In 1739 Susanna experienced "assurance of her own acceptance by God" as she received Holy Communion.[63] In recognition of this experience, Susanna's gravestone was inscribed with the words of Charles Wesley:

> The Father then revealed his Son,
> Him in the broken bread made known.
> She knew and felt her sins forgiven,
> And found the earnest of her heaven.[64]

John, Charles, and Susanna Wesley had three very different experiences of God's grace. John Wesley began to articulate his understanding of the degrees of faith based on his own religious experience, what he had witnessed in others, and the teaching of his parents. In "Principles of a Methodist" (1742), John Wesley wrote: "All I need observe is that the *first sense of forgiveness* is often mixed with doubt or fear. But the 'full assurance of faith' excludes all doubt and fear, as the very term implies. . . . 'He [or she] may not have till long after that full assurance of faith which excludes all doubt and fear.' "[65] As Collins has observed, Wesley came to distinguish the first sense of forgiveness, with its doubts and fears, from the full assurance of faith that excludes all doubt and fear; he called the former the faith of a child of God, and the latter the faith of one perfected in love.[66]

For John Wesley, conversion is a transforming act of God's grace in Christ that radically alters human lives, and ongoing growth in love of God and neighbor is sustained by the perfecting work of the Holy Spirit. In addition, John Wesley consistently linked justification and the new birth as demonstrated in his sermon "The New Birth."[67] He writes: "In order of time, neither of these is before the other. In the moment we are justified by the grace of God through the redemption that is in Jesus we are also 'born of the Spirit.' "[68] This view points to Wesley's belief that God's prevenient grace brings us to the point of repentance of our sins, justifying grace through Jesus Christ is the source of our redemption, and sanctifying grace begins a perfecting work in us at the moment of redemption. In other words, an experience of God's transforming grace in Jesus Christ leads to deepening faith as persons grow in love of God and neighbor with the help of the Holy Spirit and the support of the faith community. Through God's grace we are transformed to fully love God and neighbor in holiness of heart and life.

The Church as a Living Witness

In previous work, I have proposed that the Way of Salvation consists of a process of growth in communion with God in response to God's invitation to communion, a process that includes acts of repentance and pardon, an experience of deepening communion that involves growth in love of God and neighbor, and, finally, full communion in which one is adopted as a child of God.[69] Persons in all of these stages grow together in the church. Persons seeking salvation, those who have the faith of a servant, and those who have the faith of a child of God all share in the communion of the Trinity. The church is the context for formation in which Christians develop holiness of heart and life and bear witness to God's invitation to communion by patterning their shared life after the communion of the Trinity. The Way of Salvation is not an individual spiritual pilgrimage. In fact, Wesley indicates that the church itself is also called to the Way of Salvation in a comment on Matthew 4:17 (KJV), "Repent, for the kingdom of God is at hand." He writes: "But that phrase is not only used with regard to individuals in whom it is to be established, but also with regard to the Christian Church, the whole body of believers."[70] In other words, the church must also repent of its sin and grow in holiness as its members grow in holiness through new life in Christ.

The community and communion of the church is the environment for nurturing holiness of heart and life in preparation for God's transforming work that is both a possibility and expectation for Wesley. Among Christians, this transformation may be experienced in a variety of ways. Generally, though, Christian faith formation has two goals or phases. The first is to bring persons to the point at which they claim what John Westerhoff calls an "owned faith"—a conversion experience that involves "major change in a person's thinking, feeling, and willing."[71] Through this transformative experience, persons come to know God in Christ as the center of their lives. The second goal is to provide instruction and nurture for persons growing in their relationship with God through God's grace in Jesus Christ so that they become more Christlike in their daily living.

Both of these goals require the church to be aware that transformation is God's work. No matter how dedicated our efforts or how well-crafted our programs, the church cannot *cause* transformation. John Wesley reflects this awareness in a letter to Philothea Briggs in 1773: "All our wisdom will not even make [the children] *understand*, much less *feel* the things of God." He adds that they need to be "awakened" by God.[72] The role of the faith community, then, is to provide opportunities for participation in formative relationships, structures, and practices that provide instruction and nurture for persons seeking a saving faith. These formational nurturing activities become means of grace when God uses them to transform lives.

Conclusion: Relationships in the Ecology of Conversion

Our case study highlights the importance of relationships in a Wesleyan ecology of faith formation. The religious experiences of John and Charles Wesley did not occur in isolation. Members of the community of faith, including family members, friends, and spiritual guides such as Böhler, surrounded the Wesleys in their spiritual pilgrimages. These relationships supported both Wesleys as they struggled with questions and doubts stirred by God's prevenient grace. It was God's work that brought transformation to their lives.

Böhler became not only a vehicle of God's grace in his interactions with John and Charles Wesley; he was also a representative of the larger community of faith. Böhler relied on the teachings of his tradition and the counsel of his supervisor as he guided the Wesleys' spiritual pilgrimages. Böhler cajoled and encouraged

John Wesley into recognizing his sinful state through theological discussion, instruction, and witness. Biographer Martin Schmidt summarized Peter Böhler's role in John Wesley's conversion: "In this way Böhler brought Wesley to that state in which he wished him to be, and at the same time Wesley was prepared for it by many circumstances. . . . [Böhler] made him realize that a simple personal relationship to Jesus the Saviour is the heart of the relationship with God. . . . Wesley was now aware of the fact that faith, which trusts God for everything and the self for nothing, was the one fundamental truth of Christianity."[73] Böhler's witness was accompanied by discussions with Charles and other Methodists about the nature of salvation. Once Böhler left for the colonies, he provided spiritual companions for Charles Wesley and sent a letter that served as spiritual guidance and nurture for John Wesley.

Böhler is a good example of what I have elsewhere called "faith-mentoring."[74] Faith mentors are persons who become a vehicle of God's grace for others. Böhler's relationship with the Wesley brothers demonstrates four roles of faith-mentoring: guide, model, guarantor, and mediator. Because Böhler had already experienced a saving faith and knew what preparation was needed, he was a *guide* who "pointed the way"[75] for the Wesley's in their search for salvation. Charles Wesley's reference to Böhler as "that man of God"[76] indicates that he was a *model* of piety, providing a "living example"[77] of the kind of inner faith the Wesleys sought. Even though Böhler had questions about the Wesleys' progress in faith, he did not give up. When Böhler left England, he provided ongoing support through designated spiritual companions and correspondence. In this sense he was also a "*guarantor* for growth in a reliable relationship and accepting environment" [78] that freed the Wesleys to see themselves in need of God's transforming grace. Finally, Böhler was a *mediator,* "the one who stands between—between who we are and who we hope to be,"[79] as he helped prepare the Wesleys for the work of God's transforming power.

As faith mentor, Peter Böhler also provided a model for Christian nurture. He was no solitary charismatic but a representative of the larger faith community who provided guidance, companionship, instruction, challenge, spiritual resources, support, and comfort to the Wesley brothers. Through his witness, Böhler was used by God to prepare John and Charles Wesley for a transformative experience of God's grace, so that they might know themselves to be children of God and find the peace they were seeking.

If we accept John Wesley's view that salvation is both instantaneous and gradual, then the role of the church is critical as it prepares persons for God's transforming work. Whether we conceive of conversion as an instantaneous "point in a process"[80] or the work of God's transforming grace over time, the instruction and nurture of the faith community is critical. The role of the church is to provide the relationships, structures, and practices of a Wesleyan ecology of faith formation for those who are seeking salvation, as well as those who are trying to interpret their religious experience and translate its meaning into daily living. So the church, as a living witness to God's transforming power through Jesus Christ, has a significant ministry in faith formation. The church prepares persons to be transformed, celebrates new life that comes through God's grace, provides accountability in holy living, supports ongoing growth through instruction and nurture, and offers opportunities for loving God and neighbor through worship, formation, and service.

Chapter Twelve

From the "Works of the Flesh" to the "Fruit of the Spirit": Conversion and Spiritual Formation in the Wesleyan Tradition

Gregory S. Clapper

The Drama of Human Change and Wesleyan Theology

Both conversion and spiritual formation are all about human change. Interest in human change, though, is hardly restricted to those who occupy themselves with religious matters. Indeed, I think it is fair to say that the possibilities for human change capture the human imagination like little else. Consider, for example, the enduring appeal of Charles Dickens' *A Christmas Carol.* We see Scrooge with his odious, contemptible self-concern, totally curved in on himself, and the viewer rightly recoils. Through his fateful encounter with three different apparitions, however, Scrooge undergoes a transformation from miserly self-concern to charity and compassion; and our revulsion changes to sympathy, even a vicarious joy over his new life, that leads to a hope that such transformations can take place in others, or perhaps even in ourselves.

The drama of human change is also displayed in the movie *Forrest Gump*, but here there is another dimension, for this film not only *displays* the drama of human change, it invites the viewer to *reflect* about it. Gump's girlfriend, Jenny, undergoes all the culturally invited transformations of three decades in the twentieth century, while Gump's character remains fixed. In reflecting on the contrast between these two lives, and the strange interactions that have occurred between them, the title character asks at the end of the film, "Is it Lieutenant Dan or Mama who's right?" In other words, do we have a fixed destiny, or are we just floating on the apparently random breezes of the exigencies of life? Are we free or determined? The question is expressed symbolically in the film by a feather, which floats apparently haphazardly—but lands strategically—at both the beginning and the end of the movie.

As Christians in the Wesleyan tradition who are trying to reflect on the human change called "conversion," we need to confront this question, and the answer we give to this question must reflect both the turbulence and the providence that is seen in the movement of that feather. We must, in other words, allow that conjunctions of human freedom and God's grace *do* occur, even if at times these transformative conjunctions seem serendipitous to secular observers. Life has undeniably brutal and wounding aspects, many of which result from the misuse of human freedom (for example, the incest Jenny suffered at the hands of her father in *Forrest Gump*.) But just as undeniably, transforming grace visits us in the midst of our brokenness (as Gump's friendship is a recurrent note of grace in Jenny's life).

Finally, then, our answer to Gump's musings about freedom and determinism must be Gump's own answer: "I think it's both." Human sin can leave us, at times, with only a very limited, seemingly determined, set of options with which to exercise our human freedom, but God's grace can inhabit even the most limited options to make possible life-enhancing choices for human freedom to embrace. This understanding of the drama of human change establishes the context for our consideration of a Wesleyan perspective on conversion and spiritual formation.

In what follows, I want to show how an Arminian vision of the Christian life satisfies our deep longing to be a part of the drama of human change in a way that does full justice to both the truths of the Christian tradition and the realities of lived experience. To do this, I will first show why the Christian vocation of transforming human beings must encompass *both* conversion and the subsequent task of spiritual formation, and not only one or the other. I will then outline a few of the specific patterns of human change that are called forth in a Wesleyan program of spiritual formation, and show how this model differs from other current, competing notions of "spirituality." Finally, I will consider several impediments to capturing this vision of conversion and formation that our current intellectual culture has erected, and then I will draw some implications for our life in the church today.

Why Evangelism and Spiritual Formation Need Each Other

The United Methodist Church recently adopted a mission statement that declares that we are to "make disciples of Jesus Christ."[1] If the church is to be about making disciples, then it must be involved in doing at least three things: recruiting disciples; nurturing disciples; and sending disciples out to do God's work. Dividing the church's tasks up in this way might lead one to think that evangelism refers primarily to the first task, that of recruitment. Indeed, William Abraham has defined evangelism as "primary initiation into the kingdom of God."[2] But if we take seriously the idea that evangelistic activity is finally not about getting "decisions" but is concerned with producing *disciples,* we must see evangelism as integrally linked with the other tasks of the church, namely nurture and outreach.

In *Great Commission,* Mortimer Arias asserts that if we take seriously the "great commission" from Matthew, "our evangelism should concentrate on Christian education!"[3] Similarly, in defining evangelism as "the *demonstration* and proclamation of the gospel," Maxie Dunnam makes clear that evangelism is really an all-encompassing feature of living and working as a Christian. Speaking of the early church, Dunnam says that "every thing the church was called to be and do in its worship, witness, fellowship, and service was infused and informed by evangelism."[4]

Albert Outler also reflects this more comprehensive view of the evangelistic task. In his *Evangelism in the Wesleyan Spirit,* Outler describes Wesley's conviction that

> conversion is never more than the bare threshold of authentic and comprehensive evangelism. . . . "Never encourage the devil by snatching souls from him that you cannot nurture." . . . Thus, sanctification became the goal and end of all valid evangelistic endeavor (and this implies a lifelong process).[5]

To expand somewhat on Abraham's definition of evangelism in light of this Wesleyan emphasis on sanctification, I would say that evangelism is not just *primary* initiation into the kingdom of God, but it is any activity done in the name of fostering the journey of discipleship, whether that journey is just starting or not. Reinforcement in the faithful way of life is just as evangelistic, then, as the initial invitation into that way of life.

Adopting this broader understanding of evangelism clarifies what is already going on in unquestionably "evangelistic" contexts. For instance, it is well known that many who come forward in evangelistic crusades are coming forward to "rededicate" their lives to the cause of Christ. Caught up by gifted preachers and musicians and encouraged by the energy of the crowd, believers as well as nonbelievers sense the possibilities of starting over, of feeling again the power of conversion, and they want once again to have the "born again" experience. Such people may indeed experience spiritual growth as they dedicate themselves once more to Christ and the church. Certainly we need to attend to these "rededications" in our discussions of evangelism. Nevertheless, these experiences are clearly not "primary" points of initiation.

As is illustrated by these "rededications," the church's own practices belie a definition of evangelism that focuses only on *primary* initiation. Christian conversion, then, should be seen as a conversion *to* a lifetime of spiritual formation. Conversion does not stand alone but does, and should, lead to a subsequent disciplined pattern of new life. While exceptions occur, such as the last-minute conversion of the thief on the cross, such situations must only prove the more general rule. There can be no truly Christian formation that does not result in an embodied, ongoing, decisive commitment to leave behind the old way of life. The decisive moment we have no trouble in identifying as conversion; the ongoing commitment that results needs equal emphasis.

If it is granted that "deepening" the gospel in the life of a believer is part and parcel of the church's mission to "spread" the gospel, then particular acts of witnessing, evangelism, and conversion will not just be tasks undertaken by specialists alone, or expected only at particular moments in life. If the drama and power of conversion and spiritual formation are seen as one reality, then Christians will realize that they are *always* witnessing, as the witness of others is *always* forming them. The Christian vocation to promote positive human change is the task of all believers.

Wesleyan Spiritual Formation and Its Contemporary Rivals

"Spiritual formation" is a term of long standing in the Roman Catholic tradition, and has been adopted by increasing numbers of Protestants more recently. An ongoing, lifelong process of shaping human souls into a predetermined image is consistent with the Roman Catholic understanding of grace completing nature. Similarly, given our Arminian tradition, it should come as no surprise that Methodists should adopt this language and even develop programs for intentional spiritual growth, such as the Academies for Spiritual Formation.[6]

Some contemporary understandings of "spiritual formation," however, do not have such a clear sense of shaping, patterning, molding, and forming people along Christian lines. Particularly representative here is that loose assemblage of sometimes rambling ruminations known as "New Age" thought. Whether joined to Jungian archetypal language or on its own, the New Age approach to spirituality seeks to "discover the God within" and to create one's own plan for "realizing our potential."[7] This kind of spirituality can turn narcissistic quickly and can proceed quite readily without ever encountering the good news. "Journeying within," a person without Christ has no hope of discovering that humans are created in the image of God yet are sinful, and that each person is someone for whom Christ died, someone whose sins are forgiven, someone who is called into a very particular pattern of life marked by the fruit of the Spirit (Gal. 5:22-24). While it is important to understand the person that one has become by naming the patterns of one's loyalties, affections, loves, and hates, and by taking stock of oneself with an "internal" inventory, without an encounter with the gospel that comes from "without," the seeker will have no way of labeling and understanding her or his own heart and history, much less appropriating forgiveness and growing in the fruit of the Spirit.

For John Wesley, being a Christian meant nothing less than living an entire way of life. Wesley understood this way of life as having at least three different components that I have described as orthodoxy, orthopraxis, and orthokardia—that is, right beliefs, right action, and the right heart.[8] The way of life described by these three "orthos" is known as a "sanctified life." Such a life is grounded in the stories of the tradition, with Scripture being the key source, and not an individual's own life story. This way of life cannot be undertaken under one's own power but is a life into which people are invited by evangelism.

Again, this way of life is characterized by orthopraxis, the lifelong process of growing in holiness in the works of piety and the works of charity.[9] But these right actions will never become powerful habits unless they are guided by orthodoxy, the correct understanding of who God is and what God has done for us. Wesley was clear, though, that neither the right actions nor the right belief are enough until that metaphorical center of who we are—our "hearts"—are changed. This call to orthokardia must be heeded if the patterns for human change called "conversion" and "spiritual formation" are to yield disciples of Jesus in the Wesleyan tradition.[10]

The Competing Ways of Life of Galatians 5

By emphasizing the *continual* nature of being formed in the life marked by the three "orthos," I do not intend to downplay the important connotation of experiences of dramatic reorientation that the word conversion carries with it.

The stark contrast between the "fruit of the Spirit" and the "works of the flesh" that we find in Galatians 5 illustrates decisively both the need for conversion and the need for an intentional pattern of postconversion growth.

> For you were called to freedom, brothers and sisters; only do not use your freedom as an opportunity for self-indulgence, but through love become slaves to one another. For the whole law is summed up in a single commandment, "You shall love your neighbor as yourself." If, however, you bite and devour one another, take care that you are not consumed by one another. Live by the Spirit, I say, and do not gratify the desires

> of the flesh. For what the flesh desires is opposed to the Spirit, and what the Spirit desires is opposed to the flesh; for these are opposed to each other, to prevent you from doing what you want. But if you are led by the Spirit, you are not subject to the law. Now the works of the flesh are obvious: fornication, impurity, licentiousness, idolatry, sorcery, enmities, strife, jealousy, anger, quarrels, dissensions, factions, envy, drunkenness, carousing, and things like these. I am warning you, as I warned you before: those who do such things will not inherit the kingdom of God. By contrast, the fruit of the Spirit is love, joy, peace, patience, kindness, generosity, faithfulness, gentleness, and self-control. There is no law against such things. And those who belong to Christ Jesus have crucified the flesh with its passions and desires. If we live by the Spirit, let us also be guided by the Spirit. Let us not become conceited, competing against one another, envying one another. (Gal. 5:13-26)

To say yes to one particular pattern of formation is to say no to all competing ways of life, and that is the undeniable element of conversion in the Christian life. As Paul makes clear, there is no middle ground between the "works of the flesh" and the "fruit of the Spirit." Those who call themselves Christian have converted from the former and are called to demonstrate the latter.

When witnessing to the unconverted, it is especially important to communicate that what Christianity *affirms* as a faithful way of life (the fruit of the Spirit) and what it *rejects* (sinfulness, or the works of the flesh) are both defined *within* the Christian story. Christians need not assume that what they call "sin" is seen as such by the rest of the world. In that sense, the pattern for the Christian way of life, defined by the three "orthos," is not some sort of universally achievable insight that can be reached by mere introspection. Christianity is, instead, a very particular way of life, defined by particular narratives through which not only one's behaviors but also one's consciousness is formed. Conversion thus entails not only a positive vision of the image into which humans are to grow, but also a new understanding of what must be left behind. While the unconverted are often aware of the unfulfilling nature of their lives, they cannot fully know (and define) their way of life as "sinful." Humans do not truly know what sin is, in short, until they know what grace and salvation are.

The logic of our affections or our emotions that can be formed in either of these two competing ways I have shown in other places.[11] Briefly put, our hearts contain our spiritual and emotional history—both what has been done to us in the context of our families of origin and other significant relationships, and what we have consciously put in there ourselves. The real problem with New Age approaches to conversion is that what we will encounter "within" is basically what we have already allowed to be there. A more adequate idea of conversion involves some sort of conscious appropriation, some sort of new awareness of truth that was not there before. Accordingly, when the good news comes to us and defines us as precious in the eyes of God, created in God's image, but also fallen sinners, we have a view of ourselves that we did not necessarily have before. Some grow up thinking that they are inherently good, perhaps even superior to other people because of the attitudes instilled by their parents. In contrast, others think they are worthy only of humiliation and degradation. Either of these self-images are understandable in different contexts; however, both must be rejected when we hear the good news that we are children of God—simply because God loves us as children and neither better nor worse than any other.

What *is* important about our histories is the predisposition that they form in us. The person who is trained to think of herself or himself as superior to all others will have to undergo a particular pattern of formation and transformation. This pattern will look quite different from the pattern required by persons raised to think they are inherently worthless. The end point—the sanctified life of the fruit of the Holy Spirit leading to life eternal—will be the same for both, but the paths from their existing predispositions to that end point will be quite different, with contrasting emphases on various aspects of the good news.

A Confident Witness

One of the benefits of Wesley's construal of the gospel that emphasizes that justification necessarily leads to a sanctified life is this way of life can be proclaimed with confidence in the contemporary world. Leander Keck identifies one of the key problems in the life of the church of our day—that when the church's self-understanding is confused and its theology murky, we are prevented from speaking the good news with *confidence*.[12] However, a way of life is something that can be directly observed and is directly accessible to the world and, therefore, constitutes a peculiarly confident witness. When the Christian way of life (described not by only one or two, but all three of the "orthos") is embodied in real-life believers, it is itself the best proclamation of the gospel possible. If we employ a debatable metaphysic, a plea for a particular view of scriptural authority, a specific political rhetoric, or a narrow moralism, then our confidence will always lie in something other than the incarnated redeeming power of the Holy Spirit. If we live as God's people, the Body of Christ on earth, others will come to know and love God. There is no more powerful witness than a changed life.

Living the Wesleyan Vocation of Human Change in the Church and World Today

If anyone adopts a Wesleyan vision of changing human life and attempts to live it out in the world, she or he is sure to encounter many obstacles. Without pretending to offer a complete inventory, I would like to discuss a few of the most pernicious and persistent of these obstacles. While one would hope that these obstacles would be encountered exclusively outside of churches that count Wesley as their founder, the reality is, unfortunately, otherwise. Living out this vision will involve encountering different aspects of these obstacles both within and without the church. One word of encouragement on this score, however, is that Wesley himself often had an uphill fight within the church of his own day on many of the issues most dear to his heart!

Relativism and the Uncritical Plea for "Tolerance"

One particularly troubling feature of our current intellectual culture which can inhibit the process of disciple-making in the Wesleyan tradition is the prevailing popular attitude of relativism. In "The Problem with Relativism" John Hospers notes several specific problems with the popular idea that "values are determined by the group"—in other words, that right and wrong are defined sociologically.[13] First of all, when trying to determine what is right and what is wrong in particular settings, relativists find themselves in an insuperable dilemma because no one belongs to one group only. To which group should we look in making moral decisions? Are we to follow the values of our family, our nation, our peers, or our church? Which moral subculture is determinative and how do we negotiate the resulting conflicts of values? While this might seem to be just the sort of quandary in which relativists would want to leave us, few relativists are in the end content with the absolute nihilism and anarchy that such a view yields. For instance, if ethical relativism were true, ethical error by a majority would be impossible since, by definition, the majority of a group cannot be wrong. This, in turn, implies that reformers are by definition always wrong, since reformers typically start off as a minority in any given group. If such a democratic moralism prevails, reformers would be by necessity excluded from moral deliberation.

Second, relativists seem to depend, at least in the West, on a strong appeal to "tolerance." In the name of tolerance, they argue, we must accept a variety of definitions of "the good." The problem with this, however, is that tolerance is not a virtue in all groups, societies, or cultures. To assume that tolerance is a culturally neutral, universally accepted value is quickly disproved when one attempts to proclaim a message antithetical to the views of an authoritarian regime, whether secular or theocratic. Tolerance is embraced by the relativist as something that should have self-evidential power for all people, but tolerance turns out to be a virtue of only certain groups in certain societies. This does not mean that Christians should promote intolerance, but it simply makes the point that if all values are tied to certain stories, contexts, and cultures, then intellectually honest people cannot go the route of relativists and say that, a priori, any group's values are as good or as bad as any other's. Instead, we must take on the hard task of examining the particular and contingent claims to truth, the particular and contingent ways of life generated by different understandings of reality, and arrive at our own humble and fallible—but none the less decisive—conclusions. We must not so privilege "tolerance" language that we hide behind that shibboleth as a way of avoiding the hard and humbling task of discernment. We cannot be so afraid of intolerance that we give up the fear of error.

This is not to say that we should not remain open for further information and retain the possibility of changing our minds. One of the features of the Christian way of life, after all, is humility. But understanding that relativism offers no easy escape from the need for embracing *some* model for human change *does* mean that confident commitment to fostering change according to a particular model—Christian conversion and spiritual formation—must be a nonnegotiable feature of the life of our churches.[14] As Christians, we need to understand that there is no neutral happy medium between the fruit of the Spirit and the works of the flesh. To attempt to reach toward the former without rejecting the latter is not high-minded compromise, but the folly proscribed by Scripture when it says that those who are neither hot nor cold will be spit out (Rev. 3:15-16).

The Debilitating Fear of "Individualism"

A second obstacle to embracing and promoting a Wesleyan concept of conversion and spiritual formation is the accusation that to do so is to promote an individualistic version of Christianity. Often today, in many ecclesiastical and academic circles, one does not have to pronounce much more than the presence of a whiff of "individualism" before the approach or proposal under discussion is dismissed out of hand. The importance of recent analyses that highlight the "structural nature of sin" should not dissuade us from an emphasis on individual commitment to the faith. The community of believers is manifestly important in our traditions, in the religious life of both the Hebrews and the early Christians. Proponents of conversion and spiritual formation in the Wesleyan tradition must be clear that criticism of individualism does not touch Wesley's vision of heart religion when it is rightly perceived. It must be understood that the works of the flesh cannot whither, nor can the fruit of the Spirit grow, outside of the presence of a community. This community is necessary to interpret God's Word; to offer the sacraments of baptism and communion; to hold all of the members—and the church structure itself—accountable for their moral choices, teachings, and loyalties; and to direct the discharge of Christian love through the various works that the church discerns are needed. Orthodoxy, orthokardia, and orthopraxis are inextricably, theologically linked.[15]

The call to conversion and growth in the fruit of the Spirit is always a call to join a converting *community*, a community that has chosen to take a hand in the Lord's work of joyfully renewing not just the church, but all of creation. To be converted is not to become obsessed with oneself, for if one takes one's self as the object of one's attention, then one cannot be focusing on God and the story of Christ, which in turn points us to our neighbor. To be converted is to be freed from the self-regarding works of the flesh for a life of service marked by love, joy, peace, patience, kindness, and all of the other fruits of the Spirit. Each of these fruits—as each of the works of the flesh—is, after all, a quality that cannot be understood outside of the context of a web of relationships.

Conclusion

Finally, the most persuasive evangelistic appeal to the world is found in the quality of our lives. If the "holiness and happiness" that Wesley prescribed for humanity's ills can be seen in our lives, others will want it for themselves. When we live that vision in the midst of our broken and sinful world, conversion and growth in the image of God will occur. The final argument for the existence of God is changed lives, and changed lives are the very telos of Wesleyan theology.

Chapter Thirteen

Embodying Conversion

Philip R. Meadows

The proliferation of new books on Methodist doctrine, discipline, and worship is indicative of the present struggle to find a distinctive Methodist identity and vision: a reason for being, and its particular contribution to the church catholic.[1] The "Wesley-for-Today" project also responds to the perception of waning vitality among Methodist congregations and intends to inject new life by critically reappropriating the tradition.[2] These scholarly efforts are of central importance to the reclaiming of our Methodist identity, and yet they can never be the center of it. Our roots can provide clues for future efforts, but we must always be aware of the difference between then and now. If our roots are to provide us with any clue at all, it is the success of early Methodism in recovering authentic Christian fellowship in the context of a church institution that had disembodied the gospel. By "disembodying the gospel," I mean the failure of Christian fellowship to keep its *principles* and *practice* inseparably connected. Early Methodists embodied the gospel by living it, both personally and corporately, and this is the true meaning of practical divinity.[3]

In the spirit of many reformers before him, John Wesley perceived the people called Methodist to be continuous with, and faithful to, the principles of Christian fellowship found in the scriptural accounts of the early apostolic church. The attempt to locate Methodist identity in its *principles* should yield, therefore, a description of authentic scriptural Christianity that belongs to the whole church. Early Methodism is to be distinguished not by its principles but as a *movement* that kept its principles and practice inseparably connected, and whose life and witness embodied both the Great Commandment and the Great Commission. Early Methodism can be thought of as movement, *providentially raised* to participate in God's mission to the world; *prudentially ordered* for the salvation of humankind; *purposefully located* in its own cultural-historical context; and whose *particular charism* for the church catholic was the *embodied* reality of scriptural holiness.

It is my belief that the present crisis in Methodism, belied by the search for Methodist identity and vital congregations, lies in its disembodiment of the gospel in general, and its disembodiment of scriptural holiness in particular. Insofar as my assessment is correct, Wesley's critique of the Anglican Church of his day can be seen to fit the Methodist Church of our own.

It is also my belief that the future promise of Methodism depends upon its willingness to re-member its particular charism by re-embodying the *principles* of scriptural holiness (expressed in its doctrine, discipline, and worship) in the *practice* of authentic Christian fellowship, whose end is seeking and saving the lost in today's cultural context.

Providence, Prudence, and Church Order

One way of talking about the embodiment of the gospel in congregational life is to use the language of "church order" (or discipline), which at its best provides a rule for keeping principles and practice connected. Wesley's attitude to Anglican Church order was ambiguous to say the least. On the one hand, he claimed to be a loyal son of the Church, and to uphold its order in all points; yet on the other hand, he broke that same order many times in the course of leading the Methodist movement. It is possible, however, to discover an underlying consistency in this apparent paradox, so long as the right question is asked:

> What is the end of all ecclesiastical order? Is it not to bring souls from the power of Satan to God; and to build them up in his fear and love? Order, then, is so far valuable, as it answers these ends; and if it answers them not, it is nothing worth. Now, I would fain know, where has order answered these ends? Not in any place where I have been.[4]

Wesley clarifies his position by claiming that he "would observe every punctilio of order, except where the salvation of souls is at stake. There I prefer the end before the means."[5]

In speaking of means and end this way, Wesley is relativizing church order as a means of saving grace, whose sole end (that is, goal and reason for being) is the conversion of sinners into saints. He was convinced that the scriptural accounts of "primitive Christianity" yielded only general rules about authentic Christian fellowship, without specifying the particular concrete forms they should assume. This naturally led him to take a dynamic view of church order, capable of responding to the providential work of God in different historical-cultural contexts and, therefore, capable of providing reasonable scriptural warrant for his own innovative practices.[6] On this view, therefore, one should never treat church order as though it were an "ordinary" means of grace (that is, concretely instituted by scriptural command), but as a "prudential" means of grace (that is, provisionally adopted by the church and providentially used by God), always recognizing that God is free to act within or without any means whatsoever.

So am I suggesting that we read Wesley as a pragmatic utilitarian? Does he simply bequeath to us an attitude to church order that is endemically schismatic? Do his views provide warrant for justifying any maverick with a cause? The answer to these questions is no, and it is grounded in a proper understanding of Christian *prudence*. Romanus Cessario reminds us that prudence is not just the exercise of wisdom in the attainment of certain ends (which runs the risk of utilitarianism), but should be thought of as "virtuous activity," or the embodiment of divine wisdom in specific virtuous actions.[7] In using the language of "virtue," Cessario points out that truly prudential actions are those that flow from a unity between godly wisdom and godly habits (or dispositions). This can help us understand why Wesley's actions were simultaneously paradoxical and prudential. As a son of the Church, his wisdom and dispositions (that is, virtues) had been nurtured toward the end of holiness, through submission to its discipline. As a leader of the Methodist movement, however, he perceived that the Church failed prudentially to embody its own wisdom and end in practice.[8] This is why Wesley constantly refused to separate from the Anglican Church, preferring to remain under its discipline, while prudentially striving to renew it.[9] What we observe, then, is a renewal of *practice* rather than wisdom, or *principles*, per se: Wesley sought to lead a movement that would help Christians faithfully embody the historic scriptural tradition within the fold of the Anglican Church.[10] Defining prudence this way, as a combination of received wisdom and virtuous activity, must also be included in any adequate definition of practical divinity.

It is not true to say, therefore, that *any* new practice that can achieve certain ends is in order (that is, a pragmatic utilitarianism). The test of authenticity is first the extent to which means are subservient to the end of holiness, and second, the extent to which they are shaped by the historic wisdom of the Church. Wesley did think that, despite all its shortcomings, the Anglican Church was the finest example of faith and order to be found anywhere. Faithfulness to tradition is a matter of recognizing the enduring way that God has providentially blessed the historic faith and virtuous practice of the Church.[11]

My purpose in writing this chapter is twofold. First, to demonstrate how the early Methodist movement prudentially embodied the pursuit of scriptural holiness by having all its activities shaped, ordered, and connected by the end of converting sinners into saints. Second, to suggest how contemporary Methodism can draw upon this legacy of prudence in order to nurture vital congregations in today's world.

The Embodiment of Conversion in Early Methodism

Wesley considered Christian perfection to be the "grand depositum" of Methodism. In other words, its particular charism for the church catholic was to bear witness to the world by embodying the reality of scriptural holiness as the true end of authentic Christian life and fellowship. When Wesley writes about *The Character of a Methodist*, this is what he has in mind.

For Wesley, the Scripture way of salvation begins preveniently in the operations of conscience (through which the Spirit seeks to awaken sinners); is established in the experience of justification and new birth (when we are saved from the guilt and tyranny of sin); then continues with the process of sanctification (the transformation from sinfulness to holiness); and "ends" in Christian perfection (when we are finally saved from both the power and presence of sin).[12] Salvation is synonymous with the present experience of holiness of heart and life, which is the embodied promise of eternal life. For Wesley, the conversion from sinfulness to holiness is a process, punctuated by the defining moments of new birth and Christian perfection, which together emphasize the inbreaking, life-transforming, and perceptible presence of saving grace.[13] Wesley claims that this is nothing other than genuine scriptural Christianity, nurtured by and embodied in the people called Methodists, who not only preach the gospel but "live the gospel."[14] In response to criticisms of introducing schism by breaking church order, Wesley wrote a number of apologetic tracts in order to demonstrate that the principles, the means, and the end of the Methodist movement are consistent with plain scriptural Christianity.[15]

The Character of a Methodist

It is not by chance that Wesley brackets his tract *The Character of a Methodist* by repeatedly affirming his intention to deal with both the "*principles* and *practice(s)*" of the Methodist movement.[16] For it is, in fact, the way that the Methodist movement keeps them inseparably connected that is finally what distinguishes it from the prevailing ethos of the Anglican Church.

Wesley begins the tract by explaining that the characteristic mark of Methodism cannot be reduced to any of its particular beliefs or activities. It is not set apart by holding certain *opinions*, for they are all and only formed by Scripture.[17] Nor is it set apart by the peculiar use of *religious language* (notable for either its rhetorical or aesthetic value), unless it is to express "Scripture truths in Scripture words."[18] Nor again is it set apart on the basis of any unusual type of *activities*, for their practices only fulfil the will of God in Scripture.[19] Lastly, it is not set apart by stressing any *part of religion* (emphasizing a particular cause), because it seeks to stress the whole of religion, which is summed up as holiness of heart and life.[20]

So the distinguishing mark of the Methodists is not located in anything that they think or say or do! All its doctrines, manner of communication, and patterns of activity are simply consistent with the "common," "plain," "old," "fundamental" "principles of Christianity" as a whole.[21] As such, the Methodists should be indistinguishable from all faithful Anglicans. Rather, what distinguishes Methodists from others is that they put their *principles* into *practice*. Wesley says that "whosoever *is* what I *preach* . . . he is a Christian, not in *name* only, but in *heart* in and *life*. He is inwardly and outwardly conformed to the will of God, as revealed in the written Word. *He thinks, speaks, and lives according to the* 'method' *laid down in the revelation of Jesus Christ*."[22] Wesley describes the character of a Methodist in terms of perfect love for God and neighbor; of being justified and born again; of having the witness of the Spirit that one is a child of God; of experiencing peace, joy, and the hope of glory (which is the embodied experience of adoption and new birth);[23] of seeing God in all things, and yielding to the divine will in all circumstances (which is the embodiment of a life lived before God);[24] of a singular and consuming desire for God (which is embodied in a life of constant prayer);[25] of becoming pure in heart (which is embodied by the witness of holy living);[26] and of a universal and natural obedience to God, both in avoiding evil and doing good to all people (which is the embodiment of loving God and neighbor).[27]

Wesley's real point, therefore, is not that any of these *characteristics* actually distinguish the aim of Methodism from others, for he is simply describing what should be the high calling of all Christians. Rather, a Methodist is one whose *character* is really shaped by such scriptural holiness, who "in all his employments of every kind he not only *aims* at this . . . but actually *attains* it."[28] In short, to have the *character* of a Methodist is simply to *embody* the gospel, to *be* what one claims, to *practice* what one preaches.

What remains to be answered, then, is how such Christian character comes to be formed, that is, the means (or "method") by which sinners are thus transformed, or converted, from sinfulness to holiness of heart and life. Stanley Hauerwas expresses concern that the idea of perfection as Christian character "remains far too abstract a notion" in Wesley.[29] He goes on: "What is required is the actual depiction of lives through which we can be imaginatively drawn into the journey by being given the means to understand and test our failures and successes. . . . Thus, the only means to perceive rightly the end is by attending to the lives of those who have been and are on the way."[30] This apparent lack in Wesley only appears because Hauerwas fails to notice that the very order of Christian fellowship in the early Methodist movement embodied this end (and journey) in a whole economy of prudentially ordered practices.

The Order of Methodism

In his *Plain Account of the People Called Methodists*, Wesley sets out to give "an account of the *whole economy*" of the Methodist movement. Indeed, he continues to describe how their "virtuous activities," added and developed over time, constitute a carefully connected system for converting non-Christians into real Christians. There are two things for us to observe from this.

First, *the order of the Methodist movement itself embodies the process of conversion through which it aims at transforming sinners into saints.* In other words, the means employed by the movement are shaped by the end of holiness and Christian perfection.[31]

Wesley begins with the activity of preaching, which aims at convincing people of the truth so that they might forsake sin and seek the gospel of salvation.[32] He then united these seekers into societies where the one condition of membership was the "desire to flee from the wrath to come, and to be saved from their sins."[33] Eventually, the societies were subdivided into small "classes" so that the process of conversion could be optimized through meeting regularly for the detection and reproof of insincerity, the comfort and exhortation of genuine seekers, and the exclusion of disruptive and unrepentant sinners.[34] Those who found justifying faith and new birth in the society, through the class meeting, came to be put into separate small groups called "bands" as a "means of closer union" in fulfillment of the scriptural command to "confess your faults one to another, and pray one for another, that ye may be healed."[35] These bands also became diversified to include "penitential" bands for those real Christians who have momentarily lost sight of God,[36] and "select" bands for those desiring to "press after perfection."[37]

Here we have a way of fellowship that corresponds to, or embodies, a way of salvation. The activity of field preaching clearly embodies the dynamic of God's prevenient and convincing grace, striving to awaken the sinner from spiritual sleep and invite the response of authentically seeking the gospel of redemption. The union of seekers into a society composed of classes embodied the reality of God's convincing and repenting grace, evidenced by the fruit of resisting evil and doing good, bearing the reproach of Christ, and attending to the means of grace. The need to embody repentance according to these *Rules* was demonstrated by the stress on mutual accountability, and later in the issuing of class tickets by quarterly examination.[38] It became common practice to include those who responded to field preaching into a class on a trial basis before incorporating them in society, so that they could demonstrate their sincerity as seekers.[39] The creation of bands embodied God's justifying grace and the converting moment of new birth by maintaining a clear distinction between seekers and believers (or real Christians). The diversification of those bands also embodied God's sanctifying and perfecting grace by giving concrete shape to the believer's continuing struggle with sin in the pursuit of perfection. Not only that, but the select companies were to be an embodied "pattern of love, of holiness, and of all good works," imitable by members of the whole society.

Second, *the Methodist movement represents a prudential order, consistent with ancient Christianity, and belonging to the whole church.*[40] As Wesley gives account for every significant development in the order and practice of the people called Methodists, he makes a point of observing their continuity with ancient Christianity.[41] What is noteworthy, however, is that Wesley discovered this continuity only after the fact. In other words, Wesley was not striving to re-create the "once and future church," as though he were a prototypical church growth strategist, but expeditiously gathered and modified measures from various sources to meet the needs of his growing movement as they arose.[42] Thus, if Wesley could identify the mature Methodist movement as a successful "apostolic" strategy, it was only in retrospect.[43] What made his pragmatic approach so fruitful, however, was the high level of adaptation he applied to every measure (from field preaching to select bands) for meeting the particular needs of sinners at each stage on the way of salvation.

From those *outside* the Methodist movement, Wesley was faced with the accusation that the proliferation of his societies introduced schism and destroyed Christian fellowship in the parishes where they arose. In answer, Wesley insisted that

> the fellowship you speak of never existed. . . . Who watched over them in love? Who marked their growth in grace? Who advised and exhorted them from time to time? Who prayed with them and for them as they had need? This, and this alone is Christian fellowship. But alas! Where is it to be found? Look east or west, north or south; name what parish you please. Is this Christian fellowship there? Rather, are not the bulk of the parishioners a mere rope of sand? What Christian connexion is there between them? What intercourse in spiritual things? What watching over each others' souls? What bearing of one another's burdens? What a mere jest is it, then, to talk so gravely of *destroying* what never was! The real truth is just the reverse of this: we *introduce* Christian fellowship where it was *utterly destroyed*. And the fruits of it have been peace, joy, love, and zeal for every good word and work.[44]

There are few better metaphors of disembodiment than a "rope of sand"! A genuine rope is a thing of connection and strength, in which all the parts are intimately woven together so that neither they, nor the things that they join, can easily be separated. A rope of sand, however, implies the outward appearance of connection and strength, but without the inward reality thereof, being but a mass of disconnected particles. Just so, on the one hand, the parish church offers a mere semblance of Christian fellowship in which the churchgoing parishioners are just a loosely assembled mass, and even their outward form of religious life is an illusion; and, on the other hand, the Methodist societies introduce real Christian fellowship, through intimately connecting its members into a community that embodies the gospel, possessing both the outward form and the inward power of religious life.

From those *inside* the Methodist movement, Wesley was faced with an argument that the diversification of societies into classes and bands was neither necessary nor commanded in Scripture, but just a human invention.[45] In response to these, Wesley argued that the necessity and advantage of such small groups for promoting growth in grace was plain to both reason and experience. He also claimed that Scripture was at least indifferent to them and at best clearly supported them. As to the matter of human invention, Wesley's response is "So what?!" "You seem not to have observed that the Scripture, in most points, gives only *general* rules, and leaves the *particular* circumstances to be adjusted by the common sense of mankind."[46] Wesley argues that the order of the Methodist movement, embodied in the structure of classes and bands, is a "prudential regulation" consisting of little "prudential helps, grounded on reason and experience, in order to apply the general rules given in Scripture according to particular circumstances."[47]

In the light of our foregoing discussion, it would be a mistake to assume that Wesley thought the Anglican Church embodied some *essential* ecclesiastical order in which the *prudential* order of the Methodist movement could be accommodated. Rather, as we have seen, he considers the ordering of all real Christian fellowship to be prudential, the real distinction being whether or not any order promotes an embodiment of the gospel (both corporate and personal) which is faithful to the historic tradition of the Church. We must remember that Wesley never thought of himself, or Methodists more broadly, as anything other than faithful Anglicans. One might say he sought only to supply a deficiency in the existing order of the Church, thereby enhancing its ability to embody the gospel in his own cultural-historical context.

This enhanced church order had a threefold pattern: (1) the "great congregation" of the parish Church that supplied the need for public worship and the administration of the sacraments, prudentially ordered for the adoration of God and edification of believers; (2) the society preaching service[48] and class meetings that supplied the need for evangelistic outreach and pastoral care,[49] prudentially ordered in the service of the unchurched and awakened sinners; and (3) the society-bands that supplied the need for discipleship, prudentially ordered to nurture believers in the pursuit of holy living. For Wesley, it was only when all three were functioning together—carefully distinguished but inseparably connected—that the gospel was embodied fully and could be said to be fulfilling both the Great Commandment and the Great Commission.[50]

Keeping Order and End Connected

Church order, like any means of grace, must resist the danger of disconnecting its means from its end. This disconnection, which always amounts to a disembodiment of the gospel, typically occurs in two ways.

First, there is *the danger of making the means an end in themselves,* thus disembodying the gospel by taking the gospel out of the body. This problem occurs when a Christian fellowship identifies true religion in either what it thinks (resulting in a spiritless orthodoxy) or says (resulting in an empty liturgy) or does (resulting in a dead formalism). As we have seen, Wesley begins both *Character of a Methodist* and *Plain Account of the People Called Methodists* by denying that any of these things distinguish what it means to be Methodist. He makes it quite clear in his *Advice to the People Called Methodists,* however, that the particular "opinions," "mode of worship," and use of "ordinances," which constitute *the principles of a Methodist,* are *not a matter of indifference,* for they are upheld as the best representation of genuine scriptural Christianity, and faithful to the Anglican tradition. What is new, however, is the embodied vigor with which these *principles* are also put into *practice.*[51]

For Wesley, true religion was defined by holiness of heart manifest in holiness of life. There is an inseparable connection between this inward power of religious life and the right use of outward forms or means which serve to nurture and express it. However, unless church order serves this end, rather than being an end in itself, the Body of Christ is just a corpse! This is one reason Wesley insisted that membership of a class meeting, as well as being held accountable to the *Rules*, was the necessary condition of belonging to a society, and came to introduce class tickets for entry into the society meetings. Had he not done this, there would have been the danger of creating just another new breed of nominal Christians wearing the badge of a Methodist but having a heart and life that did not match! In short, Wesley avoided the problem of confusing means and ends by prudentially ordering Christian fellowship which embodied the conversion of its members from sinfulness to holiness of heart and life.

Second, *there is the danger of desiring ends without the appropriate use of means,* thus disembodying the gospel by disposing of the body. In Wesley's day, this manifested itself in the form of quietism (waiting for the initiative of divine grace by abandoning all human means), solitariness (thinking that one can be saved by oneself), mysticism (seeking inner union with God through renouncing all outward means), and enthusiasm (reveling in direct ecstatic experience of God). The Methodist movement has always been in danger of falling into these errors because of its particular emphases: the doctrine of personal salvation by faith alone; the unconditional and instantaneous work of divine grace; the direct inner witness of the Spirit; and holiness as the life of God imparted to the human heart. Wesley sought to avoid the problems of striving for ends without means by prudentially ordering a movement that embodied the spirituality of its members in society, with its emphasis on mutual accountability, empowerment, and growth in grace.

The danger of desiring ends without means is also inherent in the revivalist spirit of Methodism (and evangelicalism more broadly), with its tendency to reduce conversion to a personal decision for Christ.[52] When reflecting upon the limited success of his movement, the mature George Whitefield comments, "My brother Wesley acted wisely. The souls that were awakened under his ministry he joined in class and thus preserved the fruits of his labours. This I neglected and my people are a rope of sand."[53] We have heard this expression before!

We can also interpret the form of revivalism that followed Charles Finney as disembodying the gospel by either *detaching* the evangelistic function of the preaching service from the regular order of church life, or by *collapsing* the function of all church order and worship into it. A fundamental difference between Wesley's movement and the forms of revivalism associated with both Whitefield and Finney was the way he incorporated the critical element of personal decision to follow Christ into the larger context of conversion from sinfulness to holiness, embodied by the Methodist societies.

Re-Embodying Conversion in Contemporary Methodism[54]

Some of the most sustained attempts to embody conversion today can be found in those independent and mainstream congregations, including Methodist churches, who would describe themselves as "seeker-oriented." As a way to consider how contemporary Methodism might again invite Christians to embody the gospel, we will examine some points of contact between early Methodism and Willow Creek Community Church in relation to the connection between the order and end of Christian fellowship and its challenge for local congregations.[55]

Keep the End in View

We learn from early Methodism that the principles of any Christian fellowship should be shaped by its end, and those principles should be embodied in a concrete structure with practices that serve it. These principles should always reflect genuine scriptural Christianity and be faithful to the historic tradition, while the order and practice is prudentially adapted to fulfill providentially God's mission in the present cultural-historical context. This combination of revelation and adaptation reflects the nature of an incarnational faith and serves a good missiological description of the church as the Body of Christ.

Wesley described the end of early Methodism in *Character of a Methodist* as conversion from sinfulness to holiness (or Christian perfection). Willow Creek claims that its mission "is to turn irreligious [unchurched] people into fully devoted followers of Jesus Christ. . . . Our vision is to be a biblically functioning community of believers so that Christ's redemptive purposes can be accomplished in the world."[56] Whether the end be described as "the character of a Methodist" or "a fully devoted follower of Jesus Christ," such a vision is critical for the order and life of any congregation. The problem with many local churches is that they lack purpose because they lack vision: when nothing much is *aimed* for, nothing much is *attained*.

Connect Means and End

Early Methodism can teach us that the threefold order of the "great congregation," society-classes, and society-bands can be an effective way for attaining the end of scriptural holiness by embodying the way of salvation.

We can also see an "economy" of salvation embodied in Willow Creek's means for the conversion of "sinner to saint,"[57] expressing the prudential ordering of their community to seek and save the lost. At the heart of this we observe a correlation with the threefold pattern of early Methodism. First, the practice of personal evangelism coupled to a seeker service and seeker-oriented small groups. This is the prudential ordering of fellowship (not worship) for evangelism, embodied by a high degree of adaptation to meet *the needs of seekers*.[58] Second, the practice of gathering for worship, prayer, and praise, the celebration of the sacraments, and teaching from Scripture.[59] Although the "great congregation" does not exclude seekers, it is prudentially ordered to meet *the needs of believers*. Third, the practice of participating in life-changing small groups, prudentially ordered for optimizing openness to the life-transforming work of the Spirit, in the pursuit conversion and Christlikeness.[60]

This common pattern affirms the necessity of embodying the gospel by keeping evangelism, worship, and spiritual nurture *properly distinguished* yet inseparably connected.[61] It seems to me that early Methodism significantly differs from Willow Creek, however, in its emphasis on the conversion of seekers through participation in (and being held accountable to) all the means of grace (both piety and mercy), alongside the evangelical means of proclamation, persuasion, and invitation to decision. There is a sense, therefore, in which the conversion of seekers comes through embodying the practices of saints; both seekers and saints were to embody the gospel of repentance and faith.[62] So Wesleyans would always claim that the worship of the great congregation can be a means of both converting and nurturing grace,[63] and that seekers should make use of all available means. I submit, however, that these broader possibilities flourished in early Methodism only because its evangelism and spiritual nurture were fully embodied in other prudentially ordered ways.[64] It is a common failure in contemporary Methodism that all Christian fellowship gets reduced to the activity of the great congregation, which finally neglects seekers by playing to saints and neglects the saints by having no supporting small-group structure. Indeed, this amounts to a disembodiment of the gospel by failing to invite either seekers or saints to convert, to find new birth as a committed follower of Jesus Christ, or to pursue holiness of heart and life on the way to Christian perfection.

Avoid Being Disconnected

Both early Methodism and Willow Creek, however, teach us that maintaining the threefold order serves to resist the problems associated with disembodying the gospel through disconnecting means from ends, by keeping evangelism, worship, and nurture distinct but also *mutually conditioning* concerns. There are two further observations I would like to make.

First, a danger for Willow Creek lies in creating a new breed of *nominal* Christians who make some form of commitment to Christ but then fail to participate in the great congregation and accountable small groups (continuing to prefer the comfortable anonymity of the seeker service). This was also a problem for early Methodism among those who attended the society preaching services without becoming members of the society meeting proper, or those who attended the Methodist society but neglected Anglican sacramental worship. Wesley sought to avoid this problem by opening the society meetings only to sincere seekers who were prepared to be *held accountable for their seeking* through the class meeting.

Another manifestation of this problem lies in breeding *nominal* Christians who disconnect their own private spiritual journeys and discourse with God from the mutual accountability of Christian community. A criticism of the contemporary Methodist Church, therefore, would be the extent to which it nurtures people in an individualistic spirituality that perpetuates Christian fellowship as a "rope of sand." When Wesley said that there is no holiness but social holiness, he meant that a person could not become holy on his or her own. This, again, is why membership in a small group was mandatory in early Methodism. Unlike Willow Creek, Wesley considered accountable and empowering small-group fellowship necessary for both seekers and believers in the pursuit of conversion to real Christianity.[65]

Second, the challenge facing those who seek to embody salvation in any particular historical context lies in remaining faithful to the gospel while seeking to communicate it effectively through means that are prudentially adapted to the prevailing culture. The danger here is not of disconnecting means from ends, but of allowing means to be shaped (or misshaped) by the wrong ends. Willow Creek, like seeker-oriented churches in general, has been accused of compromising the gospel by an overadaptation to the felt-needs of secular culture, resulting in a message construed through the die of popular psychology and shaped by the tools of marketing technology.[66] Insofar as this is true, the language of sin, repentance, and forgiveness is typically avoided, and people are not confronted with the scriptural requirement to be holy as God is holy: *to depart* from their own ungodliness and *to be set apart* from the ungodliness of their cultural context. The temptation is to assume that cultural and psychological categories can effectively diagnose the human condition, which may then be treated by the gospel, so long as it can be swallowed comfortably. The historic wisdom of the church, however, reminds us that the language of the gospel both *describes* the human condition and *prescribes* the divine solution. Prudence, then, will recognize that authentic preaching of the gospel, while aiming at clarity, is likely to be as scandalous as it is relevant. The misshaping of the gospel by adaptation to the rhetoric and methods of the surrounding culture is also not limited to places like Willow Creek. In many mainstream liberal Methodist churches the scandalous language of "conversion" has largely been dropped in favor of less threatening models that fall under the general category of "therapy." The goal of emotional wholeness and psychological well-being is not the same as Wesley's understanding of Christian virtue and holy affections.

Exercise Prudence

The purpose of this comparison has not been to present an apologetic for the "seeker movement" or suggest that the Methodist Church should uncritically appropriate its methods. Rather, by identifying a few similarities between Willow Creek and early Methodism, I have sought to illuminate the wisdom of our own historic tradition as a challenge to contemporary Methodist congregations. That challenge is to exercise prudence in keeping means and end, principles and practice, inseparably connected and embodied in the life of its Christian fellowship. We learn two things from Wesley, however, about such prudence. First, it requires a prior submission to the discipline of the wider church, whose historic wisdom and virtues unite to maintain the end of scriptural holiness, in continuity with the primitive church. Such prudence will safeguard us from employing misshapen means attached to the wrong ends. Second, the local congregation should constantly seek to extend God's mission into the world by providentially employing means that embody the whole gospel without compromise—for the conversion of sinners, both seekers and believers, into saints.

Conclusion

Suddenly a Light from Heaven

William H. Willimon

"Now as he was going along and approaching Damascus, suddenly a light from heaven flashed around him. He fell to the ground and heard a voice." (Acts 9:3-4)

Luke begins his first volume of his Gospel assuring Theophilus that he intends to present him with an "orderly account" of the Christian movement (Luke 1:1-4). Yet when we get to Luke's second volume, the Acts of the Apostles, we soon realize that this faith is anything but orderly. A mob of scoffers is transformed into repentant believers (2:14-41), a person from the remote ends of the earth is transmuted into the baptized (8:26-40), a murderous enemy is transmogrified into "brother Saul" (9:1-31), and a despised Gentile soldier is adopted by the church (10:1–11:18). Whatever the gospel is, it is about alteration.[1] As Joel Green shows in his chapter on this theme of "darkness to light," conversion is a "cornerstone" of Luke's good news. That creator God who made something out of nothing in Genesis 1 loves to keep creating, to wrench life out of death, and delights in making a family where once there had been no people (1 Pet. 2:10).

The Christian life comes neither naturally nor normally. Little within us prepares us for the shock of moral regeneration that is occasioned by the work of Christ among us. One cannot get Christianity by being lucky enough to be born in Nashville. What God in Christ wants to do to us is nothing less than radical new creation, movement from death to life. The chapters within this book are, I suspect, more radical, disruptive, and antagonistic than even their authors may know. The United Methodists among us are awfully accommodated, well-situated, at ease in Zion, or at least disgustingly content with present arrangements. As John Tyson says in his chapter, comparing our church life to Wesley's Aldersgate experience, "our ministry bears a greater resemblance to Wesley's before Aldersgate than after." A million members lost here, a million there, what can anybody do? Everyone in mainline Protestantism is in decline, geriatric, losing members, in remission from the virus called discipleship. Sociological determinism has got us. What is to be done?

The authors in this volume, each in his or her own evangelical way, have recalled us to our originating Wesleyan expectation that God really does intend to get back what is God's, no matter the cost. As Beecher Hicks puts it, the gospel means "God is going to get back what God owns." Conversion, being born again, transformed, regenerated, detoxified, is merely God's means of getting God's way with the world, despite what that reclamation may cost God or us.

Deep in our Wesleyan once warmed hearts is a story of how a priggish little Oxford don got changed at Aldersgate and thereafter. John Wesley's life was well-formed, well-fixed by a host of positive Christian influences upon him before the evening on Aldersgate Street. Yet what happened afterward has led us Wesleyans to see his heart "strangely warmed" as nothing less than ending and beginning, death and birth, a whole new world.[2]

The essays in this volume urge us to think of Wesley's new birth, and ours, in a more nuanced, complex, sanctificationist way. They challenge a church that has become accommodated to things as they are, the cultural status quo. They present a rebuke to a church that has lost its conversionist roots, having settled comfortably into a characterization of the Christian life as continuous and synonymous with being a good person.

Scripture enlists a rich array of metaphors to speak of the discontinuous, discordant outbreak of new life: "born from above" or "born anew" (John 3:7; 1 Pet. 1:3, 23), "regeneration" (John 3:5; Titus 3:5), "putting on a new nature" (Eph. 4:24; Col. 3:10), and "new creation" (2 Cor. 5:17). Paul contrasts the old life according to the flesh with "life according to the Spirit" (Rom. 8:1-39). Baptism is one way we remind ourselves that the Christian life is at times discordant, dissonant, and disrupting. When people join Rotary, or the League of Women Voters, the organization gives them a membership card and lapel pin. When men and women join the Body of Christ, we throw them under, half drown them, strip these aspirants naked and wash them all over, and pull them forth sticky and fresh like a newborn. One might think people would get the message. But, as Luther said, the old Adam is a mighty good swimmer. A conversionist faith is disconcerting, particularly to those for whom the world as it is has been fairly good. Those on top, those who are reasonably well-fed, fairly well-off, tend to cling to the world as it is rather than risk the possibility of something new. There are certain economic, social, and political reasons Wesleyans of recent generations have said so much less about conversion—until this book.

New Creation

Paul was stunned by the reality of the Resurrection—the way God not only vindicated Jesus by raising him from the dead but also thereby re-created the whole *kosmos*. In the Easter event an old world is terminated and a new one is born, so Paul was forced to rethink everything he had previously thought, including ethics. Much of what Paul says about Christian behavior was formed as his testimony to the Resurrection, an event that he had experienced within the dramatic turnaround in his own life. Whereas Jesus did Easter at the empty tomb, Easter happened to Paul on the Damascus Road.

Yet the drama of his conversion cannot lead us to conclude that Paul's experience and its consequences for his vocation are merely subjective.[3] Paul found himself suddenly transferred to a whole new world. He changed because of his realization that, in Jesus Christ, the world had changed. Paul's key testimonial to this recreation is in his Second Letter to the Corinthians: "So if anyone is in Christ, there is a new creation: everything old has passed away; see, everything has become new! All this is from God, who reconciled us to himself through Christ, and has given us the ministry of reconciliation" (2 Cor. 5:17-18).[4]

Certainly, old habits die hard. There are still, as Paul acknowledges so eloquently in Romans 8, "the sufferings of the present time." It makes a world of difference whether or not one knows the Resurrection. Thus, making doxology to God (Rom. 11:33-36), Paul asks that we present ourselves as "a living sacrifice, holy and acceptable to God" by not being "conformed to this world" but by being "transformed by the renewing of your minds" (Rom. 12:1-2). All of this is resurrection talk, the sort of tensive situation of those who find their lives still in an old, dying world, yet also now conscious of their citizenship in a new world being born. Our lives are eschatologically stretched between the sneak preview of the new world being born among us in the church, and the old world where the principalities and powers are reluctant to give way. In the meantime, which is the only time the church has ever known, we live as those who know something about the fate of the world that the world does not yet know. And that makes us different.

Being a Sanctificationist in a World Where Lots of Folk Are Happy as They Are

To be a Wesleyan is to be someone who is always trying to keep justification and sanctification linked in a culture that, at its best, might like to have new life but, at its worst, does not want to give up anything to have it. Wade Clark Roof's massive study of contemporary American spirituality depicted a nation where there are many people on a spiritual quest, cobbling together their faith from a patchwork quilt of a little this and a little that, a nation full of people who want the benefits of adherence to a religious tradition with none of the limits.[5] This "spiritual marketplace," as Roof aptly titled it, is a world where the consumer is king, where bits and pieces are extracted from a religious tradition, and few demands are made for costly ethical transformation. Though Roof did not put the matter like this, I would characterize the new spiritual market as a place where many would like to be converted and justified, but few to be sanctified.

Sanctificationists stress the power of new life in Christ to make us more than we would have been if we had been left to our own devices. We must take up our cross *daily*. The Christian faith takes time, a lifetime, to get right. Therefore Calvin speaks of the new life in Christ as "regeneration," understanding new life as a process, as a long-term, lifelong inculcation of a set of practices that do not come naturally. Too much of American evangelical Christianity depicts the Christian life as a momentous, one-time turning, an instantaneous event that occurs in our subjective consciousness. But the Reformers were convinced that sin is so deeply rooted in our thinking and willing that only a lifetime of turnings, of fits and starts, of divine dislodgment and detoxification can produce what God has in mind for us.[6] Daily we turn. Daily we are to take up the cross and follow. Daily we keep being incorporated into the Body of Christ that makes us more than we could have been if we had been left to our own devices.[7] Thus says Calvin (to whom we Wesleyans ought to be more indebted than to Luther):

> This restoration does not take place in one moment or one day or one year; but through continual and sometimes even slow advances, God wipes out in his elect the corruptions of the flesh, cleanses them of guilt, consecrates them to himself as temples, renewing all their minds to true purity that they may practice repentance throughout their lives and know that this warfare will end only in death.[8]

Conversion, regeneration, mystical union, and *metanoia* are all attempts to speak of this turning of heart, body, and mind toward God, a turning that is occasioned by God's prior turning toward us in Christ. John Bunyan's *Pilgrim's Progress* depicts new life as a journey, a rendering that was invented by Mark for his Gospel. The appearance of Jesus made necessary a new literary form, unknown before Mark, called *gospel* that is a literary embodiment of the transformation that is occasioned by Christ. To be with Jesus is to be following Jesus, as if on a journey. We are not there yet. We fall behind, then we catch up, only to again fall back.

Hans Mol has illuminated steps within typical conversion accounts: detachment from former patterns of identity, a time of meaninglessness and anomie, a dramatic transition from darkness to light, from chaos to meaning, and finally the acceptance by the community of the initiate into a new life together.[9] The initiate is now in a new existence, a new world, having experienced a dramatic journey named as "conversion."

Yet this journey metaphor has its limits. For instance, the contemporary notion, articulated by James Fowler and others, of the Christian life as a movement, a journey, through stages of human development in the normal human life cycle, may be an inadequate metaphor for the new life in Christ.[10] Karl Barth has a wonderful survey of the history of vain Protestant attempts to make the Christian life into a series of ordered developmental moves, onward and upward.[11] Barth correctly saw all such efforts as attempts to "outline the development of the natural man into a Christian, and the Christian into an increasingly perfect Christian, in a way which can be mastered and recounted." In Barth's estimate, "this whole attempt implies an attack on the whole substance of a genuine understanding of the process."[12] A "genuine understanding" of new life in Christ surely must include some recognition of the God-initiated, human-responsive, discontinuous, surprising quality of new life. Notions of ordered development, slow, continuous movement through various stages, simply do not do justice to the jolts, bumps, fits, wallops, and starts that *metanoia* inevitably entails.[13]

Nothing so exposes the fashionable stoicism of American faith, faith in a vague God who—though generally approving of human projects—neither speaks nor acts, as the notion that our God means to change us. Conversion is a radical assault upon the conventional, officially sanctioned American faith that we are basically okay just as we are and that this world, for any of its faults, is all there is. Conversion is a statement of faith that this God means to have us—all of us—that this God will have his sovereign way with us. Whether or not one believes in even the possibility of conversion will relate in great part to one's conviction about what sort of God we have got. Or, more biblically, what sort of God has got us. Conversion is one of God's most gracious, intrusive, demanding, sovereign acts. "*By his great mercy* he has given us a new birth into a living hope" (1 Pet. 1:3*b*; my italics).

Faith is known by its subject.[14] Faith, the Christian faith, is more than the development of natural, universal human qualities. Human capacities and human development are also in the grip of sin,[15] therefore much of our "development" involves ever more sophisticated means of turning away from God toward our various gods. Very little of what it takes to be a Christian is innate. Radical turning is required, turning that is initiated by a power or source external to the person being turned.

Yet that radical turning must be embodied in a set of practices that enable remarkable transformation. Although we current Wesleyans may indeed be guilty of (in the words of Philip Meadows) "disembodying the gospel," in our failure to keep principles and practice connected in our discipleship we can be instructed by our history. Richard Heitzenrater, in his *Wesley and the People Called Methodists,* showed how Methodism was an extraordinary effort to preach to the "underclasses" of England in the eighteenth century and to form those people into "classes."[16] Those classes arose from the need of the Methodists to collect money for the paying of the debt for building houses where Methodists could gather. It was suggested that everyone in the society called Methodist contribute a penny a week (which had already been done at the Foundry Society in order to assist the poor). When someone protested that not everyone in the society could afford that much, Captain Foy suggested that each Methodist Society be divided into groups of twelve, each with a leader who would be responsible for turning in twelve pence a week, making up themselves whatever they could not collect. He volunteered to take as his group the eleven poorest.[17]

So Methodism began as a disciplined body of people to transform one another and the poor. Its theology of sanctification and perfection found its soteriology in these classes, through which Methodists made their lives vulnerable to one another so that they might move on to perfection. That is why Methodists, and in particular Wesley, always maintained that they were not saying anything different from that for which classical Christianity had always stood. Rather what they sought was the discovery of practices they could hold in common, that which made them Christians. As Stanley Hauerwas says, the Methodists of the eighteenth century were the Black Muslims of their day. They covenanted to be disciplined in terms of both their theological language and of the practices commensurate with that language to be a people who would not be forced into lives of degradation simply because they were poor.

In his codification of the examination process in order to be a member of the Methodist Society, Wesley spelled out the rules for membership: "In order to *join* a society, persons were required to demonstrate only one condition: 'a desire to flee from the wrath to come, to be saved from their sins.' Those who desired to *continue* in the societies, however, were expected 'to evidence their desire of salvation, First, By doing no harm, . . . Secondly, By doing good, . . . Thirdly, By depending upon all the ordinances of God.' "[18] These rules were fleshed out with specific examples that drew on experience Wesley had had of actually having to exclude people from the societies. Thus, for example, two had been excluded for cursing and swearing; two for habitual Sabbath breaking; seventeen for drunkenness; two for retailing liquor; three for quarrelling and brawling; one for beating his wife; three for habitual, willful lying and railing and evil speaking; one for idleness and laziness; and twenty-nine for lightness and carelessness.

Methodism grew in great part because it offered salvation by saving people from the degradation of the general habits of eighteenth-century English society. True, the Methodists reflected as much as reacted against the society in which they found themselves. However, the genius was that people were embedded into God's salvation because they were given a new way of life that saved them from the expectations of their social order.[19] As Philip Meadows notes, the particular Wesleyan charism for the church catholic was "the embodied reality of scriptural holiness."

An Agenda for Christians Who Would Be Wesleyan

Having been reminded, by the chapters in this book, of our great heritage, it is appropriate to conclude with a few suggestions about the unique tasks that the heirs of Wesley face if we would be true to his complex vision of the Christian life.

Evangelism in the Wesleyan spirit ought to mean bringing people into disciplines to save them from the world. It does not mean calling them from life in the world, though it might mean that some of our lives would become more difficult. Essential to sanctification is the cultivation of the disciplines necessary to be in the world as Christians, which is our chief ministry to the world.[20] Our great challenge, as heirs of Wesley, according to the essays in this book, is to keep together the instantaneous element that relates to our justification and the participatory element. Somehow we must do justice to both new birth and entire sanctification. An important agenda for churches within the Wesleyan tradition is to embody, in the words of Barry L. Callen, "a mutuality model of Christian conversion" that does justice to "the biblical God reaching lovingly to all persons and enabling them with the ability to respond in ways that can activate the salvation that is God's intention."

Wesley's unique "conjunctive theology"[21] manages to be rich, tensive, evangelical and catholic, conversionist and sanctificationist, stressing the triumph of the justifying and sanctifying grace of God in Christ. It is, in Ted A. Campbell's words, a movement of "sacramental Evangelicalism." We seem not to know how to speak of the movement that God wrought through the Wesley's except through conjunctions. Because of its richness and depth, few of us have been able to do justice to its conjunctive quality, but try we ought.

Wade Clark Roof has noted the need for more creative and adaptive "traditioning" of spiritually questing baby boomers. They are open to learning about the riches of our faith traditions, but are they willing to be formed, reformed by the practices within the Wesleyan tradition? Wanting simultaneously to be both fluid and grounded, longing for religious experience without religious discipline, the boomers may not be willing subjects for a sanctificationist faith. Yet the essays in this book have certainly reassured me that, buyers market or not, *any presentation of the Christian faith that would hope to be uniquely Wesleyan must somehow do justice to both justification and sanctification, the radical experience of the new birth and the morally transformative process of growth into Christ.* We heirs of Wesley are due for a debate upon the nature of the disjunctive new birth and the precise shape of the conjunctive and transformed new life, but we are not free not to attempt to be faithful to the conversionist and sanctificationist treasure that has been given to us.

In Ephesians, the same writer is able to assert the conversionist notion—"But God, who is rich in mercy, out of the great love . . . made us alive together with Christ . . . and raised us up" (Eph. 2:4-6)—

and also the sanctificationist sentiment that we have been "created in Christ Jesus for good works, which God prepared beforehand to be our way of life" (Eph. 2:10).

The church exists not for itself, but rather to save the world, to "proclaim the mighty acts of him who called you out of darkness into his marvelous light" (1 Pet. 2:9). That process can be instantaneous and dramatic as well as gradual and growing. Christ is infinitely resourceful in accomplishing his will for our lives. The joy of being a disciple of Christ is the adventure of transformation, of movement from death to life, light to darkness, all as a work of grace in our lives. *In our preparation for baptism, in our preaching, in our Christian education, images of conversion and detoxification, of relinquishment and regeneration must replace images of gradual development and nurture.*

Let Hans Küng give the charge to us preachers:

> We are to preach *metanoia*. We must entice people away from the world to God. We are not to shut ourselves off from the world in a spirit of asceticism, but to live in the everyday world inspired by the radical obedience that is demanded by the love of God. The church must be reformed again and again, converted again and again each day, in order that it must fulfill its task.[22]

And yet Kenneth J. Collins's chapter on the "standards" of conversion has served for me as a warning against depicting sanctification in a moralistic way. Moralism is an attempt at self-salvation, to be related to Christ through our earnest efforts rather than through the work of Christ in us. Wesley preached the triumph of grace, the power of grace to make us that which our earnest efforts could not. Christ means to make us not just more ethical but also more holy. Sanctification is a work of God in us, a movement from heaven, a light not of our devising, something that is due to God's grace rather than self-derived. Even for those who have yet to experience the full inbreaking of the love of Christ, if they are able to live to some degree free from the enslavement to sin, Wesley taught that their freedom is due to the work of Christ in them, whether they yet know of that work or not. Full redemption means holiness, the reception of both justifying and sanctifying grace, the accomplishment by the gospel of something the Law can never do.

When Methodism fails to stress Wesley's conviction of the powerful, even prevenient, grace of God as the source of all possibility of new life, Methodism degenerates into insufferable, sentimental moralism in which the Christian life is depicted as simply another helpful means of making nice people even nicer. Discipleship is not a sanctimonious Twelve Step program. A holy person is a testimonial not to the innate possibility within people, but rather to the insistent, transforming love of God in Jesus Christ despite our sin. *The laborious, legalistic, minutely detailed procedures and mandates in our current United Methodist* Book of Discipline *are testimonial not only to a church with too little trust, but also to a church where we attempt to do through moralistic law that which only the transforming love of Christ can do.*

Saul, church enemy number one, bloody ravager of the church, is confronted by a voice and a blinding light on his way to Damascus (Acts 9:1-19). The sudden, disjunctive quality of what happened to Saul that day makes his a paradigmatic story of conversion. The making of a murderer into a missionary is quite a testimonial to the grace of God. Saul's conversion was not the end of the story, but its beginning. The voice speaks to Ananias, explaining to him that Saul's transformation is also his vocation: "He [Saul] is an instrument whom I have chosen to bring my name before Gentiles and kings and before the people of Israel" (Acts 9:15). The light, the voice from heaven, is a sign of a dramatic transformation, a lifelong journey that begins in having a life commandeered, caught up in the loving purposes of God, nothing less than new birth that leads to new lives in Christ, the light of the world.

Abbreviations

Cragg, *Appeals* — John Wesley, *The Appeals to Men of Reason and Religion and Certain Related Open Letters*, ed. Gerald R. Cragg, vol. 11 in *Works of John Wesley* (New York: Oxford University Press, 1975).

Telford, *Letters* — *The Letters of the Rev. John Wesley, A.M.*, ed. John Telford, 8 vols. (London: Epworth Press, 1931).

Wesley, *Notes* — John Wesley, *Explanatory Notes Upon the New Testament* (London: Methodist Publishing House, n.d.; reprinted Salem, Ohio: Schmul Publishers; reprinted Grand Rapids: Baker Book House, 1981).

Works — *The Bicentennial Edition of the Works of John Wesley* (Nashville: Abingdon Press, 1984–). Begun as the *Oxford Edition of the Works of John Wesley* (Oxford: Clarendon Press, 1975–1983).

Vols. 1-4: *Sermons I, II, III, and IV*, ed. Albert C. Outler, 1984–1987.
Vol. 9: *The Methodist Societies: History, Nature, and Design*, ed. Rupert E. Davies, 1989.
Vol. 11: *The Appeals to Men of Reason and Religion*

	and Certain Related Open Letters, ed. Gerald R. Cragg, 1989. Vol. 18: *Journal and Diaries, 1735–1739,* eds. W. Reginald Ward and Richard P. Heitzenrater, 1988. Vol. 19: *Journal and Diaries, 1738–1743,* eds. W. Reginald Ward and Richard P. Heitzenrater, 1990. Vol. 25: *Letters I, 1721–1739,* ed. Frank Baker, 1980. Vol. 26: *Letters II, 1740–1755,* ed. Frank Baker, 1982.
Works (Jackson)	*The Works of John Wesley,* ed. Thomas Jackson, 14 vols. (Grand Rapids: Baker Book House, 1978).

Notes

Introduction: Conversion in the Wesleyan Tradition

1. Paul Löffler, "The Biblical Concept of Conversion," in *Mission Trends No. 2: Evangelization*, ed. Gerald H. Anderson and Thomas F. Stransky (New York: Paulist Press, 1975), 24-45.

2. William Barclay, *Turning to God: A Study of Conversion in the Book of Acts and Today* (London: The Epworth Press, 1963), 20.

3. E. Stanley Jones, *Conversion* (New York: Abingdon Press, 1959), 27.

4. According to Harran, Luther's conception of conversion developed from "his fundamental insight in the *Dictata* that the first and greatest conversion of all is God's conversion to humanity in the incarnation." See Marilyn J. Harran, *Luther on Conversion: The Early Years* (Ithaca, N.Y.: Cornell University Press, 1983), 189.

5. John B. Cobb Jr., *Grace and Responsibility: A Wesleyan Theology for Today* (Nashville: Abingdon Press, 1995), 77.

6. For a helpful treatment that explores the numerous levels of Christian conversion see Bernard Lonergan, "Theology in Its New Context: The Dimensions of Conversion," in *Conversion: Perspectives on Personal and Social Transformation*, ed. Walter E. Conn (New York: Alba House, 1978), 3-21.

7. See Kenneth J. Collins, *A Real Christian: The Life of John Wesley* (Nashville: Abingdon Press, 1999).

8. For readings of Wesley's theology that place a premium on process

to the relative neglect of the instantaneous—what can be termed "gradualism"—see Randy L. Maddox, *Responsible Grace: John Wesley's Practical Theology* (Nashville: Kingswood Books, 1994), and Hoo-Jung Lee, "Experiencing the Spirit in Wesley and Macarius," in *Rethinking Wesley's Theology for Contemporary Methodism*, ed. Randy L. Maddox (Nashville: Abingdon Press, 1998), 197-212.

9. *Works*, 2:169.

10. Theodore W. Jennings, "John Wesley *Against* Aldersgate," *Quarterly Review* 8, no. 3 (Fall 1988): 16.

11. Maddox, *Responsible Grace*, 155.

12. For example, in his contribution to this volume Henry Knight challenges the assumption that since those who have the faith of a servant are "accepted," they are therefore necessarily justified. "I would distinguish between justification and acceptance," he writes. Moreover, he observes: "If those with the faith of a servant are accepted, they seemingly must be justified as well. Yet this way of construing justification creates more difficulties than it solves." See also Kenneth J. Collins, *The Scripture Way of Salvation: The Heart of John Wesley's Theology* (Nashville: Abingdon Press, 1997), 140-42, for an explanation of what "faith of a servant" constitutes justifying faith, and what faith does not.

13. See Kenneth J. Collins, "Real Christianity as Integrating Theme in Wesley's Soteriology: The Critique of a Modern Myth," *The Asbury Theological Journal* 51, no. 2 (Fall 1996): 15-45; and Collins, *Real Christian*.

14. Heiko A. Oberman, "Quo vadis, Petre? Tradition from Irenaeus to *Humani Generis*," in *The Dawn of the Reformation: Essays in Late Medieval and Early Reformation Thought* (Edinburgh: T & T Clark, 1986), 269-96.

15. Emphasis is mine. On the necessity of conversion, the German missiologist Paul Löffler writes: " 'Fellowship' minus the passion for conversion leads to ghettoism; 'service' minus the call to conversion is a gesture without hope; Christian education minus conversion is [mere] religiosity . . . ; and 'dialogue' without the challenge to conversion remains sterile talk" (Löffler, "The Biblical Concept of Conversion," 24-45; quotation is on p. 27).

16. William James's distinction between the "healthy minded," who need to be born only once, and the "sick souls," who must be twice-born, misses the crucial element in Christian conversion that is a *necessity* for all. Indeed, the key transformation in Christian conversion has little to do with either optimistic or pessimistic outlooks on life. Nor is it principally one of moral improvement, though it includes it, of course. On the contrary, Christian conversion marks a transition that is beyond human power and which therefore must be actualized by nothing less than the

initially sanctifying grace of God—a grace whereby sinners become, for the first time, wonderfully and remarkably *holy*. This is a "supernatural work," to be sure—beyond the limits and resources of the moral self, whether this work is experienced over time (the reality affirmed, though the temporal instantiation unknown) or in a crucial, memorable, moment. It is similar to the transition from the ethical to the religious stages as amply displayed in the work of Søren Kierkegaard. See William James, *The Varieties of Religious Experience* (Harmondsworth: Penguin Books, 1982), and Søren Kierkegaard, *Stages on Life's Way* (Princeton: Princeton University Press, 1988).

17. For another helpful discussion of conversion in Luke-Acts, see Timothy E. Yates, "Christian Conversion 1902–1993: William James to Lewis Rambo," *Mission Studies* 13, nos. 1 and 2 (1996): 306-19.

18. *Works,* 18:247.

19. See Wesley's sermon "On Sin in Believers," where he makes distinctions between the *guilt, power, and being* of sin: "The *guilt* is one thing, the *power* another, and the *being* yet another. That believers are delivered from the *guilt* and *power* of sin we allow; that they are delivered from the *being* of it we deny" (*Works,* 1:328).

20. Ibid., 2:116.

21. For an example of the latter tendency, which maintains that Aldersgate represents not John Wesley's new birth or conversion but his entire sanctification, see David L. Cubie, "Placing Aldersgate in John Wesley's Order of Salvation," *Wesleyan Theological Journal* 24 (1989): 32-53.

22. Wesley, *Notes,* 379. Emphasis is mine. Bracketed material is mine.

23. For an examination of the full-orbed nature of conversion, including the moral and spiritual dimensions, which engage the entire person, see Joseph Fuchs, "Sin and Conversion," in Conn, *Conversion,* 247-62.

24. Collins, *The Scripture Way of Salvation,* 207.

25. For an excellent study of the sacrament of baptism among American Methodists, see Gayle C. Felton, *This Gift of Water: The Practice and Theology of Baptism Among Methodists in America* (Nashville: Abingdon Press, 1992).

26. Smith observes: "Any belief is legitimately called radical when it strikes at the roots of our identity, belief system, and lifestyle. To heat up any such belief and move it to center stage is so dis-easing that the fact that it ever happens makes conversion seem like a supernatural event—an interference in the laws of inertia." See Joanmarie Smith, "Teaching Toward Conversion," *Religious Education* 89, no. 1 (Winter 1994): 107.

27. For helpful discussions on the temporal aspects of conversion, see Wayne E. Oates, "Conversion: Sacred and Secular," in Conn, *Conversion*

(pp. 149-68); and F. W. B. Bullock, *Evangelical Conversion in Great Britain 1696–1845* (St. Leonards on Sea: Budd & Gillatt, 1959).

28. Recounting Billy Graham's comments about the conversion experience of Graham's wife, Stackhouse notes: "My wife, for example, cannot remember the exact day or hour when she became a Christian, but she is certain that there was such a moment in her life, a moment when she actually crossed the line" (John G. Stackhouse Jr., "Billy Graham and the Nature of Conversion: A Paradigm Case," *Studies in Religion* 21, no. 3 [1992]: 340).

29. In a more sociological perspective, Kallenberg contends: "Conversion is the emergence of a new mode of life occasioned by a self-involving participation in the shared life, language, and paradigm of the believing community" (Brad J. Kallenberg, "Conversion Converted: A Postmodern Formulation of the Doctrine of Conversion," *The Evangelical Quarterly* 67, no. 4 [October 1995]: 358).

30. Part of this dynamic is what I have called in my own work "a soteriological orientation." In other words, in Wesley's work among the poor, for example, the motivation for such labor as well as its ultimate telos had very much to do with the graces of justification and regeneration—that is, with the inculcation of holy tempers both in the minister and in those who received such ministry. See Kenneth J. Collins, "The Soteriological Orientation of John Wesley's Ministry to the Poor," *The Asbury Theological Journal* 50, no. 1 (Spring 1995): 75-92.

31. For more on the importance of Methodist class meetings, see D. Michael Henderson, *John Wesley's Class Meeting: A Model for Making Disciples* (Nappanee, Ind.: Evangel Publishing House, 1997); and David Lowes Watson, *The Early Methodist Class Meeting: Its Origins and Significance* (Nashville: Discipleship Resources, 1985).

32. For an able discussion on the nature of the faith of a servant and its relation to the larger motif of real Christianity, see Philip R. Meadows, " 'Candidates for Heaven': Wesleyan Resources for a Theology of Religions," *The Wesleyan Theological Journal* 35 no. 1 (Spring 2000): 99-129.

1. John Wesley's Conversion at Aldersgate

1. See *Works*, 18:252.

2. See Jean Miller Schmidt's treatment of this in Maddox, *Aldersgate Reconsidered*, 112. The classic treatment of this position is Maximin Piette, *John Wesley in the Evolution of Protestantism* (London: Sheed and Ward, 1938). See also Henry Rack, *Reasonable Enthusiast* (Philadelphia: Trinity Press, 1989), 581 n. 51, for a list of sources on this subject.

3. See Richard Heitzenrater's essay "Great Expectations" in Maddox, *Aldersgate Reconsidered,* in which he discusses Wesley's process of adjustment to exactly what conversion could, and could not, be expected (pp. 49ff.).

4. For an especially lively account of Wesley's Oxford years, see Stanley Ayling, *John Wesley* (Nashville: Abingdon Press, 1979), 28-43.

5. James W. Fowler, *Stages of Faith: The Psychology of Human Development and the Quest for Meaning* (San Francisco: Harper & Row, 1981).

6. *Works* (Jackson), "Plain Account of Christian Perfection," 11:366.

7. Luke Tyerman, *The Life and Times of the Rev. John Wesley, M.A.* (New York: Burt Franklin, 1872).

8. Maximin Piette, *John Wesley in the Evolution of Protestantism* (London: Sheed & Ward).

9. Bernard Lonergan distinguishes four kinds of conversion: religious, intellectual, moral, and psychic/affective (see *Method in Theology* [New York: Herder and Herder, 1972], 103-250). Walter E. Conn proposes four as well, but in a different configuration: moral, affective, critical moral, and religious (see *Christian Conversion* [New York: Paulist Press, 1986], 216-28).

10. Adherents of the Holy Living School taught that sanctification necessarily precedes justification, and that as one advances in sanctification, God is more *inclined* to grant pardon. See Alister McGrath, *Justitia Dei: A History of the Christian Doctrine of Justification* (Cambridge University Press: 1988).

11. *Works,* 25:439, 441. For a reiteration of the contents of the letter, see *Works,* 18:136-37.

12. *Works* (February 28, 1738), 18:226.

13. See Ayling, *John Wesley,* 92ff., esp. p. 94. Ayling notes that Aldersgate "of itself . . . , changed nothing [in Wesley's] theological position" but it did change Wesley. See also Martin Schmidt, *John Wesley: A Theological Biography* (Nashville: Abingdon Press, 1973), 1:222. Schmidt says Wesley was honest enough to distinguish between his perception of justification by faith and his experience of it.

14. *Works* (May 24, 1738), 18:249-50. See also Robert Tuttle, *Sanctity Without Starch* (Anderson, Ind.: Bristol Books, 1992), 15, where Tuttle discusses this moment in terms of the law of sin and death.

15. Wesley once wrote: "I am one who for twenty years used outward works not only as 'act of goodness,' but as *commutations* (though I did not indeed *profess this*) instead of inward holiness. I know I was *not holy.* But I quieted my conscience by doing such and such" (*Works,* Letter to John

Smith [December 30, 1745], 26:177, par. 6). See also ibid. (May 24, 1738; May 25, 1738; and June 6, 1738), 18:250, 251, and 254. It took him several months and a visit to Germany to begin to sort things out; and at one point, he feared he had lost his faith altogether.

16. *Works* (January 4, 1739), 19:29. This has led some to remark that Aldersgate was an experience of assurance that failed to reassure. They forget Wesley firmly believed that grace could be forfeited by sin. Wesley did not doubt that he had been justified on May 24, 1738; he feared he had temporarily lost the grace. This is consistent with his mature doctrine of sin in believers.

17. Theodore Runyon, "The Importance of Experience for Faith" in Maddox, *Aldersgate Reconsidered,* 101.

18. See Collins, *The Scripture Way of Salvation* (pp. 131ff.) for a good overview of development in Wesley's doctrine of assurance.

19. Ibid., 144.

20. *Works,* 1:131ff.

21. Ibid., "The New Birth," 2:195.

22. Ibid., 200.

23. In the index of *Works* there are more than one hundred entries for the word *conversion*. However, few of these are examples of Wesley's use of the word. Most are simply incidences of people being converted under his ministry. In Wesley's letter to Bishop Lavington in 1750, he states that he does not use the term often because it rarely occurs in the New Testament. In addition, the context shows that his avoidance of the term may be due to his reluctance to open himself to attack in theological debates because of the term's imprecision. See *Works,* 11:368-69.

24. See also J. Ernest Rattenbury, *The Conversion of the Wesleys* (London: Epworth Press, 1938), 30-31.

25. John Wesley, *The Complete English Dictionary,* 3d ed. (London: Hawes, 1777).

26. Wesley, *Notes,* 304, as cited by Kenneth J. Collins, "The Motif of Real Christianity in the Writings of John Wesley," *The Asbury Theological Journal* 49, no. 1 (Spring 1994): 54.

27. Ibid., 58. "Though Wesley eventually came to realize that the faith of a servant involves *a degree* of acceptance, such faith does not constitute justifying faith." It is also important to note that by 1768, Wesley uses the phrase "the faith of a servant" in both a narrow and a broad sense, for in exceptional cases Wesley recognizes that some may be justified and born of God yet lack the witness of the Spirit due to infirmities. See Collins, *The Scripture Way of Salvation,* 139-42.

28. *Works,* 18:214.

29. In the same journal entry for February 1, 1738, he had called himself an "heir of hell." In 1774 Wesley added in errata the pithy observation "I believe not." Wesley consistently inserted the idea that prior to Aldersgate he had the faith of a servant, though not of a son. Consistent with his more mature theology, he no longer believed that servants of God would necessarily be consigned to hell (*Works,* 18:215).

30. *Works,* "On Faith," 3:497.

31. In "Great Expectations" (in Maddox, *Aldersgate Reconsidered,* 67-69), Heitzenrater discusses Wesley's early struggle with degrees of faith.

32. *Works,* "On the Discoveries of Faith," 4:35. But note that the mature Wesley has not dropped his distinction that both justification and sanctification begin only in the moment we are justified. Servants of God are not under condemnation, but are not justified; and they have not experienced the "proper Christian salvation." See "On Working Out Our Own Salvation," ibid., 3:204.

33. Cobb, *Grace and Responsibility,* 88.

34. *Works,* 9:227.

35. William H. Willimon and Robert L. Wilson discuss denominational decline among United Methodists; see *Rekindling the Flame* (Nashville: Abingdon Press, 1987), 11-24.

36. *Works* (May 24, 1738), 18:243.

37. Ibid. (February 1, 1738), 18:214.

38. See ibid., 18:242.

39. Maddox (*Aldersgate Reconsidered)* suggests the need to interpret Aldersgate in a way that will be more useful for guiding contemporary spirituality. Although the traditional paradigm may work well for contemporary evangelicals, we need to recognize the insights of other Christian traditions in evaluating what happened to Wesley at Aldersgate, so that non-evangelicals can recognize the wisdom and power of Wesley's spiritual quest. Viewing Aldersgate as an example of transvaluing religious conversion could make Aldersgate more accessible to non-evangelicals, while retaining the decisive value and meaning of the experience, without negating the validity and insight of non-evangelical viewpoints.

2. The Transformation of the Human Heart

1. See the opening and concluding essays by Randy L. Maddox in *Aldersgate Reconsidered* for a survey of historic and contemporary viewpoints. Another survey, with a defense of Aldersgate as Wesley's conversion, is found in Kenneth J. Collins, "Twentieth-century Interpretations of

John Wesley's Aldersgate Experience: Coherence or Confusion?" *Wesleyan Theological Journal* 24 (1989):18-31. I am largely in agreement with Collins's interpretation of Aldersgate.

2. This I take to be Albert Outler's main objection to highlighting Aldersgate, although he sees the year 1738 as decisive. See Outler, *John Wesley* (New York: Oxford University Press, 1964), 14. Richard P. Heitzenrater does a fine analysis of Aldersgate, calling for an interpretation of Aldersgate from the standpoint of the mature Wesley in "Great Expectations," in Maddox, *Aldersgate Reconsidered*, 49-91. Outler and Heitzenrater seem to link Aldersgate with assurance. I agree that the later Wesley's perspective should be the appropriate lens for understanding Aldersgate, but would argue he saw it as including the gift of the faith of a child of God, justification, regeneration, and assurance.

3. See, for example, Roberta C. Bondi, "Aldersgate and Patterns of Methodist Spirituality," and David Lowes Watson, "Aldersgate Street and the *General Rules*: The Form and the Power of Methodist Discipleship," in Maddox, *Aldersgate Reconsidered*, 21-48.

4. See Henry H. Knight III, *The Presence of God in the Christian Life: John Wesley and the Means of Grace* (Metuchen, N.J.: Scarecrow Press, 1992).

5. Ole E. Borgen, *John Wesley on the Sacraments* (Grand Rapids: Zondervan Publishing House, 1972), 151.

6. Wesley, *Notes* (Acts 3:19).

7. Borgen, *John Wesley*, 150-51.

8. *Works*, "The Scripture Way of Salvation," 2:157.

9. *Works* (Jackson), Letter to Miss Bishop (October 18, 1778), 13:36.

10. Thomas Albin, "An Empirical Study of Early Methodist Spirituality," in Theodore Runyon, ed., *Wesleyan Theology Today* (Nashville: Abingdon Press, 1995), 163-65.

11. *Works*, "The New Birth," 2:187.

12. *Works*, "The Witness of the Spirit," 1:286.

13. Telford, *Letters*, Letter to Isaac Andrews (January 4, 1784), 7:202.

14. *Works* (May 24, 1738), 18:250.

15. Ibid., "The Witness of the Spirit," 1:274.

16. Ibid. (April 22, 1738), 18:234. See also Wesley's "Letter to 'John Smith' " (December 30, 1745) in *Works*, 26:175-83.

17. *Works*, Letter to "John Smith" (September 28, 1745), 26:158.

18. Ibid., 26:159.

19. *Works*, "The Scripture Way of Salvation," 2:160-61. For a thorough discussion, see Theodore Runyon, *The New Creation* (Nashville: Abingdon Press, 1988), 74-81.

20. Cragg, *Appeals*, 11:106.

21. *Works,* "On Living Without God," 4:171.

22. Ibid., 171. See also "The New Birth" in *Works,* 2:192-93; and "An Earnest Appeal to Men of Reason and Religion," in Cragg, *Appeals,* 48.

23. Cragg, *Appeals,* 48.

24. *Works,* Letter to "John Smith" (March 22, 1748), 26:290.

25. *Works* (Jackson), "Thoughts on God's Sovereignty," 10:363.

26. *Works,* "The Great Privilege of Those That Are Born of God," 1:431-32. See also "The Scripture Way of Salvation" in ibid., 2:158.

27. Ibid., "On Faith (Heb. 11:6)" I.11, 3:497.

28. Ibid., I.10, 497.

29. Ibid., I.12, 497-98. Here I use "faith of a servant" and "faith of a child" in their most normal and frequent sense in Wesley's writings. However, he did recognize exceptional cases (see n. 33 below).

30. Thus Randy Maddox argues that Wesley came to see "faith as justifying from its earliest degree" (*Responsible Grace,* 127). In contrast compare Kenneth J. Collins, *The Scripture Way of Salvation,* 103-5.

31. *Works,* Letter to the Revd. Charles Wesley (July 31, 1747), 26:255. Emphasis mine.

32. Ibid., "The Scripture Way of Salvation," 2:157.

33. Ibid., 2:158. Hence I disagree with Maddox's conclusion that Wesley came "to value the nascent faith of the 'servant of God' as justifying faith" (*Responsible Grace,* 155). In contrast with Maddox, Collins argues that Wesley uses the faith of a servant in two ways: a narrow sense (corresponding to my usage in this chapter) and a broad sense to cover those rare exceptional cases. Thus there would be a few persons truly justified and regenerated who, most likely due to ignorance or infirmities, lack the witness of the Spirit and therefore retain the faith of a servant (*The Scripture Way of Salvation,* 139-42). Maddox takes account of Wesley's unquestionable causal linkage between the witness of the Spirit and the faith of a child of God, so that the absence of one seemingly necessitates the absence of the other.

The issue is to identify what is exceptional about the exceptional cases. Clearly they are converted Christians who lack the witness of the Spirit. Do they thereby lack the faith of children of God? If so, then in these exempt cases the faith of a servant must be redefined from one who fears God and works righteousness to one who has begun to love God and neighbor, or else regeneration will have lost its normal meaning. Could they instead be justified with the faith of a servant but not regenerated? Or could they actually have the faith of a child (trusting in God) along with justification and regeneration, but lack the witness of the Spirit? Each proposal violates a claim Wesley makes about the relationship of the various elements of conversion, but that is precisely why Wesley calls the cases exceptional. The difficulty lies in discerning exactly where that breakage in relationships occurs.

34. This is in agreement with Kenneth Collins, *The Scripture Way of Salvation*, 104.

35. See *Works*, "The Witness of Our Own Spirit," 1:299-313.

36. Ibid., "On Faith (Heb. 11:6)," I.12, 3:497-98.

37. Ibid., "The Scripture Way of Salvation," III.1, 2:162.

38. Wesley, *Notes*, Acts 5:31.

39. *Works*, "The New Birth" 1, 2:187.

40. "A Farther Appeal to Men of Reason and Religion, Part I," III.6, in Cragg, *Appeals, 127-28.*

41. *Works*, "The New Birth," I.1, 2:188.

42. Ibid., 189-90.

43. Ibid., 190.

44. Ibid., 198.

45. Ibid., 194.

46. The major studies of the affections and tempers in Wesley are Gregory S. Clapper, *John Wesley on Religious Affections* (Metuchen, N.J.: Scarecrow Press, 1989); and Richard B. Steele, *"Gracious Affections" and "True Virtue" According to Jonathan Edwards and John Wesley* (Metuchen, N.J.: Scarecrow Press, 1994). Differences over how to relate the terms "affections" and "tempers" are found in Maddox, *Responsible Grace*, 68-70; and Kenneth J. Collins, "John Wesley's Topography of the Heart: Dispositions, Tempers, and Affections," *Methodist History* 36.3 (April 1998): 162-75.

47. *Works*, "The End of Christ's Coming," 2:482-83.

48. Wesley allowed for exceptions, as we have seen, considering Paul's three-day conversion to be unusually lengthy.

49. As shown by Heitzenrater in "Great Expectations," in Maddox, *Aldersgate Reconsidered.*

3. John Wesley and the Fear of Death as a Standard of Conversion

1. *Works*, 1:304.

2. *Works*, 9:78.

3. Charles Wesley, *The Journals of Rev. Charles Wesley*, ed. Thomas Jackson, 2 vols. (London: John Mason, 1949; reprinted Grand Rapids: Baker Book House, 1980), 1:89. Shortly before his own evangelical conversion, Charles Wesley questioned Mrs. Turner in the searching manner so typi-

cal of his brother: "And do you love Christ above all things?" "I do, above all things incomparably." "Then are you willing to die?" "I am; and would be glad to die this moment."

4. Schmidt, *John Wesley,* 1:217-18. Bracketed material is mine.
5. *Works,* 25:265.
6. Cragg, *Appeals,* 136. Emphasis is mine.
7. Shortly after Wesley's return to England from Holland in August 1783, he was seized with "a most impetuous flux." A grain and a half of opium was administered to him in three doses to bring about some relief. This narcotic naturally stopped the cramps that Wesley had been suffering, but it also, to use his own words, "took away my speech, hearing, and power of motion, and locked me up from head to foot, so that I lay a mere log" (*Works,* 23:287).
8. *Works,* 18:140.
9. Ibid., 18:141.
10. Ibid., 18:142.
11. Ibid., 18:143. For more on the fear of death and its connection with real, vital Christianity, see Collins, "Real Christianity," in *The Asbury Theological Journal.*
12. Ibid.
13. Ibid.
14. Ibid., 18:165.
15. Ibid., 18:169.
16. Ibid., 18:207.
17. Ibid. In this context, Wesley assumes that saving faith is inconsistent with the fear of death, the fear that has both torment and anticipates judgment. This means, then, that Wesley may have had some measure of faith during this fearful period, perhaps even the faith of a servant in a broad sense; but the point is that he did not have saving faith, that faith which makes one holy (regeneration).
18. Ibid., 18:211. Interestingly enough, while Wesley was in Georgia he tried to gauge the spiritual experience as well as the sincerity of Sophia Hopkey by questioning her along the lines of the fear of death, as demonstrated by the following: "I asked her, 'Miss Sophy, are not you afraid to die?' She answered calmly, 'No, I don't desire to live any longer. O that God would let me go now! Then I should be at rest. In this world I expect nothing but misery' " (ibid., 18:436).
19. Though the fear of death was no longer an issue for Wesley after Aldersgate, he nevertheless grappled, at least on one occasion, with the prospect of death as oblivion or as extinction. For example, in a letter to his brother Charles in 1766, Wesley wrote: "I have no more fear than love.

Or if I have [any fear, it is not that of falling] into hell but of falling into nothing" (Telford, *Letters*, 5:16).

20. *Works*, 1:110. Moreover, Wesley's later statement (on February 3, 1738)—"Hereby I am delivered from the fear of the sea, which I had both dreaded and abhorred from my youth"—does not necessarily indicate that he was free from all fear of death at this time. Indeed, one can overcome a fear of water or heights, for example, and still have a fear of death, hell, and judgment due to one's spiritual condition.

21. Ibid., 1:122-23.

22. Ibid., 18:271. For helpful treatments on the relation between the Methodist and Moravian movements, see F. Ernest Stoeffler, "Religious Roots of the Early Moravian and Methodist Movements," *Methodist History* 24, no. 3 (April 1986): 132-40; Clifford W. Towlson, *Moravian and Methodist: Relationships and Influences in the Eighteenth Century* (London: Epworth Press, 1957).

23. *Works*, 1:179. This sermon, as well as several other incidents in Wesley's life, clearly reveal that he was not a "peace at all costs" preacher. Much like his father, Samuel, when Wesley believed an important issue of the gospel was at stake, he spoke out boldly. A similar mindset can be discerned in Wesley's departure from the Fetter Lane society, in his publication of the sermon "Free Grace," which roiled George Whitefield, and in his energetic dispute with the Calvinists during 1770 and 1771.

24. Ibid., 1:162.

25. Cragg, *The Appeals*, 146.

26. *Works*, 1:257. For more on Wesley's understanding of eternal loss, see "Of Hell," ibid., 3:31ff. Indeed, the word *hell* appears more than five hundred times in Wesley's writings, a fact that has proved troubling to those modern scholars who hold what can only be termed "sentimental" and therefore unrealistic understandings of "holy love."

27. Ibid., 1:258.

28. Ibid., 1:259. Bracketed material is mine and has been inserted to indicate that the context of this sermon clearly indicates that this material is not autobiographical for John Wesley. The "I," in other words, is a literary device employed to engage the reader and to give existential force to this material.

29. Ibid., 2:19. For more on Wesley's understanding of the moral law and its role in spiritual life in convincing sinners, leading them to Christ, and in offering guidance for growth in grace, see Kenneth J. Collins, "John Wesley's Theology of Law" (Ph.D. diss., Drew University, 1984).

30. Ibid., 2:142.

31. Ibid., 2:207. A descent once more into sin, to be ensnared yet again,

and possibly to one's eternal loss, is a sobering element of Wesley's Arminian theology.

32. *Works,* 21:372.

33. Ibid., 22:357. In this context, Wesley notes that it would be well if this person were attentive to the convincing grace of the Holy Spirit until "he receives the Spirit of adoption."

34. Telford, *Letters,* 7:95.

35. See Collins, *A Real Christian.* Observe, however, that in *A Real Christian* I have reversed the terminology used in my earlier book, *The Scripture Way of Salvation.* In that setting the terms *broad* and *narrow* referred to whether or not the position included justification; that is, the terms did not refer to the numbers entailed. Though this was an apt distinction, I have reversed it in this present context simply because most people invariably think of the numbers of people entailed—and not whether the position includes or excludes justification—when the language of *broad* and *narrow* is used. Now the term *broad* means it includes many people; *narrow* means it does not. This should bring greater clarity to the discussion.

36. *Works,* 4:35-36.

37. For more on these distinctions, especially that the faith of a servant is not justifying faith in each instance, see Collins, *The Scripture Way of Salvation,* 140ff.

38. *Works,* 20:254-55.

39. Ibid., 20:255.

40. Ibid., 21:82-83. For additional details on this execution, see W. Knipe, *Criminal Chronology of York Castle* (York, England, 1867), 64-65.

41. Ibid., 2:481.

42. Ibid., 20:82-83.

43. Ibid. For additional references to assurance and deliverance from the fear of death, see ibid., 1:230-31, 261-62.

44. Ibid., 1:223. For a contemporary treatment that seeks to appropriate the art and manners of an earlier age with respect to "holy dying," see Robert Cecil, "Holy Dying: Evangelical Attitudes to Death," *History Today* 32 (August 1982): 30-34.

45. Ibid., 2:29.

46. Ibid., 4:164. Though one might suspect that Wesley would have linked freedom from the fear of death with Christian perfection, the evidence from this section clearly indicates that he most often associated it with both justification and the new birth. Such a liberty, in Wesley's mind, is entailed in the graces of a child of God and is implied in Paul's observation, "There is therefore now no condemnation for those who are in

Christ Jesus" (Rom. 8:1). In other words, with no condemnation, there is no anxious fear of death and judgment.

47. Ibid., 20:100.

48. Ibid., 19:94. Wesley also records the testimony of Henry Perronet and Charles Greenwood to this magnificent grace of God. See ibid., 22:27; 23:263.

49. Ibid., 21:207-8.

50. *Works* (Jackson), 11:190.

51. For more on the motif of real Christianity and its significance in Wesley's soteriology, see Collins, *A Real Christian*; and Collins, "Real Christianity," in *The Asbury Theological Journal.*

52. Cragg, *Appeals*, 135-36.

53. *Works* (Jackson), 10:479-80.

54. Telford, *Letters*, 6:30-31. As is also characteristic of this period, Wesley asked Ms. Cummins if she had "power over all sin." See also Wesley's journal of March 17, 1772, for an example of his ongoing use of the distinction almost/altogether Christians; his entry of August 12, 1772, for the use of the term "notional" believers; and his letter to Patience Ellison in 1777 where he links the distinction between almost/altogether Christian with being an outside/inside Christian. See *Works*, 22:311 and 345; and Telford, *Letters*, 6:274.

55. Contra Jennings, "John Wesley *Against* Aldersgate," 7. See also Kenneth J. Collins, "Other Thoughts on Aldersgate: Has the Conversionist Paradigm Collapsed?" *Methodist History* 30, no. 1 (October 1991): 10-25.

4. A Real Christian Is an Abolitionist

1. Freeborn Garrettson acquired his unusual first name from his paternal grandmother; it was his grandmother's maiden name. On the life of Garrettson, see Nathan Bangs, *The Life of the Rev. Freeborn Garrettson* (New York: J. Emory and B. Waugh, 1832); Ezra S. Tipple, *Freeborn Garrettson* (New York: Eaton and Mains, 1910); Robert Drew Simpson, ed., *American Methodist Pioneer: The Life and Journals of The Rev. Freeborn Garrettson, 1752–1827* (Rutland, Vt.: Academy Books, 1984); and especially Garrettson's own autobiography, *The Experiences and Travels of Mr. Freeborn Garrettson, Minister of the Methodist Episcopal Church in North America* (Philadelphia: Parry Hall, 1791).

2. Simpson, *American Methodist Pioneer*, 43.

3. Ibid., 42-43.

4. Ibid., 48.

5. Freeborn Garrettson, *Substance of the Semi-centennial Sermon before the New York Annual Conference, at its Session, May, 1826* (New York: Bangs and Emory), 23ff.; Simpson, *American Methodist Pioneer,* 6, 13-14, 17, 25-26, 28.

6. The name "Do-Justice" was taken from Micah 6:8.

7. Freeborn Garrettson, *A Dialogue Between Do-Justice and Professing Christian* (Wilmington, Del.: Peter Brynberg, 1820?).

8. Collins, *A Real Christian,* 102.

9. *Works,* 26:246; 3:527. See also Collins, *A Real Christian,* 87-88, 144-45.

10. Romans 8:15: "For you did not receive a spirit of slavery . . . but you have received a spirit of adoption."

11. Wesley, *Notes,* 382. See also Collins, *A Real Christian,* pp. 86, 102.

12. Garrettson, *A Dialogue Between Do-Justice and Professing Christian,* 44-45, 48-49.

13. On the sociopolitical and ecclesiastical aspects of slavery within American Methodism, see Charles Baumer Swaney, *Episcopal Methodism and Slavery, with Sidelights on Ecclesiastical Politics* (Boston: Richard G. Badger, 1926); Emory S. Bucke, ed., *The History of American Methodism* (New York: Abingdon Press, 1964), 1:251-56; Donald G. Mathews, *Slavery and Methodism: A Chapter in American Morality, 1780–1845* (Princeton: Princeton University Press, 1965); and John H. Wigger, *Taking Heaven by Storm: Methodism and the Rise of Popular Christianity in America* (New York: Oxford University Press, 1998), 125-50. Russell E. Richey reminds us that although early Methodism affirmed antislavery, it was also rife with racism. See Richey, *Early American Methodism* (Bloomington: Indiana University Press, 1991), 58-59.

14. On the concept of conversion in early American Methodism, see Bucke, *History of American Methodism,* 1:291-307; Richey, *Early American Methodism,* 84-85; Wigger, *Taking Heaven by Storm,* 106-10; Charles W. Ferguson, *Organizing to Beat the Devil: Methodists and the Making of America* (Garden City, N.Y.: Doubleday, 1971), 86-93; Dickson D. Bruce Jr., *And They All Sang Hallelujah: Plain-Folk Camp-Meeting Religion, 1800–1845* (Knoxville: University of Tennessee Press, 1974), 61-69; A. Gregory Schneider, *The Way of the Cross Leads Home: The Domestication of American Methodism* (Bloomington: Indiana University Press, 1993), 42-45; Lester Ruth, " 'A Little Heaven Below': Quarterly Meetings as Seasons of Grace in Early American Methodism" (Ph.D. diss., University of Notre Dame, 1996), 86-104.

15. Bucke, *History of American Methodism,* 1:313-15.

16. Robert Baird, *Religion in the United States of America, Or an Account of the Origin, Progress, Relations to the State, and Present Condition of the*

Evangelical Churches in the United States. With Notices of the Unevangelical Denominations (Glasgow: Blackie and Son, 1844), 605.

17. Frank Baker, *From Wesley to Asbury: Studies in Early American Methodism* (Durham, N.C.: Duke University Press, 1976), 189-97; Richey, *Early American Methodism*, 2-5, 75-80.

18. Bruce, *And They All Sang Hallelujah*, 6-89; Laura S. Haviland, *A Woman's Life-Work: Labors and Experiences of Laura S. Haviland*, 4th ed. (Chicago: Publishing Association of Friends, 1889), 15.

19. Ruth, " 'A Little Heaven Below,' " 223-43.

20. Garrettson, *A Dialogue Between Do-Justice and Professing Christian*, 44; James P. Horton, *A Narrative of the Early Life, Remarkable Conversion, and Spiritual Labors of James P. Horton* (n.p.: 1839), 85-86.

21. John G. Fee to the Kentucky Constitutional Convention [1849?], John G. Fee papers, Berea College, Berea, Ky. (Though later a Presbyterian, Fee was converted by Methodists in 1830; see John G. Fee, *Autobiography of John G. Fee* [Chicago: National Christian Association, 1891], 12.) Marcus Swift, "Address of the Wesleyan Methodist Annual Conference," *Signal of Liberty* 31 (October 1842).

22. Haviland, *A Woman's Life-Work*, 19, 27.

23. Ibid., 27, 33.

24. Francis Asbury, *The Journal and Letters of Francis Asbury*, eds. Elmer T. Clark, J. Manning Potts, and Jacob S. Payton (Nashville: Abingdon Press, 1958); entry for December 11, 1797.

25. Methodist Episcopal Church, *The Doctrines and Discipline of the Methodist Episcopal Church in America. With Explanatory Notes, by Thomas Coke and Francis Asbury* (Philadelphia: Henry Tuckniss, 1798), 86; Billy Hibbard, *Memoirs* (New York: Billy Hibbard, 1825), 99.

26. Bucke, *History of American Methodism*, 1:309.

27. Bruce, *And They All Sang Hallelujah*, 62-69; Schneider, *The Way of the Cross*, 43.

28. The uniqueness of the Methodist conceptualization of holiness faded by the 1830s when other evangelicals adopted a version of sanctification that was somewhat similar to the popular Methodist view. For the appropriation of Methodist understandings of sanctification by American Christians in the 1830s and 1840s, and especially by abolitionists, see Douglas M. Strong, *Perfectionist Politics: Abolitionism and the Religious Tensions of American Democracy* (Syracuse: Syracuse University Press, 1999), 29-40.

29. Asbury, *Journal*; entry for August 10, 1774.

30. Simpson, *American Methodist Pioneer*, 48; Haviland, *A Woman's Life-Work*, 21; Baker, *From Wesley to Asbury*, 187-88.

31. Haviland, *A Woman's Life-Work*, 28; Garrettson, *A Dialogue Between*

Do-Justice and Professing Christian, 45, 52; John McLean, *Sketch of Rev. Philip Gatch* (Cincinnati: Swornstedt and Poe, 1854), 12-13, 17-18.

32. Fee, *Autobiography*, 13, 15; Bucke, *History of American Methodism*, 1:288-89.

33. Haviland, *A Woman's Life-Work*, 35-36; Simpson, *American Methodist Pioneer*, 17, 28; Strong, *Perfectionist Politics*, 52-53, 104-5.

34. John Wesley, *Thoughts Upon Slavery* (London: 1774); Mathews, *Slavery and Methodism*, 5-8.

35. Garrettson, *A Dialogue Between Do-Justice and Professing Christian*, 41-55. Garrettson wrote (p. 48) that he had "heard many say, till the Methodists came, they never had an idea that it was a sin to keep slaves."

36. *Friend of Man* 1 (May 5, 1837): 182; *Lutheran Herald* 1 (January 8, 1845): n.p.

37. Simpson, *American Methodist Pioneer*, 234.

38. Mathews, *Slavery and Methodism*, 166.

39. Garrettson, *A Dialogue Between Do-Justice and Professing Christian*, 51; J. N. T. Tucker, ed., *Liberty Almanac, for 1844* (Syracuse: I. A. Hopkins, 1844), 15. See also Orange Scott, *The Methodist E. Church and Slavery* (Boston: O. Scott, 1844), 72-98, 126.

40. Haviland, *A Woman's Life-Work*, 15-20.

41. Ibid., 32-37; Harmon Camburn, "Early School Days: The Rise, Development, and Decadence of Raisin Seminary," Laura S. Haviland papers, Bentley Historical Library, Ann Arbor, Mich.

5. Conversion and Sanctification in Nineteenth-century African American Wesleyan Women

1. For a discussion of the belief system of the slaves, see Albert J. Raboteau, *Slave Religion: The "Invisible Institution" in the Antebellum South* (New York: Oxford University Press, 1978).

2. Julia Foote, "A Brand Plucked from the Fire: An Autobiographical Sketch by Mrs. Julia A. Foote," in *Sisters of the Spirit: The Black Women's Autobiographies of the Nineteenth Century*, ed. William L. Andrews (Bloomington: Indiana University Press, 1986), 183.

3. Foote, Smith, Lee, and Elaw wrote autobiographies. Information about Tubman comes from several biographical works. Additionally, there is an excellent biography on Smith by Adrienne M. Israel, *Amanda Berry Smith: From Washerwoman to Evangelist*, Studies in Evangelicalism, no. 16 (Metuchen, N.J.: Scarecrow Press, 1998).

4. Jarena Lee, *The Life and Religious Experiences of Jarena Lee* (Philadelphia: Jarena Lee, 1836), 1.

5. Ibid.
6. Ibid., 2.
7. Ibid., 4.
8. Ibid., 4-5.
9. Ibid., 5.
10. Ibid., 7-8.
11. Ibid., 9.
12. Ibid., 11.
13. Zilpha Elaw, "Memoirs of the Life, Religious Experience, Ministerial Travels, and Labors of Mrs. Zilpha Elaw: An American Female of Colour," in Andrews, *Sisters of the Spirit, 54.*
14. Ibid., 55.
15. Ibid., 56.
16. Ibid., 56-57.
17. Ibid., 57.
18. Ibid., 66-67.
19. Julia A. Foote, "A Brand Plucked from the Fire: An Autobiographical Sketch by Mrs. Julia A. Foote," in Andrews, *Sisters of the Spirit*, 169-70.
20. Ibid., 177.
21. An experience common to Holiness revival religion in which a person is believed to be overpowered by the Holy Spirit to the point that he or she becomes totally conscious of God and loses consciousness of the material world and falls to the floor. The experience, which lasts from a few moments to several hours, is so called because the person often takes on the appearance of a dead or gravely ill person.
22. Foote, "A Brand Plucked from the Fire," 180.
23. Ibid., 182.
24. Ibid.
25. Ibid., 183.
26. Ibid.
27. Ibid., 184-85.
28. Ibid., 186.
29. Ibid., 191.
30. Ibid., 186-87.
31. Amanda Berry Smith, *An Autobiography: The Story of the Lord's Dealing with Mrs. Amanda Smith, the Colored Evangelist* (Chicago: Afro-American Press, 1969), 43.
32. Ibid., 29.
33. Ibid., 27-28.
34. Ibid., 42.

35. Ibid., 44.
36. Ibid.
37. Ibid., 45-46.
38. Ibid., 46-47.
39. Ibid., 49.
40. Ibid., 76.
41. Ibid., 79.
42. Ibid., 84.
43. Even though all four women were married at some point, only Jarena Lee and Amanda Berry Smith experienced anything like a normal home life. Lee was married to an AME preacher. Smith's first husband went off to fight in the Civil War and never returned. Her second husband was an ordained deacon in the AME church. Harriet Tubman's husband refused to accompany her on her journey to freedom, and upon her return she found that he had married someone else. She never remarried. Elaw had married a man who previously professed Christianity but after the wedding attempted to get her to renounce her religious beliefs.
44. Cornel West, *Prophesy Deliverance: An Afro-American Revolutionary Christianity* (Philadelphia: Westminster Press, 1982), 35-36.
45. Ibid.
46. Smith, *An Autobiography*, 80.
47. Andrews, *Sisters of the Spirit*, 15.

6. "To Turn from Darkness to Light" (Acts 26:18)

1. Most recently, see Thomas M. Finn, *From Death to Rebirth: Ritual and Conversion in Antiquity* (Mahwah, N.J.: Paulist Press, 1997); and Philip Rousseau, "Conversion," in *The Oxford Classical Dictionary*, 3d ed., ed. Simon Hornblower and Antony Spawforth (Oxford: Oxford University Press, 1996), 386-87. The difficulties inherent in defining terms in a study of "conversion" in the New Testament are often acknowledged—for example, Beverly Roberts Gaventa, *From Darkness to Light: Aspects of Conversion in the New Testament*, Overtures to Biblical Theology 20 (Philadelphia: Fortress Press, 1986), esp. 1-16; Richard V. Peace, *Conversion in the New Testament: Paul and the Twelve* (Grand Rapids: Wm. B. Eerdmans, 1999), 1-14.
2. Jacques Dupont ("Conversion in the Acts of the Apostles," in *The Salvation of the Gentiles: Essays on the Acts of the Apostles* [New York: Paulist Press, 1979], 61-84) claims that conversion in Acts belongs to the moral category, as opposed to the cognitive category, of conversion. Charles H. Talbert ("Conversion in the Acts of the Apostles: Ancient Auditors'

Perceptions," in *Literary Studies in Luke-Acts: Essays in Honor of Joseph B. Tyson*, ed. Richard O. Thompson and Thomas E. Phillips [Macon, Ga.: Mercer University Press, 1998], 141-53) modified this conclusion by insisting that both moral and cognitive types of conversion are found in Acts. The possibility of such a distinction is exploited in the work of J.-W. Taeger (*Der Mensch und sein Heil: Studien zum Bild des Menschen und zur Sicht der Bekehrung bei Lukas*, StNT 14 [Gütersloh: Gerd Mohn, 1982]), for whom the human situation in Lukan thought is ignorance needing correction, not sin needing forgiveness (see now the important counterproposal of Christoph W. Stenschke, *Luke's Portrait of the Gentiles Prior to Their Coming to Faith*, WUNT 2:108 [Tübingen: J.C.B. Mohr (Paul Siebeck), 1999]). My formulation questions whether Luke would allow for any meaningful line to be drawn between the cognitive and the moral.

3. Cf. Acts 2:38; 3:17-20; 5:31; 13:38-41. Martin Dibelius ("The Speeches in Acts and Ancient Historiography," in *Studies in the Acts of the Apostles* [London: SCM Press, 1956], 138-85 [165]) observes that the exhortation to repentance is stereotypical in the speeches in Acts; cf. Petr Pokorny, *Theologie der lukanischen Schriften*, FRLANT 174 (Göttingen: Vandenhoeck & Ruprecht, 1998), 122-24.

4. Cf. Jeremiah 3:12-16; 7:3-25; 14:6-7; Ezekiel 18:30; Zechariah 1:3; 7:8-10; Malachi 3:7; Odil Hannes Steck, *Israel und das gewalstsame Geschick der Propheten*, WMANT 23 (Neukirchen-Vluyn: Neukirchener, 1967).

5. This has also been observed by Hans F. Bayer, "The Preaching of Peter in Acts," in *Witness to the Gospel: The Theology of Acts*, ed. I. Howard Marshall and David Peterson (Grand Rapids: Wm. B. Eerdmans, 1998), 257-74 (262-65).

6. To what degree is a conversion from idolatry the same for Jew and Gentile? For the Gentile, such conversion had immediate and far-reaching social consequences, since this entailed withdrawal from pagan, and thus separation from, ordinary social life (see Martin Goodman, *Mission and Conversion: Proselytizing in the Religious History of the Roman Empire* [Oxford: Clarendon Press, 1994], 104-5). This was less true for the Jew, at least in the period covered by Luke's narrative.

7. See *Joseph and Aseneth* 8:10; 15:12; 1 Thessalonians 5:4-7; Colossians 1:12-13; Ephesians 5:8; 1 Peter 2:9; Dennis Hamm, "Sight to the Blind: Vision as Metaphor in Luke," *Biblica* 67 (1986) 457-77. See also Isaiah 42:7, 16 and Luke 2:32. Some scholars (for example, Luke Timothy Johnson, *The Acts of the Apostles*, Sacra Pagina 5 [Collegeville, Minn.: Liturgical Press, 1992], 436-37) take Luke's εἰς οὓς as a reference to the Gentiles alone, but a Pauline mission inclusive of Gentiles and Jews is supported by the Isaianic echoes, by Luke 1:78-79, and by Acts 26:20, 23. See Jacob

Jervell, *Die Apostelgeschichte*, KEK 3 (Göttingen: Vandenhoeck & Ruprecht, 1998), 594.

8. This point is underscored in Gaventa, *From Darkness to Light*, 52-129. See also Robert F. O'Toole, *The Unity of Luke's Theology: An Analysis of Luke-Acts*, Good News Studies 9 (Wilmington, Del.: Michael Glazier, 1984), 191-224. Contra Ulrich Wilckens, *Die Missionsreden der Apostelgeschichte: Form- und traditionsgeschichtliche Untersuchungen*, 3d ed., WMANT 5 (Neukirchen-Vluyn: Neukirchener, 1974), 180-82.

9. See also Luke 3:10-14. Dupont ("Conversion," 62-69) argues that a prerequisite to conversion is a "sense of sin," and finds the impetus for such questions as these in a kerygma oriented toward addressing the "ugliness of sin." To the contrary, as is most evident in Luke 3:1-20 and Acts 2:1-41, the fundamental kerygmatic concern is with God's restorative initiative; what is at stake is a radical reformation of worldview. John's message, like Peter's, is that his audience, while thinking that they were living in ways congruent with the ancient purpose of God, have actually failed to understand that purpose; persuaded that this is the case, they inquire, "What, then, shall we do?"

10. See Ronald D. Witherup, *Conversion in the New Testament*, Zaccaheus Studies: New Testament (Collegeville, Minn.: Liturgical Press, 1994), 44-47.

11. Cf. Leviticus 14–15; Isaiah 1:16-17; Zechariah 13:1; *Jubilees* 1:22-25; *Sibylline Oracles* 4.162-70; 1QS (*Serek Hayahad*) 3:6-9. On the question of Jewish precursors to John's baptism, it is telling that the ambiguous evidence for proselyte baptism leads two recent studies to completely disparate conclusions. Robert L. Webb (*John the Baptizer and Prophet: A Socio-Historical Study*, Journal for the Study of the New Testament—Supplement Series 62 [Sheffield: Sheffield Academic Press, 1991]) insists that the immersion of proselytes does not antedate the baptisms of John and the earliest Christian communities, while Joan E. Taylor (*The Immerser: John the Baptist Within Second Temple Judaism*, Studying the Historical Jesus [Grand Rapids: Wm. B. Eerdmans, 1997]) takes the opposite view. See the summary in David S. Dockery, "Baptism," in *Dictionary of Jesus and the Gospels*, ed. Joel B. Green and Scot McKnight (Downers Grove, Ill.: InterVarsity Press, 1992), 55-58.

12. Arnold van Gennep, *The Rites of Passage* (London: Routledge & Kegan Paul, 1960); see also the helpful discussion of this and related issues in Ellen Juhl Christiansen, "Taufe als Initiation in der Apostelgeschichte," *Studia theologica* 40 (1986): 55-79.

13. The incomplete nature of the act of conversion is emphasized in

Francis S. Hegel, " 'Conversion' and 'Repentance' in Lucan Theology," *The Bible Today* 37 (1968): 2596-602.

14. See the helpful discussion in Wayne A. Meeks, *The Origins of Christian Morality: The First Two Centuries* (New Haven, Conn.: Yale University Press, 1993), 18-36.

15. Meeks, *Origins of Christian Morality*, 36.

16. See George Panikulam, *Koinonia in the New Testament: A Dynamic Expression of Christian Life*, Analecta biblica 85 (Rome: Biblical Institute, 1979), 111-12; Lindy Scott, *Economic Koinonia Within the Body of Christ* (México: Kyrios, 1980) 70, 108.

17. See Friedrich Wilhelm Horn, *Glaube und Handeln in der Theologie des Lukas*, 2d ed., GTA 26 (Göttingen: Vandenhoeck & Ruprecht, 1986), 46.

7. New Creation or New Birth?

1. See Ben Witherington III, "Praeparatio Evangelicii: The Theological Roots of Wesley's View of Evangelism," in *Theology and Evangelism in the Wesleyan Heritage* , ed. J. Logan (Nashville: Abingdon Press, 1993), 51-80.

2. See Ben Witherington III, "The Waters of Birth: John 3:5 and 1 John 5:6-8," *New Testament Studies* 35 (1989): 155-60.

3. John Wesley, *Sermons on Several Occasions* (London: Wesleyan Methodist Book Room, n.d.), 236; emphasis added.

4. The old debate of whether *anothen* in John 3 means "again" or "above" is not finally a matter that can be settled, though the former rendering makes better sense in the context of the discussion between Jesus and Nicodemus. The author makes clear by other means that he is referring to a birth that comes from God.

5. Wesley, *Sermons*, "The Marks of the New Birth," 248-49.

6. Ibid., 247.

7. It is an interesting fact that in the Standard Sermon entitled "The Means of Grace," Wesley lists prayer, searching the Scriptures, and receiving the Lord's Supper, but *not* baptism. This cannot be because he assumed every one in his audience was baptized as an infant, for there were non-Conformists in his audience for whom this was not true. It rather reflects where the heart of the matter was with Wesley; namely, it had to do with spiritual experience that comes through faith.

8. I. H. Marshall, *The Epistles of John* (Grand Rapids: Wm. B. Eerdmans, 1978), 186.

9. Wesley, *Sermons*, "The Great Privilege," 248.

10. Ibid., 249.

11. Ibid., 252.

12. Ibid., 258.

13. Marshall, *Epistles*, 184-85.

14. See Ben Witherington III, *Paul's Narrative Thought World: The Tapestry of Tragedy and Triumph* (Louisville: Westminster Press, 1994), 23-28, where another form of these observations appears.

15. See, for example, E. P. Sanders, *Paul and Palestinian Judaism* (London: SCM Press, 1977), 474ff.

16. See K. Stendahl's famous influential article, "The Apostle Paul and the Introspective Consciousness of the West," *Harvard Theological Review* 56 (1963): 199-215.

17. Here I am relying on the telegraphic exposition of Romans 7 found in Wesley's *Notes*, ad loc.

18. Emphasis added.

19. See "Salvation by Faith," in *Works*, 1:109-30.

20. For another form of this argument see Witherington, *Paul's Narrative Thought World*, 258-60.

21. Wesley, *Sermons*, "Justification by Faith," 62-63.

8. A Mutuality Model of Conversion

1. See Paul S. Fiddes, *The Creative Suffering of God* (Oxford: Clarendon Press, 1988).

2. See Barry L. Callen, *God as Loving Grace: The Biblically Revealed Nature and Work of God* (Nappanee, Ind.: Evangel Publishing House, 1996).

3. Gilbert W. Stafford, "Salvation in the General Epistles," in John E. Hartley and R. Larry Shelton, eds., *Wesleyan Theological Perspectives: Salvation* (Anderson, Ind.: Warner Press, 1981), 209-10.

4. John Sanders, *The God Who Risks: A Theology of Providence* (Downers Grove, Ill.: InterVarsity Press, 1998), 244. If God were completely unconditioned, it surely would be necessary to reinterpret radically our traditional understandings of divine promising and covenanting, since the usual approach to these concepts entails conditionality in God. See Nicholas Wolterstorff, *Divine Discourse: Philosophical Reflections on the Claim That God Speaks* (New York: Cambridge University Press, 1995), 97-103.

5. This trajectory is affirmed by theologians like Clark H. Pinnock. See Barry L. Callen, *Clark H. Pinnock: Journey Toward Renewal* (Nappanee, Ind.: Evangel Publishing House, 2000) for an extensive recounting of Pinnock's intellectual journey away from a scholasticized Calvinism, including his insistence that this journey has been inspired biblically at every point.

6. Norman Geisler, *Chosen But Free: A Balanced View of Divine Election* (Minneapolis: Bethany House Publishers, 1999), 209ff.

7. Kenneth J. Collins, "The New Birth: John Wesley's Doctrine," *Wesleyan Theological Journal* 32, no. 1 (Spring 1997): 59-60.

8. From John Wesley's sermon "The New Birth."

9. See Stanley Hauerwas and William H. Willimon, *Resident Aliens: Life in the Christian Colony* (Nashville: Abingdon Press, 1989).

10. See Harold Bender, "The Anabaptist Vision," *Mennonite Quarterly Review*, 18 (1944): 67-88.

11. John Oyer, *Lutheran Reformers Against the Anabaptists* (The Hague: Martinus Nijhoff, 1964), 212.

12. Note that Randy L. Maddox (*Responsible Grace*) views the whole of the theological burden of John Wesley within this emphasis of Menno.

13. Howard Snyder, *The Radical Wesley and Patterns for Church Renewal* (Downers Grove, Ill.: InterVarsity Press, 1980), 147.

14. Hymn "O Church of God," in *Worship the Lord: Hymnal of the Church of God* (Anderson, Ind.: Warner Press, 1989), 289.

15. Menno Simons, *The True Christian Faith* (c. 1541), as in *The Complete Writings of Menno Simons* (Scottdale, Pa.: Herald Press, 1956), 343.

16. Clark Pinnock, *Flame of Love: A Theology of the Holy Spirit* (Downers Grove, Ill.: InterVarsity Press, 1996), 113-14.

17. The intellectual journey of Clark H. Pinnock is chronicled in a biography written by Barry L. Callen and titled *Clark H. Pinnock: Journey Toward Renewal* (Nappanee, Ind.: Evangel Publishing House, 2000).

18. Mildred Bangs Wynkoop, "John Wesley: Mentor or Guru?," *Wesleyan Theological Journal* (Spring 1975): 7. See Appendix D of Callen, *Clark H. Pinnock*, where Pinnock reflects on the trauma experienced as he has sought to renew in more relational categories the view of God's nature and way with humans. He observes: "Had I been a Wesleyan, I might have had an easier time of it."

19. Philip R. Meadows, "Providence, Chance, and the Problem of Suffering," *Wesleyan Theological Journal* 72 (Fall 1999): 62-63.

20. Henry H. Knight III, *A Future for Truth: Evangelical Theology in a Postmodern World* (Nashville: Abingdon Press, 1997), 172.

21. Randy L. Maddox, "John Wesley and Eastern Orthodoxy," *Asbury Theological Journal* 45, no. 2 (1990): 39.

22. Note H. Ray Dunning, *Redefining the Divine Image: Christian Ethics in Wesleyan Perspective* (Downers Grove, Ill.: InterVarsity Press, 1998). He writes chapters on the "image of God" as relation to God, others, the Earth, and self.

23. Randy L. Maddox, review of Pinnock's *The Scripture Principle* (1984), in the *Wesleyan Theological Journal* (Spring/Fall 1986): 204-5.

24. Clark Pinnock, *The Scripture Principle* (San Francisco: Harper & Row, 1984), 101-3.

25. Clark Pinnock, "Evangelicals and Inerrancy: The Current Debate," *Theology Today* 35, no. 1 (April 1978): 68. Pinnock points with appreciation to the example of the letter of Timothy L. Smith to *The Christian Century* (March 2, 1977).

26. For the record of Clark Pinnock's own theological journey, see Barry L. Callen, *Clark H. Pinnock.*

27. See Randy L. Maddox, "Reading Wesley as a Theologian," *Wesleyan Theological Journal* 30, no. 1 (Spring 1995): 7-54. Also see Maddox, "The Recovery of Theology as a Practical Discipline," *Theological Studies* 51, no. 4 (December 1990): 650-72.

28. Clark Pinnock, "The Great Jubilee," in Michael Bauman, ed., *God and Man: Perspectives on Christianity in the 20th Century* (Hillsdale, Mich.: Hillsdale College Press, 1995), 97.

29. Colin Williams, *John Wesley's Theology Today* (New York: Abingdon Press, 1960), 44. Wesley remained on the edge of Calvinism in that he also attributed all good to the free grace of God and denied the presence of all natural free will and human power antecedent to divine grace.

30. William J. Abraham, *The Coming Great Revival: Recovering the Full Evangelical Tradition* (San Francisco: Harper & Row, 1984), 65-66.

31. Clark Pinnock, "From Augustine to Arminius: A Pilgrimage in Theology," in Clark Pinnock, gen. ed., *The Grace of God and the Will of Man* (Minneapolis: Bethany House Publishers, 1989), 19.

32. See Daniel B. Clendenin, *Eastern Orthodox Christianity: A Western Perspective* (Grand Rapids: Baker Books, 1994); and Bishop Kallistos Ware, *The Orthodox Way,* rev. ed. (Crestwood, N.Y.: St. Vladimir's Seminary Press, 1995).

33. Maddox, "John Wesley and Eastern Orthodoxy," 35. Maddox develops Wesley's whole theological vision around the concept of "responsible grace" in *Responsible Grace.*

34. See, for example, Albert C. Outler, "The Place of Wesley in the Christian Tradition," in K. A. Rowe, ed., *The Place of Wesley in the Christian Tradition* (Metuchen, N.J.: Scarecrow Press, 1976), 30.

35. It is to be recalled that the teachings of John Calvin himself and what later was formalized as "Calvinism" (for example, at the Synod of Dort in 1618–1619) are not always identical.

36. Clark Pinnock was influenced by I. Howard Marshall's examination of the security issue (Marshall, *Kept by the Power of God,* [London: Epworth Press, 1969]).

37. See Barry L. Callen, *Faithful in the Meantime: A Biblical View of Final*

Things and Present Responsibilities (Nappanee, Ind.: Evangel Publishing House, 1997), 77-81. Callen affirms the both/and synergism of the saving grace of God and rejects on biblical grounds the claim that God enters into unconditioned covenants with individuals or nations, including Israel (p. 78).

38. Clark Pinnock, "From Augustine to Arminius," 18. Pinnock's colleague and friend John Sanders was traveling a similar road. The shift in theistic view first came to him through Bible reading, especially in relation to petitionary prayer. Why pray in a petitionary way if God already has determined everything? To the contrary, he observed, there is a divine-human mutuality (see Sanders, *The God Who Risks* [Downers Grove, Ill.: InterVarsity Press, 1998]). While Pinnock was supplementing his Bible reading with Wesleyan, Pentecostal, and Process sources, and finding there much support for an open free-will theism, Sanders was finding the same support by reading select Dutch Reformed sources, especially Vincent Brümmer.

39. Pinnock, *Flame of Love*, 113.

40. *Works* (Jackson), 10:364.

41. R. Larry Shelton, "A Covenant Concept of Atonement," in *Wesleyan Theological Journal* 19, no. 1 (Spring 1984): 91. Emphasis added.

9. Conversion and Baptism in Wesleyan Spirituality

1. I have used the expression, for instance, in an article relevant to the current study ("Baptism and New Birth: Evangelical Theology and the United Methodist 'Baptismal Covenant I,' " *Quarterly Review* 10, no. 3 [Fall 1990]: 34-45), but the idea is not original. (See Robin Maas, "Wesleyan Spirituality" in Robin Maas and Gabriel O'Donovan, O.P., eds., *Spiritual Traditions for the Contemporary Church* [Nashville: Abingdon Press, 1990], 303-19, esp. the first paragraph on p. 303.) I would note that Charles R. Hohenstein published a helpful article in response to mine ("New Birth Through Water and the Spirit: A Reply to Ted A. Campbell," *Quarterly Review* 11, no. 2 [Summer 1991]: 103-12), and this article is, among other things, an attempt to continue that discussion in a different context.

2. My use of a lowercase *c* for "catholic" is simply to avoid the identification of the catholic tradition in spirituality solely with Roman Catholic spiritual traditions. Here I have reference to a broader set of spiritual and theological traditions that include Eastern Christian traditions and, with respect to the issues considered here, appear in both Lutheran and Anglican traditions in their own ways.

3. Bernard G. Holland, *Baptism in Early Methodism* (London: Epworth Press, 1970), the title of the first chapter (p. 3).

4. John Baillie, *Baptism and Conversion* (New York: Scribner, 1963), cited in Holland, *Baptism in Early Methodism*, 9.

5. Council of Trent, "Decree Concerning Justification," chapter 7, in John Leith, ed., *Creeds of the Churches: A Reader in Christian Doctrine from the Bible to the Present*, 3d ed. (Atlanta: John Knox Press, 1982), 412.

6. Martin Luther, "The Babylonian Captivity of the Church," trans. A. T. W. Steinhäuser, in *Martin Luther: Three Treatises*, 2d rev. ed. (Philadelphia: Fortress Press, 1970), 178-206.

7. *Book of Common Prayer* (1662), service for the "Publick Baptism of Infants"; in W. M. Campion and W. J. Beamont, eds., *The Book of Common Prayer Interleaved with Historical Illustrations and Explanatory Notes Arranged Parallel to the Text*, 10th ed. (London, Oxford, and Cambridge: Rivingtons, 1880), 186.

8. *Works*, 1:242-43. I acknowledge the controversy over whether or not Wesley's Aldersgate experience should be described as a "conversion" experience, but Wesley's own language in the conclusion to the previous fascicle of the journal—which acknowledges that at the time of the writing of the first and second fascicles he did not consider himself to have been "converted unto God" (see February 1, 1738 journal entry, ibid., 1:214) "makes it quite natural to see the account of Aldersgate as a "conversion" experience; however, Wesley may have altered his views as to whether he then received the "assurance of pardon" at that time.

9. *Works*, "The New Birth," 2:197.

10. See Holland, *Baptism and Early Methodism*, 53-71; Williams, *John Wesley's Theology Today*, 116-19; Collins, *The Scripture Way of Salvation*, 126-27.

11. Frederick Hockin, *John Wesley and Modern Methodism* (London: Rivingtons, 1887), 85ff.; cited in Holland, *Baptism in Early Methodism*, 6-7.

12. William H. Willimon, *Remember Who You Are: Baptism, a Model for Christian Life* (Nashville: Upper Room, 1980), 60, 82-93; see also Willimon's *Worship as Pastoral Care* (Nashville: Abingdon Press, 1979), 149-51.

13. Hohenstein, "New Birth Through Water and the Spirit," 105.

14. See Willimon's "How to Be Born Again," in *Remember Who You Are* (pp. 82-93) and his discussion of baptismal "death" (pp. 94-104).

15. See Ted A. Campbell, *The Religion of the Heart* (Columbia: University of South Carolina Press, 1991), 88-91 and 121-24.

16. August Hermann Francke's sermon "If and How One May Be Certain That One Is a Child of God" (1707), cited in Peter C. Erb, ed., *Pietists: Selected Writings*, Classics of Western Spirituality (New York: Paulist Press, 1983), 147.

17. This is one of the most frequent points for pugnacious, and I think misguided, allegations between advocates of Evangelical and catholic spiritualities. Advocates of sacramental spiritualities accuse Evangelicals of contempt for the objective power of God available in the sacraments, and an arrogant bending of Christianity to their own experience. Internally, Evangelical spirituality appears quite different, stressing the objective power of God (outside of the individual) as the only transformative power that can deliver one from self-love. On their part, however, Evangelicals have often accused advocates of sacramental spirituality of relying on mere human works and ecclesial institutions as a ruse for avoiding the direct encounter with the divine. Neither of these sorts of polemics reveals much deep understanding of the spiritual traditions of the other. I think I am right in saying that both traditions, in their own ways, stress the objective power of God but locate this power in quite different areas.

18. *Works*, "The New Birth," 2:196, 197.

19. Ibid., 2:196-97. Wesley cites the catechism.

20. Ibid., "On the Great Privilege of Those That Are Born of God," 1:431-43. Wesley mentions that the new birth is "not barely the being baptized" (ibid., 432).

21. Ibid., "The Original, Nature, Properties, and Use of the Law," 2:16.

22. Ibid., "The Marks of the New Birth," 1:417-30; and "The First Fruits of the Spirit," ibid., 1:234-47. In the former sermon Wesley notes that regeneration is "ordinarily annexed to baptism" (Introduction, par. 1, ibid., 417).

23. Holland, *Baptism in Early Methodism*, 7. For Wesley's revision of the *Prayer Book* service for infant baptism, see Charles R. Hohenstein's "The Revisions of the Rites of Baptism in the Methodist Episcopal Church, 1784–1939" (Ph.D. diss., University of Notre Dame, 1990), pp. 52, 248-53. The prayer in question is given on p. 253.

24. Robert A. Prichard, *A History of the Episcopal Church* (Harrisburg, Pa.: Morehouse Publishing, 1991), 89.

25. William R. Cannon, *The Theology of John Wesley, with Special Reference to the Doctrine of Justification* (Nashville and New York: Abingdon-Cokesbury Press, 1946), 129. See also Holland, *Baptism in Early Methodism*, 9. Collins makes much the same point in *The Scripture Way of Salvation*, 129.

26. Holland, *Baptism in Early Methodism*, 151.

27. Williams, *John Wesley's Theology Today*, 115-22; Holland, *Baptism in Early Methodism*, 53-71 ("Infant Baptism and the Two Regenerations"). I would also avoid Randy L. Maddox's attempt to distinguish between

"new birth" and "regeneration" (*Responsible Grace,* 159-60, 176-77). The distinction seems forced and is contrary to the meaning of *regeneratio,* literally "rebirth," and to Wesley's own writings, which typically equate the two. For instance, Wesley's "On God's Vineyard" (1787) takes "born again," "born from above," and "born of the Spirit" to be synonyms for *regeneration* (*Works,* 3:506).

28. Wesley, *Notes,* John 3:5.

29. Holland, *Baptism in Early Methodism,* 5-6. See the concluding quotation of Luther on p. 151; there are several references to Luther in Holland's work, none to Calvin.

30. On the influence of Reformed theology and spirituality in eighteenth-century Anglicanism, see John Walsh and Stephen Taylor, "The Church and Anglicanism in the 'Long' Eighteenth Century" (in John Walsh, Colin Haydon, and Stephen Taylor, eds., *The Church of England, c. 1689–c. 1833: From Toleration to Tractarianism* [Cambridge: Cambridge University Press, 1993], 29-45), where Walsh and Taylor point out that eighteenth-century Anglicans could be Tories with respect to politics, and yet Reformed with respect to their theological convictions.

31. Westminster Confession 28, in Leith, *Creeds,* 224-25.

32. Anglican Articles of Religion, no. 27, in ibid., 275-76.

33. Even the expression "they that receive Baptism rightly" in the Anglican Article may indicate an acknowledgement of the "receptionist" tendency of Reformed sacramental theology (seen explicitly in Article 29, which had been added to the original 38 Articles in 1571). There is a longstanding question of whether John Wesley himself was responsible for all the alterations of the Articles of Religion (and the same issue applies to the revisions of the *Prayer Book*) in the *Sunday Service* book that accompanied Whatcoat and Vasey to America in 1784. This question itself will probably not be easily (if ever) resolved, but the case I advocate here is that the Reformed understanding of baptism illuminates trends reflected in the revisions in the 1784 *Sunday Service* on the part of the Methodist movement in Wesley's day, if not by Wesley himself.

34. F. Ernest Stoeffler, *The Rise of Evangelical Pietism,* Studies in the History of Religion, no. 9 (Leiden: E. J. Brill, 1965). See also Campbell, *Religion of the Heart,* 44-53, 70-75, 78-98.

35. On this point, see Collins, *The Scripture Way of Salvation,* 129.

36. *Works,* "Prophets and Priests" (or, "The Ministerial Office"), 4:75-84. See also Ted A. Campbell, *John Wesley and Christian Antiquity: Religious Vision and Cultural Change* (Nashville: Abingdon Press, 1991), 82.

37. *Works,* "On God's Vineyard," 3:504-8.

38. See "Prophets and Priests," pars. 9-11 in *Works,* 4:78-79. See also Campbell, *John Wesley and Christian Antiquity,* 81-82.

39. A letter to the editor of the *Wesleyan-Methodist Magazine,* 1824, pp. 238ff.; cited in Holland, *Baptism in Early Methodism,* 4-5.

40. On the latter, Ted A. Campbell, "Charismata in the Christian Communities of the Second Century," *Wesleyan Theological Journal* 17, no. 2 (Fall 1982): 7-25.

10. The Epistemology of Conversion

1. This book was originally his Gifford Lectures of 1901–1902 and was published in 1902. See William James, *The Varieties of Religious Experience* (New York: Longmans, Green, and Co., 1902).

2. Charles Taylor illustrates this tendency nicely in a recent publication. Noting that William James attempts to define religion as the feelings, acts, and experiences of individuals in their solitude so far as they apprehend themselves to stand in relation to whatever they consider the divine, he writes: "This experience is seen as feeling; the most important thing is seen as feeling. . . . Although thoughts . . . and formulations may vary, feelings and conduct that flows from feeling are the same among religions. There's a short circuit, as he says, between feeling and conduct, and it's on this short circuit that she—that is, religion—carries on her principal business, while ideas and symbols and institutions are not to be regarded as organs with an indispensable function necessary for religious life to go on." Taylor goes on to attribute this conception of feeling to the Pietist and Methodist tradition within Protestantism. ("Transformations in Religious Experience," *Harvard Divinity Bulletin* 28 [1999]: 18).

3. It is fascinating that Wesley did not particularly like the term "conversion," using it very sparingly, in that he did not think it was a biblical concept. The issue here, however, is entirely semantic, for Wesley more than covers the territory marked out by conversion in his treatment of the Christian life.

4. Wesley proved helpful not just in sorting out my spiritual and intellectual pilgrimage, but also in becoming acquainted with Christian doctrine, the sacraments, and the crucial place of the church in the life of faith.

5. This applies equally to the much despised Pietists, as recent work on Kant and Schleiermacher is beginning to show. If anything, the Pietists became much too captive to their philosophical musings.

6. See Scott Jones, *John Welsey's Conception and Use of Scripture* (Nashville: Kingswood Books, 1995).

7. See Rex Dale Matthews, "Religion and Reason Joined, a Study in the

Theology of John Wesley" (Th.D. thesis, Harvard University, 1986). This remains a landmark study of Wesley's religious epistemology.

8. *Works,* 2:480-81.

9. Ibid.

10. Wesley, of course, was not alone in appealing to both divine revelation and the spiritual senses and yet failing to show how these might be coherently integrated. One thinks immediately of Jonathan Edwards, a thinker whose philosophical reflections are more sophisticated than Wesley's.

11. See William J. Abraham, *Waking from Doctrinal Amnesia: The Healing of Doctrine in The United Methodist Church* (Nashville: Abingdon Press, 1995).

12. See W. Stephen Gunter, et al., *Wesley and the Quadrilateral: Renewing the Conversation* (Nashville: Abingdon Press, 1997).

13. By foundationalist I mean someone who insists on absolutely certain foundations for all claims to knowledge. Such a position is to be contrasted with that of the coherentist, who holds that all our beliefs are grounded on at least one other belief. There are, of course, more moderate forms of foundationalism.

14. See his "A Clear and Concise Demonstration of the Divine Inspiration of the Holy Scriptures" (date uncertain) in *Works* (Jackson), 11:484.

15. See the much discussed unit in John Calvin, *Institutes of the Christian Religion,* 2 vols., ed. John T. McNeill (Philadelphia: Westminster Press, 1960) 1:74-92.

16. This can be taken either as a form of inner revelation, in which case revelation is used to validate revelation, and we want to know how this new revelation can be validated; or it can be taken as an appeal to a particular kind of inner experience, in which case we have a new foundation in religious experience. The matter is hotly disputed in debates within Calvin scholarship.

17. I am assuming here that it is possible to read the inner witness in Calvin as a form of religious experience.

18. Matthews, "Religion and Reason Joined," 245.

19. We still await a comprehensive study of religious experience in early Methodism.

20. This judgment stands whatever Wesley may have borrowed from the Eastern tradition.

21. The classical exploration of a mechanistic account of conversion in Wesley's ministry is to be found in William Walters Sargant, *Battle for the Mind: The Physiology of Conversion and Brain-Washing* (Garden City, N.Y.: Doubleday, 1957).

22. This is the deep insight that has surfaced in particularist, as opposed to Methodist, theories of knowledge. For this crucial distinction see Roderick Chisholm, "The Problem of the Criterion," in *The Foundations of Knowing* (Minneapolis: University of Minnesota Press, 1982), 61-75.

23. Wesley was very aware of this in the case of both reason and perception.

24. This proposal has been developed for sense perception in a splendid way by William P. Alston in his *The Reliability of Sense Perception* (Ithaca, N.Y.: Cornell University Press, 1993).

25. This way of thinking about knowledge and warrant has been brilliantly developed in the work of Alvin Plantinga; see his *Warrant the Current Debate* (New York: Oxford University Press, 1993); and *Warrant and Proper Function* (New York: Oxford University Press, 1993).

26. Richard Swinburne's *The Existence of God* (Oxford: Clarendon Press, 1979) is the best in the field in the last generation, deploying the resources of probability theory.

27. William P. Alston, *Perceiving God: The Epistemology of Religious Experience* (Ithaca, N.Y.: Cornell University Press, 1991) is a landmark study in this vein.

28. Basil Mitchell's *Justification of Religious Belief* (London: Macmillan, 1973), remains the crucial pioneering work in this tradition. The truly great hero of this tradition is, of course, John Henry Newman.

29. See Alvin Plantinga's magisterial *Warranted Christian Belief* (New York: Oxford University Press, 2000).

30. I have argued this case at length in my *Canon and Criterion in Christian Theology: From the Fathers to Feminism* (Oxford: Clarendon Press, 1998).

31. This dimension of epistemology is currently receiving extended attention in contemporary philosophy. For one of the standard works in the field, see Alvin Goldman, *Knowledge in a Social World* (New York: Oxford University Press, 1999). The implications of this work in epistemology for knowledge of God have yet to be explored.

32. Matthews, "Religion and Reason Joined," 321-22.

11. Conversion: Possibility and Expectation

1. I developed this proposal for a Wesleyan ecology of faith formation in *Making Disciples: Faith Formation in the Wesleyan Tradition* (Nashville: Abingdon Press, 2000).

2. *Works,* "Witness of the Spirit I" (1746), 1:274.

3. John Wesley's use of an educational method of instruction in the midst of practicing a holy life is discussed in "How to Teach: Structures for Teaching" in Matthaei, *Making Disciples.*

4. Horace Bushnell, *Christian Nurture,* 1847, reprint ed. (Grand Rapids: Baker Book House, 1984).

5. Various approaches to Christian education are discussed in Jack L. Seymour, ed., *Mapping Christian Education: Approaches to Congregational Learning* (Nashville: Abingdon Press, 1997).

6. A discussion of the church's participation in deepening lives of faith can be found in Charles R. Foster, *The Future of Christian Education: Educating Congregations* (Nashville: Abingdon Press, 1994); Maria Harris, *Proclaim Jubilee: A Spirituality for the Twenty-First Century* (Louisville: Westminster/John Knox, 1996); Maria Harris and Gabriel Moran, *Reshaping Religious Education: Conversations on Contemporary Practice* (Louisville: Westminster/John Knox, 1998); Mary Elizabeth Moore, *Ministering with the Earth* (St. Louis: Chalice, 1998); Jack L. Seymour, Margaret Ann Crain, and Joseph V. Crockett, *Educating Christians: The Intersection of Meaning, Learning, and Vocation* (Nashville: Abingdon Press, 1993); and Linda J. Vogel, *Teaching and Learning in Communities of Faith* (San Francisco: Jossey-Bass, 1991).

7. Richard P. Heitzenrater, *Mirror and Memory: Reflections on Early Methodism* (Nashville: Kingswood Books, 1989), 106.

8. Ibid.

9. This summary of Piette and Lee is based on Towlson, *Moravian and Methodist,* 2.

10. Ibid., 3.

11. Ibid., 4.

12. Ibid.

13. Heitzenrater, *Mirror and Memory,* 107.

14. Towlson, *Moravian and Methodist,* 4-5.

15. Heitzenrater, *Mirror and Memory,* 107-8.

16. In "Great Expectations" (in Maddox, *Aldersgate Reconsidered,* 51), Heitzenrater notes three questions that concerned John Wesley: "How is 'Christian' *defined*?" "How does one *become* a Christian?" "How does one *know* that he or she is a Christian?"

17. *Works,* "Principles of a Methodist," 9:51.

18. Ibid., 9:60. Maddox observed Wesley's beginning awareness of exclusive language when he changed "Christian men" to "Christian" in an edited work. Although Wesley remained a man of his time, his language will be changed to be more inclusive in this text if it does not alter his meaning. See Maddox, *Responsible Grace,* 259 n. 22.

19. Towlson, *Moravian and Methodist*, 48.
20. *Works* (February 7, 1738), 18:223.
21. Ibid., 18:224.
22. Towlson, *Moravian and Methodist*, 48.
23. Letter from Peter Böhler to Count Zinzendorf (February 17, 1738), in Towlson, *Moravian and Methodist*, 50.
24. Charles Wesley, *Journal* (February 24, 1738), 1:82.
25. *Works* (March 4, 1738), 18:228.
26. Ibid.
27. Ibid. (March 6, 1738).
28. Letter from Peter Böhler to Count Zinzendorf (March 23, 1738), in Towlson, *Moravian and Methodist*, 53.
29. *Works* (March 23, 1738), 18:232.
30. Letter from Peter Böhler to Count Zinzendorf (April 22, 1738), in Towlson, *Moravian and Methodist*, 55.
31. Ibid.
32. Ibid.
33. *Works* (April 22, 1738), 18:233-34.
34. Ibid., 18:234.
35. Ibid.
36. Ibid. (April 23, 1738).
37. Ibid.
38. Towlson, *Moravian and Methodist*, 57.
39. Charles Wesley, *Journal* (May 17, 1738), 1:88.
40. Ibid. (May 21, 1738), 1:90.
41. Ibid., 1:91.
42. Ibid., 1:92.
43. *Works* (May 10, 1738), 18:239.
44. Ibid.
45. *Works* (May 24, 1738), 25:550.
46. *Works* (May 24, 1738), 18:250.
47. Collins, *The Scripture Way of Salvation*, 131.
48. *Works*, "Salvation by Faith" (1733–1735), 1:117.
49. *Works*, Letter from Susanna Wesley to John Wesley (August 28, 1725), 25:179.
50. *Works* (Jackson), Letter from John Wesley to Miss Bolton (January 9, 1789), 12:486.
51. In his spiritual pilgrimage account of May 24, 1738, John Wesley reflects on his struggle with this question; see *Works*, 18:242-51.
52. Heitzenrater, "Great Expectations," 66.
53. *Works* (May 29, 1738), 18:253.

54. Ibid. (June 6, 1738), 18:254.

55. Ibid.

56. Ibid., n. 3.

57. Ibid. (June 13, 1739), 19:68.

58. Ibid.

59. Ibid, 19:69.

60. Susanna Wesley (October 19, 1738), *Susanna Wesley: The Complete Writings*, ed. Charles Wallace Jr. (Oxford: Oxford University Press, 1997), 174.

61. Ibid. (December 6, 1738), 176.

62. Ibid., 177. Emphasis mine.

63. *Works* (August 1, 1742), 19:284 n. 58.

64. Ibid., 19:283-84.

65. Ibid., "Principles of a Methodist" (1742), 9:61.

66. Collins, *The Scripture Way of Salvation*, 141.

67. Ibid., 103.

68. Ibid.

69. Matthaei, "Community and Communion: Vision and Context of Formation for Holiness of Heart and Life," in *Making Disciples*.

70. Wesley, *Notes*, Matthew 4:17 (1755 reprint ed. [Naperville, Ill.: Allenson, 1958], 27).

71. John Westerhoff, *Will Our Children Have Faith?* (New York: The Seabury Press, 1976), 98.

72. Letter from John Wesley to Philothea Briggs (September 18, 1773), Telford, *Letters*, 6:39.

73. Schmidt, *John Wesley*, 1:241.

74. Sondra Higgins Matthaei, *Faith Matters: Faith-Mentoring in the Faith Community* (Valley Forge: Trinity Press International, 1996).

75. Ibid., 56.

76. Charles Wesley, *Journal* (April 19, 1738), 1:84.

77. Matthaei, *Faith Matters*, 57.

78. Ibid., 69.

79. Ibid., 76.

80. Rattenbury, *The Conversion of the Wesleys*, 18.

12. From the "Works of the Flesh" to the "Fruit of the Spirit"

1. See *The Book of Discipline of The United Methodist Church*, 1996, 114.

2. William Abraham, *The Logic of Evangelism* (Grand Rapids: Wm. B. Eerdmans, 1989), 13.

3. Mortimer Arias, *Great Commission: Biblical Models for Evangelism* (Nashville: Abingdon Press, 1992), 19.

4. Maxie Dunnam, *Congregational Evangelism: A Pastor's View* (Nashville: Discipleship Resources, 1992), 2. Emphasis mine.

5. Albert C. Outler, *Evangelism in the Wesleyan Spirit* (Nashville: Tidings, 1971), 23.

6. For more information, see the Upper Room website (http:www.upper-room.org) and go to the "Academy for Spiritual Formation."

7. For a recent overview of this free-floating approach to spirituality, see the cover story of *USA Today* (December 23-26, 1999), where author Cathy Lynn Grossman asserts that current trends show that "self-defined 'spirituality' is replacing a church-based faith."

8. See Gregory S. Clapper, *John Wesley on Religious Affections*; and also Clapper, "*Orthokardia*: The Practical Theology of John Wesley's Heart Religion" *Quarterly Review* 10, no. 1 (Spring 1990): 49-66.

9. See my *As If the Heart Mattered: A Wesleyan Spirituality* (Nashville: Upper Room, 1997), pp 88-97, where I explain in more depth what Wesley meant by these terms.

10. For more on how the three "orthos" can be embodied today, see my *As If the Heart Mattered.*

11. See Clapper, *John Wesley on Religious Affections;* and "*Orthokardia.*"

12. Leander Keck, *Church Confident* (Nashville: Abingdon Press, 1993).

13. See John Hospers, *Moral Problems in Human Conduct* (New York: Harcourt Brace Jovanovich, 1961).

14. The easy, popular acceptance of relativism does show some signs of cracking. Regarding certain issues that some constituencies regard as nonnegotiable, the problems with relativism have come to the surface. See the recent discussion about female circumcision in Africa and whether or not speaking out against such practices is "culturally imperialistic" and "paternalistic," or whether such interventions on behalf of women are morally justified. For example, see Carolyn Fluehr-Lobban, "Cultural Relativism and Universal Rights," in *Virtue and Vice in Everyday Life*, 4th ed. (Fort Worth: Harcourt Brace, 1997), 220-25.

15. See Clapper, *John Wesley on Religious Affections; "Orthokardia"*; and *As If the Heart Mattered.*

13. Embodying Conversion

1. See the United Methodist Church bishops' document, *Vital Congregations—Faithful Disciples: Vision for the Church* (Nashville: Graded Press, 1990).

2. For an analysis of the "Wesley-for-Today" movement, see Philip R. Meadows, "Following Wesley," *Christian Century* 116, no. 5 (February 17, 1999): 191-95.

3. The work of scholars like Geoffrey Wainwright (British Methodist) and Stanley Hauerwas (United Methodist) has helped us to see the necessity of embodying our theology and ethics in the ecclesial practices of worship and mission. See Geoffrey Wainwright, *Doxology: The Praise of God in Worship, Doctrine, and Life* (New York: Oxford University Press, 1980); and, more recently, Stanley Hauerwas, *Sanctify Them in the Truth* (Nashville: Abingdon Press, 1998), esp. chaps. 4 and 7.

4. *Works* (Jackson), Letter to John Smith (June 25, 1746), 12:80-81. Here we see in the one end an inseparable connection between the Great Commission (to bring souls from the power of Satan to God) and the Great Commandment (to build them up in God's fear and love). See also Geoffrey Wainwright, "The End of All Ecclesiastical Order," *One in Christ* 27, no. 1 (1997): 34-48. Albert C. Outler argued that Wesley's "concept of the Church grew out of his Aldersgate experience. He eventually came to believe that every ecclesiastical obligation was subservient to the salvation of souls" (*John Wesley*, 332).

5. *Works* (Jackson), Letter to Rev. Mr. D. (April 6, 1761), 12:264.

6. See George G. Hunter, *To Spread the Power: Church Growth in the Wesleyan Spirit* (Nashville: Abingdon Press, 1987), 39ff. Hunter refers to Wesley's method as "sanctified pragmatism."

7. See Romanus Cessario, *The Moral Virtues and Theological Ethics* (Notre Dame: University of Notre Dame Press, 1991), 76.

8. Thomas Aquinas tells us that "prudence, which is right reason about things to be done, requires that a man be rightly disposed with regard to the ends; and in this depends on rightness of appetite [that is, disposition/virtue]," quoted from Cessario, *The Moral Virtues*, 87.

9. See Durward Hofler, "The Methodist Doctrine of the Church," *Methodist History* 6 (1967), 25ff. Also Reginald Kissack, "Wesley's Concept of His Own Ecclesiastical Position," *London Quarterly & Holborn Review* 186 (1961): 57-60.

10. Wesley did, of course, bring fresh emphasis to neglected doctrine in the Church, especially the need for justification and new birth; the experience of assurance; and the way that these things support the pursuit of holiness.

11. See Cessario, *The Moral Virtues*, 92: "Prudence extends divine providence so that it reaches even to the most particular of moral actions."

12. In speaking of Christian perfection as the "end" of sanctification, I mean to imply its telos (or goal) with respect to the conquering of sin, not

that it represents a final and static state in the Christian life, for Wesley makes it clear that even the perfect continue to grow in grace and love.

13. In other words, the way of salvation is not reducible to a process, for it is defined by the punctuating marks of conversion as justification/new birth and Christian perfection, which bring the sinner into radically new states of Christian life and experiences before God. While these moments belong to a continuum of God's activity in salvation, they represent major turning points in the Christian life that continue to express the insufficiency of human effort and the triumph of God's unconditional grace. Wesley was not a gradualist.

14. For examples of Wesley's use of this expression, see *Works* (Jackson) (December 8, 1744), 1:478; and ibid. (December 15, 1770), 3:423. For the way that this characterises the Methodists, see *Works* ("A Plain Account of the People Called Methodists"), 9:260; ibid. ("A Short History of Methodism"), 9:367, par. 16; and ibid. ("The Principles of a Methodist Farther Explained"), 9:195. He also uses this idea to demonstrate the failure of enthusiasm (*Works* [Jackson], Letter to Rev. Mr. Potter [November 4, 1758], 9:94, par. 14), and those whose preaching for conversion was disconnected from discipleship (ibid., Letter to Rev. Mr. G [April 2, 1761], 12:263). In defense of field preaching, though it be technically contrary to Church order, Wesley claims that "this preaching is not subversive of any good order whatever. It is only subversive of that vile abuse of the good order of our Church, whereby men who neither preach nor live the Gospel are suffered publicly to overturn it from the foundation; and, in the room of it, to palm upon their congregations a wretched mixture of dead form and maimed morality" (*Works* [Jackson], Letter to a Friend [April 10, 1761], 13:233, par. 2).

15. These included *The Principles of a Methodist* (1742–1789) and *The Principles of a Methodist Farther Explained* (1746–1771), or *A Plain Account of the People Called Methodists* (1749–1786) and *A Short History of Methodism* (1765–1789).

16. *Works*, "The Character of a Methodist" (1742–1791), 9:32, 42, pars. 1, 2, and 17.

17. Ibid., 9:33, par. 1.

18. Ibid., 9:34, par. 2.

19. Ibid., par. 3.

20. Ibid., 9:35, par. 4.

21. *Works*, 9:41, par. 17. Emphasis added.

22. Ibid., 9:41, par. 17.

23. Ibid., 9:35, par. 6.

24. Ibid., 9:36, par. 7.

25. Ibid., 9:37, par. 8.

26. Ibid., 9:38, par. 10.
27. Ibid., 9:38-39, pars. 11-13.
28. Ibid., 9:39, par. 14. Wesley continues: "His business and refreshments, as well as his prayers, all serve to this great end. Whether he sit in his house or walk by the way, whether he lie down or rise up, he is promoting in all he speaks or does the one business of his life . . . to advance the glory of God by peace and goodwill among men."
29. Hauerwas, *Sanctify Them in the Truth*, 127.
30. Ibid., 128.
31. Geoffrey Wainwright claims that "the relationship between growth in grace and order in the Church is in fact—or at least in principle—reciprocal" (*The End of All Ecclesiastical Order*, 35). To put it another way, conversion should be constitutive of church order. Colin Williams said that "Wesley's view of holiness was woven into his ecclesiology. He believed that the gathering together of believers into small voluntary societies for mutual discipline and Christian growth was essential to the Church's life" (Williams, *John Wesley's Theology Today*, 151). Clarence Bence claims that "the most striking and ever-relevant feature of Wesley's ecclesiology is its soteriological focus, an emphasis that shaped almost every aspect of his thought and action" ("Salvation and the Church: The Ecclesiology of John Wesley," in: Melvin E. Dieter and Daniel N. Berg, *The Church* [Anderson, Ind.: Warner Press, 1984], 299).
32. *Works*, "A Plain Account of the People Called Methodists," 9:255-58.
33. Ibid., 9:257.
34. Ibid., 9:260-62.
35. Ibid., 9:266-67.
36. Ibid., 9:268-69.
37. Ibid., 9:269-70. Relatively speaking, the life of the band meetings was rather short, petering out toward the end of Wesley's life. Rupert Davies notes, however, that "Wesley himself never ceased to urge their establishment and retention" (p. 13).
38. See ibid., 9:69ff., "The Nature, Design, and General Rules of the United Societies." Here, Wesley claims that a society is "no other than 'a company of men—having the form, and seeking the power of godliness,' united in order to pray together, to receive the word of exhortation, and to watch over one another in love, that they may help each other work out their salvation' " (par. 2). For a detailed study of the society-class meeting, see Watson, *Early Methodist Class Meeting*.
39. See Watson, *Early Methodist Class Meeting*, 106ff.
40. For accounts of the apostolicity of early Methodism, see Wainright, *The End of All Ecclesiastical Order*, esp. pp. 37ff.; and Henry D. Rack,

"Religious Societies and the Origins of Methodism," *Journal of Ecclesiastical History* 38, no. 4 (1987): 588.

41. See also Campbell, *John Wesley and Christian Antiquity.*

42. So Wesley begins by saying, "I must premise, that as they had not the least expectation at first of anything like what has since followed, so they had no previous design or plan at all, but everything arose just as the occasion offered. . . . At . . . times they consulted on the most probable means, following only *common sense* and *Scripture*—though they generally found, in looking back, something in *Christian antiquity*, likewise, very nearly parallel thereto" (*Works,* 9:254, par. 2).

43. This must cause us to proceed with caution in reading Wesley as a "strategist," either of the apostolic or church growth kind. See George G. Hunter, "John Wesley as Church Growth Strategist," *Wesleyan Theological Journal* 21, no. 2 (1986); "The Apostolic Identity of the Church and Wesleyan Christianity," in Logan, *Theology and Evangelism in the Wesleyan Heritage.*

44. *Works,* "A Plain Account of the People Called Methodists," 9:259.

45. These may have been a resistance to the invasive nature of such accountable fellowship (among seekers or believers), or those with a view of Scripture that rejected the use of means not explicitly authorized by the text. The latter argument could, of course, support the former.

46. *Works,* "A Plain Account of the People Called Methodists," 9:263. Wesley continues: "The Scripture (for instance) gives that *general* rule, 'Let all things be done decently and in order.' But common sense is to determine, on *particular* occasions, what order and decency require. So, in another instance, the Scripture lays it down as a *general* standing direction, 'Whether ye eat or drink, or whatsoever ye do, do all to the glory of God.' But it is common prudence which is to make the application of this, in a thousand *particular* cases."

47. Ibid., 9:268.

48. For a detailed study of the early Methodist society preaching service, see Adrian Burdon, *The Preaching Service: The Glory of the Methodists* (Nottingham: Grove Books, 1991). Burdon notes that "when the service took place in public the intention was evangelistic, to awaken the sleeping sinner to the need for inner holiness. When the service was an event on the timetable of the Methodist Society, added to this intention was that of encouraging those already awakened" (p. 19). He goes on to claim that "every Methodist Preacher aimed at enabling all who would listen to commit themselves to Christ. . . . An important aspect of the Methodist Sermon was the way in which it would be connected to real life. . . . The message was delivered through the medium

of his daily life. . . . The hymns of Charles Wesley served to heighten the emotion of the worshippers, to drive home the theology which had been preached" (pp. 23-24). The "liturgical" pattern of the preaching service included a simple combination of music, prayers, and Bible text geared to making effective the communication of the gospel in popular language (pp. 20-23).

49. Henry Rack notes that "the new doctrinal emphasis on justification by faith experienced in conversion turned the whole orientation of the Methodist societies outwards towards aggressive evangelism, even while they provided for more intensive pastoral care" ("Religious Societies and the Origins of Methodism," 587).

50. Charles Edward White captures the spirit of this in the essay "John Wesley's Use of Church Discipline," *Methodist History* 29 no. 2 (1991): 112-18. Consider his concluding remark: "Perhaps Wesley exaggerated when he said that if only Christians would exercise proper church discipline the world would be converted. But then again, perhaps not."

51. Wesley says: "Your *principles* are new, in this respect, that there is no other set of people among us (and possibly not in the Christian world) who hold them all in the same degree and connexion. . . . And perhaps there is no other set of people (at least not visibly united together) who lay *so much,* and yet *no more* stress than you do, on rectitude of *opinions,* on outward *modes of worship,* and the use of those *ordinances* which you acknowledge to be of God—" (*Works,* "Advice to the People Called Methodists," 9:125, par. 9). Later, he adds: "You will give offence to the *bigots for* opinions, modes of worship, and ordinances, by laying *no more* stress upon them; to the *bigots against* them, by laying *so much;* to *men of form,* by insisting so frequently on the inward *power* of religion; to *moral men* (so called) by declaring the absolute necessity of *faith* in order to acceptance with God . . ." (p. 127, par. 14).

52. This results in an unbalanced emphasis on the first part of the Great Commission ("Go therefore and make disciples of all nations") to the neglect of the second ("teaching them to obey everything that I have commanded you").

53. Quoted from Ayling, *John Wesley,* 201.

54. For an useful critique of The United Methodist Church bishops' vision statement in *Vital Congregations,* see L. Gregory Jones and Michael G. Cartwright, "Vital Congregations: Toward a Wesleyan Vision for The United Methodist Church's Identity and Mission," in Alan G. Padgett, ed., *The Mission of the Church in Methodist Perspective* (Lewiston: The Edwin Mellen Press, 1992), chap. 5.

55. This comparison really deserves a much more detailed study, not

possible in the space of a single chapter. I have, however, included some more detailed discussion in the footnotes that follow. For an in-house account of both the history and thinking behind the church, see Lynne and Bill Hybels, *Rediscovering Church: The Story and Vision of Willow Creek Community Church* (Grand Rapids: Zondervan Publishing House, 1995). See also Anthony B. Robinson, "Learning from Willow Creek," *Christian Century* 108 (January 23, 1991): 68-70. From a British Anglican perspective, see Paul Simmonds, *Reaching the Unchurched: Some Lessons from Willow Creek* (Nottingham: Grove Books, 1992).

56. Paul Braoudakis, ed., *Willow Creek Community Church: Church Leaders Handbook* (Barrington, Ill.: Willow Creek Association, 1997), 55. Henceforth, this text will be referred to as *CLH*. See "Growing Fully Devoted Followers," in Hybels, *Rediscovering Church*, chap. 13. I am convinced that Wesley would have approved of Willow Creek's description of the character of a Creeker, marked by "The Five G's": grace ("the individual appropriation of the saving work of Christ"), growth (*"the ongoing evidence of a changing life and pursuit of Christlikeness"*), group ("participation in the body of Christ and connection with others in significant relationships"), gifts ("serving Christ's body"), good stewardship ("honoring God with one's material resources") (*CLH*, 62). Emphasis is mine.

57. *CLH*, 57ff. For a narrative account, see "A Mission and a Strategy," in Hybels, *Rediscovering Church*, chap. 11.

58. "The purpose of the seeker service is to communicate biblical truth in a way that prepares and persuades seekers to receive the message of the gospel. . . . The seeker service is a tool that Willow Creek provides for believers to use as they reach out to their seeking friends" (*CLH*, 77). These services are held on Saturday evenings and Sunday mornings, rather than midweek, in order to attract seekers. It is important to remember that Willow Creek does not consider these services to constitute "worship." Those who criticize the concept of the seeker service for confusing the activities of worship and evangelism typically proceed from a wrong assumption. For an instance of this mistake, see (ironically) Bart Swaim, "The Great Assumption," *Regeneration Quarterly* 3 (1997): 15-16. From the perspective of liturgical studies, see Gordon W. Lathrop, "New Pentecost or Joseph's Britches? Reflections on the History and Meaning of the Worship Ordo in the Megachurches," *Worship* 72, no. 6 (1998): 521-38. Lathrop traces the liturgical order of the seeker service back through the revivalism of nineteenth-century America to the camp meeting, noting its pragmatic emphasis on conversion, and raising some serious questions for the church. It is certainly true that Willow Creek's use of the arts to "direct" emotions to increase receptivity to persuasive preaching is

characteristic of revivalism (see G. A. Pritchard, "Artful Evangelism: Strengths and Weaknesses in the Use of Arts at Willow Creek Community Church," *Touchstone* 8, no. 1 [1995]: 23-33; James L. Brauer, "The Role of Music in Seeker Services," *Concordia Journal* 24 [1998]: 7-20). I would argue that the seeker service actually bears close similarity in order and function to the preaching service of the early Methodist movement (which was, of course, a form of revivalism). A common weakness with many critiques of Willow Creek, including this one, is that they attempt to evaluate the seeker service without carefully situating its part in the community's whole strategy to embody the gospel, especially with regard to the role of worship. The seeker service differs significantly from revivalism, however, by taking the view that making a commitment to Christ (let alone becoming a fully devoted follower) is a long process. So it does not aim at inducing personal crises for an instant "harvest," typical of revivalism. What differentiates both early Methodism and Willow Creek from the excesses of revivalism, however, is that the seeker/preaching service is seen as bridge to full participation in the breadth of activities offered by a life-transforming Christian fellowship. Making a decision for Christ is not embodied by an "altar call" but by incorporation into the worship, ministry, and small-group life of the community.

59. Willow Creek's great congregation is called "New Community" and meets on a Wednesday or Thursday night. "We meet together to develop lives that are filled with worship [that is, private and corporate], with the understanding that that includes times of teaching and learning, times of fellowship and celebration, times to observe sacraments like Communion and baptism, times of prayer and confession, and extended times of praising God through music and song" (*CLH*, 83).

60. "The purpose of small groups is to connect people relationally in groups (four to ten individuals) for the purpose of growing in Christlikeness, loving one another, and contributing to the work of the church, in order to glorify God and make disciples of all nations" (*CLH*, 115). There remains, of course, the question of how Willow Creek and Methodism understand what it constitutes "Christlikeness." The goal of emotional wholeness and psychological well-being (so prevalent at Willow Creek) is very different from Wesley's understanding of characterizing Christian perfection through the formation of virtue and holy affections. It is interesting to note that whereas Wesley was a trained theologian, John Ortberg (Willow Creek's teaching pastor) is a trained clinical psychologist.

61. Lester Ruth has offered a critique of the distinction between the

liturgical nature traditionally associated with the great congregation and that of seeker services. He claims that the traditional order of *lex orandi, lex credendi* (that order of belief shapes order of worship) has been substituted for *lex agendi, lex orandi* (that the evangelistic "agenda" shapes worship). There are two problems with this. First, as Ruth admits, Willow Creek would not see the seeker service as worship (since worship is the prudential ordering of the great congregation) and speak of it with this kind of liturgical language. Second, in concentrating on the seeker service, he tends to miss the subtle dynamic obtaining between the seeker service and the believers' service, which are inseparably connected and mutually conditioning concerns. As such, we might say more fully that the *lex agendi* of the seeker service (in fulfillment of the Great Commission) cannot be separated from the *lex orandi* of the believers' service (in fulfillment of the Great Commandment), both of which serve to embody the *lex credendi* in the church community as a whole. See Lester Ruth, "Lex Agendi, Lex Orandi: Toward an Understanding of Seeker Services as a New Kind of Liturgy," *Worship* 70 (1996): 386-405.

62. For Willow Creek, being a seeker and becoming committed to Christ does tend to follow the revival mode of intellectual persuasion and personal "emotional" experience (albeit construed over a period of time). In the class meeting, however, sincere seeking was embodied by, and held accountable to, the practices of repentance and faith, according to the society *Rules*.

63. Early Methodism differs from Willow Creek, however, in that manditory membership of a society-class meeting also held seekers accountable for their participation in all the means of grace, that is, the worship of the great congregation and through personal acts of both piety and mercy. Tony Maan has an interesting discussion, from a Reformed perspective, in his article "Should Seekers Be Invited to the Table?" *Reformed Worship* 48 (1998): 22-25. It is also important to remember, however, that there was no such thing as an anonymous but sincere seeker in the Methodist order of Christian fellowship. In early Methodism, the small group function of mutual accountability and empowerment belonged to classes that combined both seekers and believers. Indeed, the genius of the class-band structure meant that seekers and believers would meet together in class, with a high degree of peer-ministry, while reserving the band-meetings for those converts pressing on to perfection. The class, perhaps even more than the field preaching/preaching service, was the real locus of evangelism and conversion.

64. Some seeker-oriented congregations opt out of a separate seeker service in favor of making the great congregation "seeker-friendly,"

which often means redefining worship (and therefore the church's witness) according to the mores of the unchurched. In a convincing exegesis of 1 Corinthians 14:16-25, Jeffrey Peterson argues that the biblical concept of openness to the presence of seekers among believers in worship is about effective communication rather than compromising accommodation: "Paul's major concern is for *clarity* when the Christian confession is proclaimed in worship; when Christians gather for worship, the faith is to be exhibited with sufficient clarity that the interested non-member can respond to the living God who has brought salvation through his Son. . . . Paul insists that worship be *intelligible* to pagans, not that it be *attractive.* He knows that the gospel, clearly stated, scandalizes non-Christians. . . . The unbeliever can say 'Amen,' expressing assent to the Christian vision of God and his saving work, only when our worship clearly articulates and embodies the Gospel" ("How Shall the Seeker Say Amen?" *Christian Studies* 13 [1993]: 28-29, 31). On the other hand, "the leaders of Willow Creek Community Church do not believe it is possible to minister optimally to both seekers and believers within the confines of one service. . . . In honoring the needs of both groups, Willow Creek has chosen to minister to each group through separate services" (*CLH*, 77). For the variety of ways that churches seek to embody a seeker-orientation, see Ruth, "Lex Agendi, Lex Orandi." See especially "The Use of Seeker Services: Models and Questions," *Reformed Liturgy & Music* 30, no. 2 (1996): 48-53. Ruth prefers the Willow Creek model to that of "seeker-friendly" worship, but concludes that it should be more rigorously defined by excluding seekers from the worship of the great congregation in order to protect its distinctive sacramental order. From a Wesleyan perspective, this misses the point of the threefold pattern by collapsing the productive tension between catholicity and prudential order that can exist in both seeker services and the great congregation, thereby denying seekers access to all the means of grace. It is only the function of believers' small groups (like society-bands) to embody the *separate gathering* of saints in the broad order of Christian fellowship. See also John H. Tietjen, "The Megachurch: Who We Are Shapes What We Do," *Word & World* 13 (1993): 415-17. The problem with not carefully distinguishing seeker and believer services is articulated in Tietjen's fear that a widespread move to making Sunday mornings "seeker-friendly" will eventually cause a general redefinition of what constitutes authentic Christian fellowship through the redefinition of its worship.

65. It is clear from Willow Creek's "Five G's" and "Seven Steps" that belonging to a small group of believers is normative for being a fully devoted follower of Jesus Christ. Hybels comments that Willow Creek

has grown from being a church *with* small groups to being a church *of* small groups. Unlike early Methodism, however, participation in a small group is not normative for their definition of seeking.

66. See especially G. A. Pritchard, "Evaluating the Willow Creek Way of Doing Church," in *Willow Creek Seeker Services: Evaluating a New Way of Doing Church* (Grand Rapids: Baker Books, 1996), pt. 2, 187ff. Pritchard's analysis is extremely helpful in identifying some of the potential dangers in the life of this Christian community (not that it is necessarily remarkable in many respects). The study is based on research performed over a decade ago, however, and Willow Creek has continued to developed significantly in its principles and practice. Over this time, Bill Hybels has continued to modify and clarify the position of Willow Creek in response to such criticisms, as any leader of a young movement must do, including Wesley's defense of the people called Methodists. See Hybels' response to critics of the seeker-church movement in "Selling Out the House of God?" *Christianity Today* 38 (July 18, 1994): 20-25; "Values That Distinguish a Movement" and "Commonly Asked Questions About Willow Creek Community Church," in *Rediscovering Church*, 183ff. and 205ff. See also the defense of Mark Mittelberg (evangelism trainer at Willow Creek), and a critique by Douglas Groothius in "Pro and Con: The Seeker-Church Movement," *Christian Research Journal* 18 (1996): 54-55. For a helpful review of Pritchard's book, see David S. Lueke, "Is Willow Creek the Way of the Future?" *Christian Century* 114 (May 14, 1997): 479-85.

Conclusion: Suddenly a Light from Heaven

1. Gaventa, *From Darkness to Light*. Ben Witherington's chapter on conversion in the Johannine and Pauline literature is a wonderful contribution to the literature that stresses the conversionist theme in the New Testament.

2. Theodore Jennings dismissed Aldersgate as a "non-event" (see "John Wesley *Against* Aldersgate," 7). Those who are reasonably well-situated in this world as it is, have a stake in denying the possibility of radical change. For an informed critique of anticonversionist literature in Methodism, see Collins, "Other Thoughts on Aldersgate," 10-25.

3. The accounts of Paul's "conversion" are more properly interpreted as stories of vocation rather than conversion. To be called, according to Paul, is to be changed, transformed, converted. To be converted is to be called. See William H. Willimon, *Acts: Interpretation* (Atlanta: John Knox Press, 1988), 73-83.

4. Verse 17, in the Greek, lacks both subject and verb, so it is best rendered by the exclamatory, "If anyone is in Christ—new creation!"

5. Wade Clark Roof, *Spiritual Marketplace: Baby Boomers and the Remaking of American Religion* (Princeton: Princeton University Press, 1999).

6. David Steinmetz, "Reformation and Conversion," *Theology Today* 35 (1978): 25-32.

7. Jim Wallis, *Call to Conversion* (New York: Harper & Row, 1982).

8. John Calvin, *Institutes of the Christian Religion,* The Library of Christian Classics, vol. 20, ed. John T. McNeill, trans. Ford Lewis Battles (Philadelphia: Westminster Press, 1960), 3.3.9. "Viewing Wesley's doctrine of salvation through the interpretive lens of John Calvin will render the former's doctrines of justification and grace, at least in some respects, remarkably clear" (Collins, *The Scripture Way of Salvation,* 206).

9. Hans J. Mol, *Identity and the Sacred* (New York: Free Press, 1977), 45-53.

10. Fowler, *Stages of Faith;* Donald Capps, *Life-Cycle Theory and Pastoral Care* (Philadelphia: Fortress Press, 1983).

11. Karl Barth, *Church Dogmatics,* vol. 4, pt. 3, second half, trans. G. W. Bromiley (Edinburgh: T. & T. Clark, 1962), sec. 71.2, 504-6.

12. Ibid., 506-7.

13. After discussing the limits of the organic, developmental notions of "faith development" in Fowler and Capps, Craig Dykstra says that any faithful account of the Christian faith must include "the tradition's emphasis on the priority of the activity of God as the source of faith and on the nature of faith, as response to God in history, makes it wary of organic metaphors, which suggest that faith is a structure built into human beings that undergoes evolutionary or developmental transformation. . . . The tradition has usually been hesitant to put too much emphasis on progress in the life of faith or to stake out any stages by which such progress might be marked . . . hesitant to define or describe maturity in faith and in the life of faith too exactly" (*Growing in the Life of Faith: Education and Christian Practices* [Louisville: Geneva Press, 1999], 36).

14. John Calvin defines faith this way: "We shall possess a right definition of faith if we call it a firm and certain knowledge of God's benevolence toward us, founded upon the truth of the freely given promise in Christ, both revealed to our minds and sealed upon our hearts through the Holy Spirit" (*Institutes of the Christian Religion,* 3.2.7).

15. If I were to indicate the major way that contemporary heirs of Wesley deviate from Wesley's anthropology, it would be in our inadequate assessment of human sinfulness. The late Thomas Langford, won-

derful Wesleyan theologian, once told me that he conducted a survey of twentieth-century theological writings by Methodists and was struck by how few of them even mentioned the word *sin*. Perhaps this omission of *sin* is one of the reasons we no longer speak much of prevenient, justifying, and sanctifying grace. Who needs the grace of God when we are basically good people capable of progress?

16. Richard P. Heitzenrater, *Wesley and the People Called Methodists* (Nashville: Abingdon Press, 1995).

17. Ibid., 192.

18. Ibid., 138.

19. Stanley Hauerwas and I attempted to stress the centrality of Christian practice for Christian holiness in *Where Resident Aliens Live: Exercises for Christian Practice* (Nashville: Abingdon Press, 1996).

20. In his chapter on the ministry of Freeborn Garrettson, Douglas Strong depicted the implications of the radical inner change with a radical social critique.

21. Collins, *The Scripture Way of Salvation*, 207.

22. Hans Küng, *The Church* (Garden City, N.Y.: Doubleday & Co., 1976), 438.

DATE DUE